essential guide to

o'ahu

INCLUDING **WAIKĪKĪ** AND **HONOLULU**

Virginia Wageman

ISLAND HERITAGE

Published and
distributed by
Island Heritage
ISBN 0-89610-084-7

Printed in Hong Kong
First edition, first printing,
2002

Maps by Stephen Downes

Designed by Jim Wageman

Address orders and
correspondence to:

Island Heritage
94-411 Ko'aki Street
Waipahu, HI 96797
Phone 800-468-2800;
808-564-8800
Fax 808-564-8888
www.islandheritage.com

Page 1 (background):
19th-century hula dancers
with traditional instruments.

Pages 2–3: Honolulu and
Diamond Head from Tantalus.

contents

maps

top ten **essentials**
for a great vacation on oʻahu

- Go surfing in the fabled gentle waves of Waikīkī, taking a surfing lesson from a beachboy, a Waikīkī tradition since tourists started coming to the islands in the '30s and '40s. The beachboys at Aloha Beach Service at the Moana Hotel are, as the locals would say, da best (see page 162).

- Eat at one of Oʻahu's great restaurants. Alan Wong's, Chef Mavro, La Mer, and Hōkū's top the list (pages 278–301).

- Visit Oʻahu's great museums, especially the Bishop Museum, with ethnographic treasures of Hawaiʻi and the Pacific; the Honolulu Academy of Arts, a gem of an art museum; and the Contemporary Museum, where art since 1940 is displayed amid stunning surroundings (pages 143–51). Each offers a different perspective on these exotic islands and the people who live here.

- Have a leisurely and very civilized afternoon tea, a throwback to the Victorian age of Hawaiʻi's royalty. Enjoy flaky fresh-baked scones, dainty

Top to bottom: Surfing off Waikīkī; Chef Mavro prepares a meal; untitled stoneware sculpture by Arnold Zimmerman on the grounds of the Contemporary Museum (a gift of the Honolulu Advertiser Collection at Persis Corporation); tea at the Halekūlani; Mandara Spa.

Opposite, top to bottom: Visitors in an outrigger canoe; windward Oʻahu mountains; ʻIolani Palace; Maunawili Falls; Auntie Genoa Keawe.

sandwiches, and scrumptious pastries with a pot of refreshing mango tea. Our favorite is the tea served daily at the Halekūlani (see page 279).

● Treat yourself to a massage or other spa treatment (page 210). Hawai'i is famous for its *lomilomi* massage, passed down to practitioners by *kūpuna,* using both gentle and vigorous kneading strokes and body manipulations to ease muscle pain and increase circulation.

● Go for an outrigger canoe ride, launched from the beach at Waikīkī (page 192). The thrill of riding the waves by canoe and the sights of Waikīkī from offshore make for an unforgettable experience.

● Take a round-the-island helicopter tour (page 217), which provides awesome sights as well as gives the visitor a totally new perspective of the island and its towering mountains, majestic waterfalls, and beautiful coastline.

● Visit 'Iolani Palace (page 73) and the Mission Houses Museum (pages 83–84)

for a step back in time. You'll see the grand throne room and other artifacts of Hawai'i's royal past as influenced by Great Britain, at the palace, and the houses built by the early missionaries out of New England that reflect America's colonial influence.

● Take a hike (pages 197–207)! Walking allows you to see just how much beautiful flora and fauna are left amid the ever-growing built environment. Maunawili Falls (page 200), on the windward side off the Pali Highway, usually has few people on the trail.

● Take in such legends of local entertainment (see pages 235–46) as Auntie Genoa Keawe (page 241), Henry Kapono (page 239), or the incomparable Don Ho (page 240), now appearing at times with his daughter Hoku, a recording artist in her own right. Among other relative newcomers are Daniel Ho, Ten Feet, and Colón. For those with an ear for jazz, pianists Rich Crandall, Betty Loo Taylor, and David Swanson deliver a variety of hip, sophisticated sounds.

o'ahu *at a glance*

"Nothing had prepared me for Honolulu. It is so far away from Europe, it is reached after so long a journey from San Francisco, so strange and so charming associations are attached to the name, that at first I could hardly believe my eyes. . . . Though the air is so soft and the sky so blue, you have, I know not why, a feeling of something hotly passionate that beats like a throbbing pulse."

— W. SOMERSET MAUGHAM, "HONOLULU," 1916

few have not heard of the beautiful and exotic Hawaiian islands. Hawai'i has been immortalized in music, in poetry and novels, in films, and in paintings and prints. It has become a global legend. Can its reality live up to its myth? Despite the changes in this once-Polynesian kingdom, few of the millions of tourists who visit these islands each year leave disappointed. Many return again and again; nearly half of Hawai'i's tourists are repeat visitors.

Page 10: *A View in the Bay at Woahoo, Sandwich Islands* (detail), 1786. From Nathaniel Portlock, *A Voyage round the World* (London, 1789).

Page 11: Surfing off Waikiki.

Opposite: Waikiki Beach and Diamond Head.

Nearly every visitor to Hawai'i comes to O'ahu at some time, either passing through for a few days visit or to stay for a week or more. Some don't go away at all. Known as "the Gathering Place," O'ahu is home to a cosmopolitan city with towering skyscrapers, and it is here that the business of government takes place and that 72 percent of Hawai'i's population of 1.2 million lives—about half of whom live in Honolulu. Military personnel and their dependents comprise nearly 15 percent of the state's population, and almost all of them reside on O'ahu (less than 4 percent on the other islands).

Contrary to modern myth, however, the name O'ahu does not mean "gathering place." The name is so ancient that both its origin and its meaning are lost in the mists of time. It is best not to attempt a translation, simply accepting it as the name given this island by the ancients. In modern Hawai'i, though, O'ahu is definitely a gathering place, the focal point of most of the state's educational, artistic, business, and social activities.

The University of Hawai'i's main campus (Mānoa) is on this island, as are four of its associated colleges. There are several small private universities, including Hawai'i Pacific University and Chaminade University of Honolulu, and a large number of secondary and primary schools, both private and public. Most of the state's museums, libraries, art galleries, theaters, and other entertainments are here, as are the greatest number and diversity of restaurants. Major festivals, concerts, and sporting events are frequent on O'ahu.

At about 600 square miles, O'ahu is the third largest of the Hawaiian islands. Ninety percent of O'ahu's hotels are in Waikīkī, and there is still a lot of agricultural and undeveloped countryside, even on this most populous island, with a great deal of spectacularly beautiful scenery.

Though O'ahu's—indeed Hawai'i's—main source of revenue is tourism, with military expenditure in second place, agriculture is still important on O'ahu as on the other principal islands. Pineapples, coffee, papayas, bananas, corn, lettuce, and tropical flowers are among O'ahu's crops.

Opposite top:
A tree-shaded walk-way at the University of Hawai'i, Mānoa.

Opposite bottom:
Sweet-potato farmers in Waikāne Valley, windward coast of O'ahu.

The television and movie industry provides notable revenue and local employment, as our islands offer an enormous variety of popular film locations, even for stories that are set elsewhere, especially in southeast Asian countries, such as Vietnam. Classic feature films shot in Hawai'i include *From Here to Eternity, Tora! Tora! Tora!, Raiders of the Lost Ark, Jurassic Park, Waterworld,* and, most recently, *Pearl Harbor.* Major successful television series that have been O'ahu based include *Hawaiian Eye, Hawaii Five-O, Magnum P.I.,* and the critically dismal *Baywatch Hawaii.* Made-for-television mini-series *War and Remembrance, The Thornbirds,* and *Blood and Orchids* were all shot in the islands. MTV's *Real World* shot a segment in Honolulu a few years ago, setting up house in a Diamond Head mansion, and *Good Morning America* regularly broadcasts from the islands.

O'ahu has both sophisticated urban glamour and idyllic rural retreats, both upscale luxury and rustic camping—and lots of offerings in between. With the exception of certain condominium complexes, bed-and-breakfast homes, vacation rentals, and rural campsites, most of O'ahu's visitor accommodations are in Waikīkī. Honolulu, the most populated area, is on the island's south shore and includes Waikīkī. The rest of the island—with the exception of the largely military residential suburbs of Pearl Harbor, the new planned communities in central O'ahu, and the windward-side towns of Kailua and Kāne'ohe—is relatively undeveloped.

The largest number of visitors come to the islands in the months of February and August. However, there is no single "good" or "bad" time to visit.

Waikīkī

The area now known as Waikīkī has become a self-contained metropolis where most of O'ahu's transient population resides. An ordinary day finds more than 93,000 people dwelling on these 450 acres (smaller in area than Honolulu airport's reef runway), about 70 percent of whom are visitors. The remaining 30 percent—Waikīkī's "permanent" population—are overwhelmingly Caucasian (64 percent) newcomers who were born outside Hawai'i (81 percent). Most are unmarried (63 percent) and live in high-rise buildings (98 percent). These statistics are not typical of Hawai'i or O'ahu in general. Nothing about Waikīkī is typical.

Waikīkī has always been a special place with a special appeal. The nature of this appeal has changed radically over the years, but it hasn't diminished. The glitz and

Below (background): Diamond Head by moonlight, circa 1940.

Opposite: Beachfront hotels, Waikiki.

Waikiki

Warm perfumes like a breath from vine and tree

Drift down the darkness. Plangent, hidden from eyes,

Somewhere an ukulele thrills and cries

And stabs with pain the night's brown savagery.

And dark scents whisper; and dim waves creep to me,

Gleam like a woman's hair, stretch out, and rise;

And new stars burn into the ancient skies,

Over the murmurous soft Hawaiian sea.

—Rupert Brooke (british, 1887–1915), 1913

the glamour in this languorous tropical paradise provide a dreamlike context for vacationers from all over the world.

The Waikīkī lifestyle is not the normal routine. A most unlikely and eclectic mix of humanity throngs the streets, (usually) in blissful harmony: honeymooners, teenagers, conventioneers, business people, retirees, beach bums, even local residents out for a night on the town, the cast of thousands constantly changing. Waikīkī is a fantasy world—exciting and relaxing, fleeting and eternal.

Neighbor Islands

O'AHU IS ONE OF EIGHT MAIN ISLANDS in the Hawaiian chain. One of the islands, **Kaho'olawe**, which lies off Maui's leeward coast, is not inhabited. Until recently, the 45-square-mile Kaho'olawe was used by the military as a target for bombing practice. In 1994 ownership of the island was officially transferred by the U.S. Navy to the state of Hawai'i, specifically to people of native Hawaiian descent. Workers are now removing ordnance from enough of the island so that it might at least be visited. The eventual use of the island has yet to be determined, though many native Hawaiians are hopeful that it will become a place for a separate nation of Hawai'i to exist.

The tiny island of **Ni'ihau** is privately owned by the Robinson family of Kaua'i. It has no tourist facilities and can be visited by nonresidents only by invitation. Situated 17 miles west of Kaua'i across the Ka'ie'ie Channel, Ni'ihau, owing to its fierce protection from outside influence, is the last stronghold of Hawaiian culture (its entire population is of at least part-Hawaiian blood), and it is the only place on earth where Hawaiian is still spoken as the mother tongue. Most residents never leave the island. The only authorized visits there are those by a few state government leaders who go to assure themselves that educational funds and other state monies are being properly dispensed and utilized. Ni'ihau is known for its small shells that are strung into lovely lei and sold at premium prices in stores throughout the islands.

That leaves the islands of Kaua'i, O'ahu, Moloka'i, Lāna'i, Maui, and Hawai'i (commonly known as the Big Island)—in that order, northwest to southeast and chronologically in age—for visitors to explore. Each of the main Hawaiian islands has its own special magic, and the *Essential Guides* to Maui (including Lāna'i and Moloka'i), Kaua'i, and Hawai'i (the Big Island) provide the same in-depth coverage of those islands as does this guidebook. We hope you can visit all of our islands and discover for yourself the unique charm—past and present—of each.

Native Hawaiians living on Ni'ihau have been creating shell ornamentation since before Captain Cook's arrival in 1778. Because few flowers grow in Ni'ihau's dry soil, the residents consider the delicate shells to be their flowers. The shells found on Ni'ihau are sometimes referred to as the gems of the Pacific because they are the only shell jewelry in the world that a licensed appraiser may appraise; they are insurable as a precious gem. Among *kama'āina*, owning a Ni'ihau shell lei is like owning a string of pearls.

Shell jewelry is an evolving art form, and lei makers are constantly creating new color patterns and styles of stringing. Lei patterns are usually named for the island blossoms of Kaua'i, such as *pīkake* (jasmine), *helekonia* (heliconia), and *lokelani* (rose). Shell-gathering season lasts only five or six months a year, and it may take up to six or seven years to collect the shells for an intricate lei.

Interisland air service is frequent and excellent. There are no boats providing regular passenger service from O'ahu, though one can travel via ferry between Maui and Lāna'i and Moloka'i. Flights are short, the longest taking only 30 minutes. Prices are kept reasonable by a high level of traffic. Oahuans alone make half a million trips to the neighbor islands each year.

The island closest to O'ahu is **Moloka'i**, nearly 26 miles across the Kaiwi Channel. Moloka'i and her people embody much of the traditional Hawaiian spirit and prefer to keep to the old ways as much as possible. This sleepy island has a handful of hotels, including one luxury resort, the Moloka'i Ranch, with an inland lodge and beachside "tentalows." The island remains uncrowded, with few tourists adding to the population of 7,000. The northwestern coast contains the peninsula of Kalaupapa where, in the 1860s, those suffering from leprosy were forced ashore in isolation. Today this settlement is the home of a dwindling number of those afflicted with Hansen's disease. Remote, windswept, and quiet, Kalaupapa receives an occasional

Queen Emma, wife of Kamehameha IV, in Victorian dress, wearing multiple strands of Ni'ihau shell lei in a photo made sometime after 1856.

visitor, who must be accompanied by a guide. Children under the age of sixteen are not permitted in the settlement. Kalaupapa contains a memorial to the Belgian priest, Father Damien, who died a martyr serving the lepers on this peninsula.

Only 9 miles from Moloka'i, across the Kalohi Channel, is the rural island of **Lāna'i**, mostly owned by Castle and Cooke. At one time pineapple was the only major industry until the opening of two elegant luxury hotels in the early 1990s. One, the Lodge at Kō'ele, is styled after an English country manor and set on 21 acres in the central uplands skirting Lāna'i City. The other, the Mānele Bay Hotel, is a splendid beachfront resort on the cliffs overlooking Hulopo'e Bay. A Greg Norman–designed championship golf course, the Experience at Kō'ele, is adjacent to the Lodge, situated in a forested setting surrounded by tall pines and lush mountain vegetation. The Mānele Bay Hotel has a spectacular Jack Nicklaus–designed 18-hole course called the Challenge at Mānele, built on 350 acres atop a natural lava outcropping and set among native *kiawe* and *'ilima* trees. Its signature hole plays from atop a cliff rising 150 feet above the sea and requires a 200-yard tee shot across the ocean.

Maui, to whose county Moloka'i and Lāna'i belong, is the next in the chain. From the towering grandeur of the volcano Haleakalā—still considered active though it's been over two hundred years since it erupted—to the sweeping beaches of Kā'anapali, Maui in all its variety truly fulfills the dreamer's fantasy of what a tropical paradise should be. It is here that the visitor may discover both the charming, sleepy village of Hāna and the fast-paced resort area of West Maui. Bustling Lahaina, the center of the whaling industry of yesteryear, is today the capital of the whale-watching industry. Maui is considered by many to be the best island in the world. It's not hard to see why. There are miles of pristine beaches, the largest dormant volcano anywhere, hiking trails to challenge even the most experienced outdoors person, lush valleys, and cool, green pastureland. And, there are nightclubs, world-class golf courses, luxury hotels, superb restaurants, art galleries, and plenty of opportunities for shopping. Each year 2.3 million visitors come to this idyllic island.

Nearly 30 miles southeast of Maui, across the 'Alenuihāhā Channel, lies the island of **Hawai'i**, referred to as the **Big Island**. Youngest in the island chain, its active volcano, Kīlauea, on the flanks of Mauna Loa, is still building the coastline. Hawai'i is so big that all the other islands would fit into its borders with room to spare. This island is a place of great variety, from the sleepy, plantation-town atmosphere of east Hawai'i (the tropical Hilo side) to the bustling west side, site of Kailua-Kona and the barren stretches of lava rock on which the luxury "gold coast" resorts of Kahala sparkle. In the center of the island are the two highest peaks in the Pacific, Mauna

The Belgian priest Joseph Damien de Veuster, known as Father Damien, ministered to the lepers at Kalaupapa until he himself succumbed to the disease in 1889.

Kea and Mauna Loa, each rising to almost 14,000 feet. Here too is the enormous and privately owned Parker Ranch, more than 200,000 acres dotted with beautiful, healthy cattle and home to the Hawaiian *paniolo*, or cowboy. The Big Island was the birthplace of the conqueror Kamehameha the Great, who united the islands into one kingdom. The monarch died in Kona, and his remains are hidden forever, as was the custom for great *ali'i* in Hawai'i.

One hundred miles northwest of O'ahu is the oldest inhabited island in the chain, **Kaua'i**. Known as "the Garden Isle," Kaua'i is an island of flowers and slow ways, but it is highly experienced in handling masses of visitors while protecting this breathtaking paradise. Hanalei, located on the north shore of the island, is one of the world's most beautiful valleys. The spectacular Waimea Canyon tends to dwarf everything else on the island. Sometimes referred to as the Grand Canyon of the Pacific, it is not quite as large as its namesake but is every bit as stunning.

Telephone

O'AHU'S AREA CODE IS 808, as for the rest of Hawai'i. When calling from a neighbor island, it is necessary to dial the area code along with the number. See also page 248.

Climate *and* Weather

CURRENT O'AHU WEATHER CONDITIONS are available by calling the National Weather Service at 973-4381; for Honolulu weather only, call 973-4380. For a recreational forecast from the National Weather Service, call 973-4382. Also, O'ahu weather is available on the Worldwide Web: www.hawaiiweathertoday.com/mwt.

Hawai'i's pleasant climate doesn't change much throughout the year. The temperature ranges between a daytime high near 90°F (about 30°C) in "summer" and a nighttime low near 60°F (about 18°C) in "winter." There are no distinct seasons as such. Even in winter the daytime temperature is usually in the 80s. The comfort factor that this involves depends on what you're used to. Residents start to shiver and bundle up when the mercury plummets to 75°F (24°C). The coldest months are February and March and the hottest August and September.

Despite this lack of strong seasonal variation, Hawai'i is home to an extraordinary diversity of microclimates—from desert to rainforest. The temperature drops about 3°F for every thousand feet of increased altitude, a factor that sometimes produces seasonal snow on the upper slopes of Haleakalā on Maui and the Big Island's Mauna Kea.

Rainfall varies dramatically in different parts of each island—from a mere 10 inches annually in some leeward areas to more than 40 feet at the summit of Kaua'i's Mount Wai'ale'ale (the wettest spot on Earth), where it virtually never stops raining. Hawai'i's lush tropical foliage requires a lot of rain, yet drought is not unheard of—there was a prolonged period of drought in the late 1990s. The state's heaviest rains are brought by storms between October and April. Fortunately, most local rain showers are short, except in the upper reaches of valleys where the rain clouds never leave for long. Downtown Honolulu has on rare occasions had as much as 17 inches of rainfall in a single day, though its annual average is only 24 inches. The windward areas get far more rain than their leeward counterparts.

The Waikīkī district, on O'ahu's south shore, has among the fairest weather patterns in the islands—a fact that has contributed greatly to its popularity. There have been only a few damaging storms in Hawai'i, the most devastating in recent years being Hurricane 'Iniki ("strong wind"), in September 1992. 'Iniki hit the island of Kaua'i dead on with winds measuring up to 175 m.p.h. and left behind a path of destruction and property loss estimated at $1.6 billion. Hurricane Iwa in 1982 brought gusts of 100 m.p.h. to the islands.

While most natural disaster–type events such as hurricanes and tsunamis and even volcanic flows are usually predicted well in advance, the one natural event that is unpredictable is a tsunami caused by an earthquake in the immediate area. If you happen to be near the coast and you feel the earth start to shake, leave immediately for higher ground. This means run, and don't stop for anything. Such disasters are rare—just one or two in a century—but they can happen.

Time *and* Daylight

BECAUSE OF HAWAI'I'S TROPICAL LOCATION, the length of daylight doesn't vary greatly from one time of year to the next, and so Hawai'i has never felt a need to save daylight time. Hawai'i Standard Time is in effect year round. In June, with the longest days, the sun rises about 5:45 A.M. and sets about 7 P.M. In the shorter days of December, sunrise is about 7 A.M. and sunset about 5:45 P.M.

Hawai'i Standard Time is 5 hours behind New York, 4 hours behind Chicago, 3 hours behind Denver, and 2 hours behind San Francisco. It is also 11 hours behind London, 19 hours behind Tokyo, 20 hours behind Sydney, and 22 hours behind Auckland and Suva. Add an hour to all of these when daylight savings time is in effect elsewhere.

The popular local phrase "Hawaiian time" simply means "late."

For the current time on O'ahu, call 983-3211.

The Hawai'i state flag.

State Flag *and* Anthem

THE HAWAI'I STATE FLAG has served kingdom, republic, and state. It was designed sometime prior to 1816 for King Kamehameha I, who had been presented with a British Union Jack in 1794 by Captain George Vancouver. It is said that Kamehameha combined the Union Jack, found in the upper-left quadrant of Hawai'i's flag, with the stripes of the United States flag so that pirates at sea might mistake Hawaiian ships for either British or American and allow them to pass without incident. The eight horizontal stripes represent the archipelago's eight main islands.

Hawai'i Pono'ī

Hawai'i pono'ī,
Nānā i kou mō'ī,
Ka lani ali'i,
Ke ali'i.

Makua lani ē,
Kamehameha ē,
Na kāua e pale
Me ka ihe.

Hawai'i's own,
Look to your king,
The royal chief,
The chief.

Royal father,
Kamehameha,
We shall defend
With spears.

—King David Kalākaua, 1876

Hawai'i's state anthem, "Hawai'i Pono'ī," is its former national anthem and was written by King David Kalākaua in 1876, with music by Henry Berger, conductor of the Royal Hawaiian Band. Kalākaua was a gifted writer, musician, and *bon vivant* who reigned from 1874 to 1891. "Hawai'i Pono'ī" is still sung at ballgames and public assemblies.

The flamboyant King David Kalākaua, known as the Merrie Monarch, in the military dress he so loved.

Language

English became the common language of Hawaiian commerce very early in the era of immigration and economic investment by Americans and other foreigners. And so it has remained. The missionaries made sweeping and now irreversible changes in the Hawaiian language when they hurriedly transliterated and transcribed it for print in order to produce Bibles. Subsequent efforts to suppress the native tongue were very successful. By the second half of the 20th century, only a few hundred native speakers were left, most of whom were either very old or from Ni'ihau. However, a strong grass-roots movement to save the language has taken hold, and a few schools even offer Hawaiian-language immersion programs.

Virtually everyone in the islands today speaks the American variety of English, with a few local variations on the theme. Perhaps the most important variation for tourists is the local way of giving directions. The cardinal points of the compass on an island are far less relevant than the obvious "toward the mountain" and "toward the sea." A contracted form of the Hawaiian words for these directions is universally used in Hawai'i. "Toward the upland *(uka)*" is *mauka;* "toward the sea *(kai)*" is *makai*. For the other directions, major landmarks are used. On the island of O'ahu, they are Diamond Head and *'ewa* (for the town of 'Ewa, past Pearl Harbor).

Some people have difficulty with Hawaiian place names and street names. The Hawaiian language is beautiful and only looks intimidating to non-Polynesians who are not accustomed to seeing so many vowels in a row. Basically, if you just pronounce all the letters individually, you'll be fine. The glottal stop (written ') is a pause created by stopping between vowel sounds; for example, a double "o" is pronounced like "oh-oh" in English. In Hawaiian, this is called an *'okina*. Just stop talking, then start immediately again. The macron (written as a long mark over a

The Hawaiian hand wave, with the thumb and little finger extended and the three middle fingers folded to the palm, called the *shaka*, is a unique way of greeting, as common here as waving.

vowel), called a *kahakō* in Hawaiian, simply means that the vowel is held a little longer. The meaning of many words varies according to the presence or absence of a *kahakō*.

Consonants are pronounced the same as in English except that "w" sounds like "v" when it immediately precedes a final single vowel and occasionally at other times. Vowels are pronounced as in Spanish or Italian (ah, eh, ee, oh, oo). The vowel combinations—ai, ae, ao, au, ei, eu, oi, and ou—are stressed on the first member and sounded as single units, though the second vowel in the set is truly pronounced and not lost in the combination.

Multisyllabic words are almost always accented or stressed on the next-to-last syllable. No matter how many times you hear it differently along the tourist trail, the very special and wonderfully soft Hawaiian word "aloha" is not correctly pronounced with the accent on the last syllable.

You will often see Hawaiian words written without the *kahakō* or *'okina*. This was the custom of English-speaking people who first transcribed the language and was common practice until fairly recently. The markings are necessary for correct pronunciation of many words and for discerning between similarly spelled words with quite different meanings.

The other feature of local language that visitors are bound to encounter is Hawai'i's own brand of pidgin English. It is spiced with words from the rich linguistic heritage brought by people of many lands, but, basically, it is English with a bit of Hawaiian, and, if you listen carefully, you'll catch on. The idiom and the lilt are peculiar to Hawai'i, but the pronunciation of most words is recognizable.

A list of commonly used Hawaiian and pidgin English words along with their meanings is in the glossary at the end of this book.

Troubles *in* Paradise

THERE ARE FEW WORRIES in our island paradise, but wise travelers should be aware of a few things that could possibly cause annoyance or difficulty during their stay.

Unfortunately, on O'ahu theft tops the list. Anyone leaving belongings unattended on the beach is inviting their removal. Parked cars are particularly preyed upon, especially obvious rental cars. Valuables are not safe even when locked in the glove compartment or trunk. Camping areas may also be subject to hostile invasion, so camping alone is not recommended; nor is hiking alone, especially, sad to say, if you are a woman. Purse-snatching has become an annoying and sometimes dangerous method of theft in recent years, even in broad daylight. Be especially vigilant in shopping centers, parking lots, and parks, where distracted tourists are easy prey for bold purse-snatchers.

You might be offered incredible bargains for dinner shows, tours, car rentals, and other attractive propositions. The bargains are real, but in exchange for the savings you may be required to attend a sales presentation for timeshare condominium vacation units. Most of these are an hour or more in duration, and the saving is often well worth the time spent. The catch is that there is a high-pressured sales pitch. Don't be intimidated into buying something you don't want.

Ladies of the Night congregate in several areas of Waikīkī. They are harmless, just practicing their trade.

FROM *"Glamour's Gone"* BY Don Blanding

If all the lingering sweetness of white ginger blooms
has lost its subtle thrill . . .
if scented moonlight, vibrant with the throbbing song
of hot native voices can not raise the rhythm of your
heart one beat . . .
. . . .
if all these things have lost their power . . . for they
are not gone . . . then romance is dead, beauty is a
hag, love is an idle tale, blood can know no sultry
fevers of desire . . .
and glamour's gone from Hawaii
and from all the world . . .
for you!

So wrote poet and artist Don Blanding in *Vagabond's House,* a book of poems about Hawai'i published in 1928. This poem is addressed "to a Tourist Who Could Find No Lure or Charm in Hawaii." Blanding, a native of Oklahoma, moved to the Honolulu of his dreams in 1921 and quickly established himself as the islands' poet laureate. He published over fifteen books, mostly of sentimental poems with his own deco-inspired illustrations.

island *geography, history, environment*

Fairly recently in the history of the Earth (only 25 million years ago), a series of cracks began to open in the ocean floor of the north Pacific. In tumultuous explosions followed by fiery rivers of magma and molten lava, land began to build up underneath the surface of the sea. In time, the land broke the surface and lay barren and exposed to winds and the pounding sea. The rise and fall of ice caps thousands of miles away helped raise or lower the level of the sea. Still the land remained, buffeted by winds, clawed by seas that broke over the exposed shoreline. Then there was a time of quiet.

When the Polynesians arrived in the Hawaiian islands, they brought their own versions of how the land came to be. In one account, a mischievous Polynesian demigod named Māui fished the land up from the bottom of the ocean.

Māui had gone fishing in the vast ocean with his brothers. When they were far from their own island, Māui told his brothers to turn around and paddle slowly back toward their home. He gave them strict instructions not to look back at him and to paddle with all their strength when he gave the word. Then he cast his fishhook into the water. The brothers felt a powerful pull and, forgetting Māui's words, turned around to see what he had caught. To their amazement, he was pulling up islands. "See what you have done!" cried Māui angrily. "I was going to pull up a great land, but because you stopped paddling I have only these islands."

Dietrich Varez, *Māui the Fisherman,* linocut.

Right: Ka'a'awa Beach and Valley, windward O'ahu.

Page 28: Lei made from vines, flowers and leaves, seeds, and *kukui* nuts.

Page 29: Louis Choris, *Vue du Port Hanarourou,* 1816. From his *Voyage Pittoresque autour du Monde* (Paris, 1822).

Today the islands are but the tops of volcanic mountains, enormous when measured from the ocean floor up. They lie across 1,523 miles of ocean and are made up almost entirely of lava.

Hawai'i is uniquely isolated at about 1,000 miles from its nearest neighbors—the Line Islands at the equator to the south and the Marshall Islands to the southwest. Nothing but ocean lies between Hawai'i and California, 2,390 miles to the east-northeast; Japan, 3,850 miles to the west-northwest; and Alaska, 2,800 miles to the north. The Marquesas—from which at least some of the early Polynesian migrants came—are 2,400 miles to the south-southeast.

The Hawaiian archipelago includes 132 islands, reefs, and shoals strewn across the Tropic of Cancer—from Kure Atoll in the north to Nīhoa in the south. Many of the northwestern islands are uncharted, and reefs can rip out the bottoms of unsuspecting ships. The 84 million underwater acres of the northwestern islands are the largest nature preserve in the U.S., with fishing and other activities limited to help conserve the area's coral reefs and wildlife.

A new island, Lo'ihi—which means "prolonged in time"—is being created by volcanic eruptions southeast of Hawai'i island; visitors ten thousand or so years from now are likely to find that island. All the islands are included in the state of Hawai'i except the Midway Islands, which are administered by the U.S. Fish and Wildlife Service. Hawai'i's major islands share their tropical latitudes with such urban centers as Mexico City, Havana, Mecca, Calcutta, Hanoi, and Hong Kong. The 158th meridian west, which passes through O'ahu's Pearl Harbor, also crosses Point Barrow on Alaska's north coast, Atiu Island in the South Pacific's Cook Islands, and Cape Colbeck near the edge of Antarctica's Ross Ice Shelf.

While Hawai'i's land surface adds up to only 6,425 square miles (at that, still larger than Connecticut, Delaware, or Rhode Island), the archipelago, including its territorial waters, covers a total of about 654,500 square miles—an area considerably larger than Alaska and more than twice the size of Texas.

Cultural History

IN ANONYMITY AND OUT OF ASIA, the ancestors of the Hawaiians began millennia ago to work their way across the vast, trackless Pacific. They journeyed from central Asia to Southeast Asia, poised on the brink of a great adventure: the people of the land were about to become the people of the sea and ultimately the people of "many islands," for that is what the word Polynesia means. As they moved, they changed, altering their gods to the demands of new places, subtly reworking their myths and legends and genealogies to make them compatible with the enormous seas and the evolution of their canoes. Their mode of dress changed; their physical statures altered as they adapted to life on, and in, the water.

At some point during these long and epic voyages, perhaps as long ago as AD 400, the Polynesians stood offshore in the lee of a group of islands at the apex of a triangle formed by New Zealand, Tahiti, and Hawaiʻi. Some anonymous Polynesian sailor would have shouted excitedly to the rest of the crew and pointed out islands that would mark the crowning achievement of the long voyages. That sailor and the rest of the crew are believed to have been from the Marquesas island group far to the southeast, though new theories as to the origins of the original settlers are still being put forth.

Because the windward sides of the islands have numerous rivers, abundant rainfall, and fertile lands, the earliest settlements are believed to have been there. However, excavations in Waipahu, in the vicinity of Pearl Harbor, indicate that leeward Oʻahu's well-watered lowlands attracted settlers by AD 600, very early in Hawaiʻi's history.

More voyages back and forth followed. One day, a new group of energetic islanders, the Polynesians from Kahiki (probably Tahiti), made the journey. In all likelihood they came to escape war or famine. Or perhaps it was merely the

Dietrich Varez, *Waʻa Kaulua,* linocut. Capable of withstanding heavy seas, the *waʻa kaulua,* or double-hulled canoe, was used by Polynesians for long voyages of discovery and migration.

dominance of a strong, aggressive race that led to their voyage. Whatever the cause, by about AD 1200 the people from Kahiki had surfaced as the unquestioned masters in a magnificent new home. They gave it a name: Hawai'i. Later some would say the name had no significance, while others believed it was a variation of Hawaiki, the legendary homeland of all Polynesians.

Other newcomers had made landfall here over the centuries. Seeds came in the bellies of birds; coconuts washed ashore on the beaches and took hold. Windblown pollen and insects bumped up against the islands' high mountains. Natural springs and rivers formed.

Left to right: bananas, bamboo, breadfruit, and *kukui* nuts.

The Polynesians added variety to the indigenous plants, introducing bananas, sweet potatoes, bamboo, ginger, yams, breadfruit, and *kukui* trees. They also brought dogs, chickens, and pigs to Hawai'i. In time, a new civilization developed as the settlers adapted to their new home.

The life of the average Polynesian Hawaiian was ordered, based on major rituals and practices brought to Hawai'i by the Polynesians. The *ali'i,* or royalty, were absolute masters. A second group, the *kāhuna,* or priests, cast a long shadow, dealing in both the natural and supernatural worlds. As *kāhuna,* the priests were known to talk with the gods and interpret their powers. The ordinary men and women were *maka'aīnana,* in many cases born to a time and place that locked them into a pattern from which they could not escape.

But it was not an altogether grim life. The *maka'aīnana* lived in a healthy, uncrowded, and stunningly beautiful archipelago where they arose to brilliant mornings and retired awash in sunsets of great beauty. They had their *makahiki,* a festival time following the fall harvest when they played traditional games, and they revered their old people, the *kūpuna.* They cared about the family unit and about their *'ohana,* or extended family. By the time Westerners arrived, Hawaiian society had become complex and colorful, yet infused with a strict sense of order.

The great English explorer and navigator Captain James Cook came upon these remote north Pacific islands on January 18, 1778. European diseases and Western weapons followed, dramatically changing the lives of the Hawaiians.

Captain James Cook.

The islands impressed Cook, who was surprised to find that the inhabitants spoke a variation of the languages he had heard earlier in the South Pacific. He wrote of the natives' generosity and worried over their tendency to steal; he watched with both understanding and dismay as native girls, the *wāhine,* came aboard his two ships. He knew such liaisons with his men were inevitable, but he also knew some of his sailors were infected with venereal disease.

Cook was killed by Hawaiians on the beach at Kealakekua, on the southernmost island, after a misunderstanding. Had he lived, he would have seen diseases decimate the Hawaiian population from an estimated 800,000 in 1778 to fewer than 40,000 a century later. And by 1878 other forces had diminished the influence of the Hawaiians in their own land.

In Kamehameha's lifetime, Hawaiian power reached its zenith. Tough and energetic, intelligent and implacable, Kamehameha had inherited as his personal god the war god Kūkā'ilimoku from his uncle, Kalani'ōpu'u, ranking chief at Kealakekua. He also inherited a tall frame and a tactician's approach to problem solving. When Kamehameha saw the superior firepower of European guns and the logic of European tactics in war, he immediately appropriated English advisors and set out to buy guns. He wanted to become the person who linked the islands, each under one or more chieftains, into a true kingdom with himself as its head. By craft and treachery, by bravery and a modicum of luck, Kamehameha fulfilled his dream. A series of bloody wars and a bit of diplomacy with the king of Kaua'i brought all the islands under his rule.

Under Kamehameha, trade and interaction with the West were extensive. When he allowed, ships from abroad filled Hawaiian harbors. But he also was careful to maintain the old ways among his people. The *kapu* system that allowed the *ali'i* to

**Louis Choris,
*Kamehameha in
Red Vest*, 1816,
watercolor. Honolulu
Academy of Arts, gift
of Edith B. Williams.**

lay an edict over any person, place, or thing remained in effect at Kamehameha's death. If the Hawaiians did not fully understand the concept of nationhood, they certainly understood the power of authority. Kamehameha ruled as much by force of personality as by force of arms.

Upon his death on May 8, 1819, at the end of years of peace and stability, Kamehameha was buried in a secret place on the island of Hawai'i. It is a secret that endures. Today no one knows the burial site of the greatest of all Hawaiians.

Almost immediately Kamehameha's influence began to dissipate. A week after the king's death, his favorite wife, Ka'ahumanu, declared Kamehameha's son, Liholiho, the next ruler, adding, however, that she would rule with him. In time she pressured Liholiho into abandoning the *kapu* system and the old religion, and momentous changes inevitably followed. About the time Kamehameha died, word flashed around the maritime nations that there were enormous herds of whales in the Pacific. The news galvanized seamen, who knew the Atlantic grounds held fewer and fewer whales, and Hawai'i assumed a new importance. Within three years, up to sixty whaling ships at a time anchored in Honolulu Harbor alone, and the waters of Lahaina on Maui were dark with the timbers of ships. Sailors came to rely on Hawai'i's ports for women, grog, and provisions. There was, they said, "no God west of the Horn," and they seemed bent on proving it. Whaling became an important industry to Hawai'i; whaling men became a prime nuisance.

Whaling meant money. Goods were transshipped, ships were repaired, and the activity attracted nonwhaling merchant vessels as well. Whaling also brought bewilderment and confusion to the *maka'āinana,* who saw the sailors indulging themselves without punishment. By now the Hawaiians had no strong system of their own to turn to for faith, and they were finding it difficult to make sense of their lives and times.

A second group of foreigners, or *haole,* brought more than a little confusion to the Hawaiians as well. The missionaries had arrived in 1819 with their stern visages and rigid lifestyles as well as their talk of Trinity and damnation. Between the whalers and the missionaries, battles raged over the land, bodies, and souls of the native Hawaiians.

In their way, the missionaries turned out to be as tough as the oak planking of the whaling ships. Arriving first on the brig *Thaddeus* on October 23, 1819, the missionaries found Hawaiian society in chaos following Kamehameha's death. They also found a dearth of new ideas and moved quickly to fill the vacuum. Liholiho came to be regarded as a friend. The missionaries converted Keōpūolani, the queen mother, then the powerful chiefess Kapiʻolani. Within two years, the missionaries had created a written form of Hawaiian, printed Bibles, and opened schools. They became a powerful force in the islands, and their descendants would become powerful leaders of Hawaiʻi society, business, and industry.

Hawaiʻi attracted more and more foreigners. Americans, Britons, French, Germans, and Scots traveled to Hawaiʻi, drawn to the image of a tropical paradise, held by the opportunities they found.

In the United States in 1859, an oil well went into production in Pennsylvania, signaling the end of the whaling industry, with whales no longer the only source of the precious oil for which they were slaughtered. War broke out between the Union and the Confederacy, and many whaling ships were pressed into service as merchant-men, decreasing markedly the whaling fleet. Finally, in the fall of 1871, ice trapped thirty-three whaling ships in Arctic waters north of the Bering Strait and remorse-lessly crushed the last hope of a whaling industry.

In Hawaiʻi, new industries flourished, one of them sugar. Planters needed cheap agricultural labor and had to look to foreign countries because diseases had vastly reduced the Hawaiian population. Plantation owners turned first to China, then Japan, then Portugal, the Philippines, and other places. This marked the beginning of Hawaiʻi as a multiethnic society.

Land ownership, which before Cook's arrival was reserved only for the *aliʻi,* became an increasingly perplexing problem. The Hawaiian government ulti-mately gave up rights to all property except certain lands set aside for the king and the government. Commoners now were permitted to buy land, and foreigners could lease it. The *haole,* having come from civilizations that prized land ownership, reached for as much as they could get. The average Hawaiian, at sea with all the attendant bureaucracy, just got more confused. On the one hand, he could lease or cultivate his land, rights he never before possessed, while on the other hand, it became easy to sell land to the *haole.* The Great Mahele, the movement that began in the 1840s with attempts to tie the Hawaiians closer to their land by reappor-tioning it among various groups, ended in their losing it in great quantities.

In the 1890s conflicts grew between Queen Liliʻuokalani, destined to be the last Hawaiian monarch, and a group of businessmen who objected to the queen's push for a new constitution that would have restored much of the Hawaiian royalty's lost powers. On January 17, 1893, the monarchy was toppled, and the Republic of Hawaiʻi was formed with a new constitution.

Queen Kapiʻolani.

Five years later, on August 12, 1898, spectators jammed the area around ʻIolani Palace in Honolulu to hear the Hawaiian national anthem played and watch the Hawaiian flag slowly lowered to the ground and the American flag raised in its place. America's national anthem was played, and Sanford Ballard Dole, a leader in the monarchy's overthrow, was sworn in as first chief executive officer of the Territory of Hawaiʻi, a possession of the United States.

Stability and social change followed. A society emerged in which racial groups were proud of their ancestry but also proud of their Americanization. It seemed there was a little Hawaiian blood in almost everyone. For more than four decades, the largely agricultural society went about its business, attracted a few visitors, and never dreamed it would be the target of a sudden attack that became the impetus for the United States to enter World War II.

Below: The USS *Nevada* under attack by Japanese aircraft, Pearl Harbor, December 7, 1941.

Opposite: Barbed wire barricades the beach at the Royal Hawaiian Hotel.

On Sunday, December 7, 1941, Japanese aircraft swarmed in from a fleet that had crept unseen and unheard across the Pacific to a point north of the islands. The devastating raid on Pearl Harbor plunged America into the war and brought quick changes to Hawaiʻi. Martial law was declared, a military government was installed in ʻIolani Palace, and thousands of young servicemen turned up in the islands. Some never left. The number of intermarriages soared. By the end of the war, the whole fabric of Hawaiʻi society had changed with the interweaving of the new *haole* immigrants. The end of the war also saw the return of the young *nisei*—the second-generation Japanese—who had fought bravely for their new country and who now thirsted for political power. They were determined to put an end to the long rule of the entrenched Republican establishment of the day.

The Japanese attack on Pearl Harbor on December 7, 1941, the date that would "live in infamy," in the words of President Franklin D. Roosevelt, startled Hawai'i islanders in the early morning hours. By the time Japanese planes had withdrawn, nineteen ships had been sunk or damaged and 3,000 Americans, including 68 O'ahu residents, had lost their lives. During the attack, Howell M. Forgy, chaplain on the U.S. cruiser *New Orleans*, kept up the spirits of the sweating sailors with the phrase "praise the Lord and pass the ammunition," words that would become a popular wartime song.

To ward off invasions by sea, barbed wire was stretched along O'ahu's beaches. Martial law was declared, and all authority was turned over to the military. For three years the people of Hawai'i lived without civil liberties. Every person was fingerprinted, and the property of Japanese aliens was confiscated by the military. Letters sent to the mainland were examined by military censors, and everyone was under suspicion. Every word printed in the newspapers or announced on the radio had to be cleared by the censors.

Nearly 2,000 Japanese Americans were arrested by military intelligence and sent to internment camps on the mainland for the duration. Meanwhile, Japanese allowed to remain in Hawai'i volunteered for the war effort, with the men of the Japanese American 100th Battalion establishing themselves as loyal and brave soldiers. Among its members was Daniel J. Inouye, who has represented Hawai'i in the U.S. House and Senate since 1959.

On August 14, 1945, when the people of Hawai'i learned that the war was over, there were wild celebrations in the city of Honolulu. However, the war had irrevocably altered life in Hawai'i, bringing an influx of *haole* to the islands and politicizing the Japanese American population. In 1988 the United States Congress issued a formal apology to Japanese Americans who had been detained in the camps.

With their GI Bill for education, the veterans went off to colleges and came back as lawyers, doctors, accountants, and other professionals. They were politically oriented and hard working. Their enthusiasm inspired other young men in Hawai'i equally fired by ambition. In 1954, in a thunderous victory, the Democrats, led by the veterans, took over the top political positions in Hawai'i and forced a new equality on the establishment.

In another five years statehood marked the beginning of still another era of change. Statehood meant stability for investments. The advent of the jet plane, a surge in the influx of tourists, and international publicity about America's newest state turned Hawai'i into a magnet for those seeking a new life in a paradisiacal setting. Its capital, Honolulu, is today a thriving business and academic center—the gateway for commerce and cultural exchange with Asia, Australia, and the South Pacific.

Tourism rapidly edged out agriculture as the primary source of revenue, which it remains to this day. Nearly 7 million visitors are drawn to Hawai'i's islands each year, spending over $10 billion a year. About a quarter of the local labor force has jobs in the visitor industry; by contrast, agriculture—which once dominated Hawai'i's economy —today claims only 2 percent of the total workforce.

O'ahu, *the* Capital Island

O'AHU IS THE CAPITAL ISLE, but this was not always so. In ancient times, the island of Hawai'i—known today as the Big Island—was preeminent in island affairs, both in contemporary life and in legend and oral tradition. The conquering Kamehameha was from that island and ruled his newly unified kingdom from there much of the time. In the 1820s, the nation's official capital was established at Lahaina, Maui, where the Pacific fleets of the whaling industry based their activities. The seat of national government was moved to Honolulu, O'ahu, in 1845, and this city was officially declared the capital in 1850.

Three times as many people live on O'ahu as on all the other islands combined. Governed by one mayor as the City and County of Honolulu, the county includes not only all of O'ahu but all of the far-flung northwestern islands except Midway.

Waikīkī

Waikīkī has always been popular. Prior to the arrival of Europeans, it was the center of power for the ruling chiefs of O'ahu. Its reefs provided fish, shellfish, octopus, sea urchins, and other marine delicacies; the marshy inland floodplain provided perfect conditions for wetland agriculture; the wide, sandy shoreline was perfect

This thatch-roofed house, the beach residence of Kamehameha V, circa 1863, is today the site of the Royal Hawaiian Hotel.

Below: Hula dancers practice with *pūʻili*, slit-ended bamboo sticks used as rattles, circa 1930s.

for beaching canoes; its surf was ideal for the most Hawaiian of recreations; and its weather was idyllic.

With the advent of European trade via large deep-draught sailing ships, Waikīkī was left to the farmers, and commerce and government shifted toward Honolulu Harbor, where European vessels could dock with far greater ease in its calm, sheltered waters.

However, Waikīkī remained a favored spot for the local aristocracy to escape the bustle of urban life, and well-heeled immigrant merchants and planters followed suit. Cottages and, later, more substantial dwellings became clustered along the Waikīkī shoreline, and some of these eventually began to offer paid lodging to visitors.

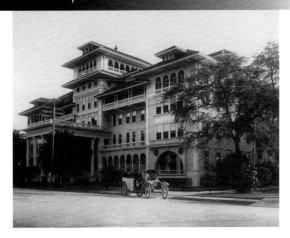

Waikīkī's first resort hotel—the now venerable Moana—opened its doors to guests in 1901, followed in 1927 by the "pink palace" of the Royal Hawaiian. The pair were for decades the second most prominent feature in the district, both dwarfed by the looming brow of Laeʻahi, now called Diamond Head.

The most substantial changes to the face of Waikīkī were made possible by the construction of the Ala Wai Canal, a drainage channel that converted the former marshes *mauka* of Kalākaua Avenue into terra firma. Waikīkī's centuries-old agricultural system had been made possible by the Kuʻekaunahi, ʻĀpuakēhau, and Piʻinaio streams, flowing to the sea from the Pālolo, Mānoa, and Makiki valleys and crossing the beach at points near the present end of ʻŌhua Avenue, between the Moana and Royal Hawaiian hotels, and at the present site of Fort DeRussy Beach.

Opposite top left: The Moana Hotel, circa 1910.

Opposite top right: The original Royal Hawaiian, demolished in 1926, was located on Hotel Street in downtown Honolulu.

Left: A surfer surveys the Waikiki shoreline, circa 1930s. From left to right are the Royal Hawaiian, the Outrigger Canoe Club (now in a location closer to Diamond Head), and the Moana.

Plant *and* Animal Life

ABUNDANT, HIGH-QUALITY WATER AND CLEAN AIR bless this environmental wonderland. Plant life in Hawai'i also is a naturalist's dream. More than 2,500 kinds of plants grow only in Hawai'i. Because of Hawai'i's long isolation, evolution of

plant life was rapid and diverse. Conversely, many plants that are found throughout the Pacific were not present in Hawai'i until man brought them—such as the banyan, *kalo,* and figs. Most of the myriad orchids that grace Hawai'i today came from other places. Of the many varieties found here, there is only one native palm tree.

Because Hawai'i is so far from other land, very few animals arrived under their own power. The hoary bat *(Lasiurus)* is an exception. The Hawaiian bat is smaller than its distant relatives but strong enough to fly long distances. The Hawaiian monk seal *(Monachus schauinslandi),* a species related to seals in the Caribbean and the Mediterranean, also arrived from afar. It may have been the first mammal to live in Hawai'i and today is found nowhere else. The Polynesian rat *(Rattus)* stowed away aboard Polynesian voyaging canoes and, like the Polynesians themselves, originated in Asia. The Polynesians valued the domestic dog *(Canis)* as pet, food source, and a part of religious rituals. By all accounts, the Polynesian dog was highly dependent and nonaggressive; as new breeds of dogs came to the islands, the original version disappeared.

Above: The *nēnē,* Hawai'i's state bird.

Below: The monk seal is native to Hawai'i.

The importation of pigs *(Sus scrofa)* to the islands turned out to be a mixed blessing. They were an important food source, but when they began to run wild in the lush forests, they became a nuisance. Today feral pigs are blamed for destroying much of the islands' watershed areas by digging up the forest floor and the aquifer, the natural filter through which a lot of island water flows.

Captain Cook released goats in Hawai'i, and others who came after him brought sheep, cattle, and horses. These large animals were extremely destructive to Hawaiian plants. By 1900 many native plants below roughly the 1,200-foot level had been eradicated, some replaced by heartier species. Today these large animals are considered an asset, not a menace, except for wild goats, which continue to ravage remote mountain areas.

Hawai'i's isolation also gave rise to a unique bird life. Today, however, more than half the native birds have become extinct in Hawaiʻi. They have succumbed to hunters, to introduced predators such as the swift mongooses brought to Hawaiʻi to combat rats, and to urban encroachment.

Many birds live near streams, marshes, or ponds; the largest number inhabit the deep forests. Perhaps the most dramatic to watch are the long-winged seabirds. Twenty-two different species spend their nonbreeding time flying over the open ocean, scavenging for food and resting on the water, coming back to Hawaiʻi to breed. Millions of them nest in the sanctuary of uninhabited small islands northwest of the occupied islands of Hawaiʻi. Some birds that were introduced to the islands from elsewhere and thrive here include pigeons, doves, mynahs, cardinals, and sparrows.

The state bird is the *nēnē (Branta sandvicensis),* a goose that lives high on the rugged slopes of the volcanoes. The *nēnē* has battled back from near extinction. Many of Hawaiʻi's native birds are found only on specific islands; the *ʻio,* or hawk *(Buteo solitarius),* for example, is found only on the island of Hawaiʻi.

Long before any land mammals came, before plants or even birds, marine mammals swam in the surrounding seas. In fact, the ancestors of some of the whales and dolphins now found in Hawaiian waters may have been here even before the islands arose from the sea. They include the humpback whales, which are seasonal visitors, several varieties of dolphins, killer whales, sperm whales—in all, at least twenty types. On Oʻahu, whales may be sighted from November through the end of April off Makapuʻu and Koko Head on the south shore and off Kaʻena Point on the northwest side of the island. Whale-watching cruises in season are a favorite activity.

Humpback whales ply Hawaiʻi's waters from November through May. Each whale has a distinctive tail fluke, visible when they breach, or leap out of the water, and individual whales can be identified from their markings.

Other marine life became important to the Hawaiians not only for food but in rituals, legends, myths, and *mele* (chants). Hawaiian fishermen had their own god, Kuʻulakai, and small *koʻa* (fishing shrines) near the ocean were dedicated to the god. The shrines often were no more than stacked rocks, but they were significant to the fishermen, who offered the first of their catch at the *koʻa*. A fish—particularly a shark—that frequented the waters near their homes was often considered an *ʻaumakua,* or family god, by the Hawaiians.

Each wave of newcomers brought its own fishing mystique, taste, and style. Today the fishing practices of Hawaiʻi's people reflect the state's multiracial populace and preserve the islands' reputation as a top marine center.

exploring **o'ahu**

The magnificent
Ko'olau Mountains,
at Kualoa Ranch.

*T*here are many sights to be seen on O'ahu, too many for just a day
or so. Here we present an overview of the places you may want to visit so that you
can select those that especially appeal to you. Descriptions follow a counterclockwise
sequence around the island, beginning with Waikīkī and Diamond Head, followed
by greater Honolulu—which encompasses downtown, Chinatown, and Nu'uanu
Valley—then around to the windward coast, to the north shore, to the leeward
coast, and back to Honolulu by way of the Leilehua Plateau, the last stronghold
of pineapple cultivation on O'ahu.

As you travel,
watch for the
warrior signs put
up by the Hawai'i
Visitors Bureau to
mark historic and
cultural sites (above).
Presumably, the signs
were designed to
point toward the
attraction, but
many have ended
up pointing in the
opposite direction.

Pages 46–47:
Kahana Bay,
where the north
shore begins.

Sacred sites of interest to visitors include memorials and cemeteries as well
as distinctive houses of worship of a diversity of religious and spiritual traditions.
The houses of worship mentioned in this section are of particular historical or
architectural interest.

Hawai'i was the first state in the nation to adopt an Art in Public Places program,
by which one percent of construction appropriations are set aside to provide funding
for the acquisition of works of art. Since 1967, the state's buildings have been
enhanced by visual arts in all media, especially those expressive of the multicultural
heritage of Hawai'i. We have included references to the more easily accessible artworks,
including earlier commissions, in our descriptions of buildings.

Larger museums are listed in a separate section (see pages 143–51), since visiting
museums generally commands large expenditures of time, often not available during
a sightseeing tour. Hiking, another means of exploration, is covered under Activities
(see pages 197–207), though several shorter walks are included in this section.

O'ahu Facts and Figures

- With a land area of about 600 square miles, O'ahu is just a little more than half the size of the state of Rhode Island, which is 1,067 square miles.

- The population of O'ahu according to the 2000 census is 876,156, making up 72 percent of Hawai'i's total population.

- Caucasians make up 25 percent of O'ahu's population, Japanese 21 percent, and native Hawaiians 16 percent.

- The most recent volcanic eruption on O'ahu was 1.3 million years ago.

- At 4,003 feet, Mount Ka'ala, in the Wai'anae Mountains, is O'ahu's highest peak.

- Waves over 50 feet high have occasionally been observed on O'ahu's north shore.

- The average temperature on O'ahu is between 84°F during the day and 70°F at night.

- There are forty golf courses on O'ahu; many consider the Ko'olau Golf Club the world's most challenging course.

- The USS Arizona Memorial at Pearl Harbor is Hawai'i's most often visited site.

the island of o'ahu

Sunset Beach

Pūpūkea

Waimea Bay

Waimea Falls Park

Ka'ena Point

Mokulē'ia

Dillingham Airfield

HALE'IWA

930

83

99

803

Yokohama

Mākua

930

Wai'anae Mountains

Schofield Barracks

Mākaha

93

WAI'ANAE

75

Lualualei

Mā'ili

780

0   Miles   4

0   Km   4

NĀNĀKULI

H1

Kō 'Olina

93

KAPOLEI

N

Barbers Point

Turtle
Bay

*Kahuku
Point*

83

Kahuku

Mālaekahana

LĀʻIE

*Polynesian
Cultural Center*

Koʻolau Mountains

Hauʻula

Punaluʻu

Crouching Lion

83

*Dole
Pineapple
Pavilion*

KAʻAʻAWA

WAHIAWĀ

Kualoa Point

*Wheeler
Army Airfield*

Waiāhole

Mōkapu Point

MILILANI

H2

KAHALUʻU

Heʻeia
Park

*Marine Corps
Base Hawaiʻi*

83

99

830

H3

H1

KĀNEʻOHE

Kāneʻohe
Bay

Kailua

*Pearl
Harbor*

63

83

Lanikai

90

61

KAILUA

78

Bellows Air Force Station

H1

WAIMĀNALO

ʻEWA

76

*Keʻehi
Lagoon*

92

ʻEwa

*Sand
Island*

HONOLULU

H1

HAWAIʻI KAI

72

Makapuʻu Point

*Honolulu
International
Airport*

*Honolulu
Harbor*

Waikīkī

*Koko
Head*

Hanauma Bay

Diamond Head

Walking Tours

Several groups lead walking tours of the downtown area. A 2-hour tour sponsored by the Honolulu chapter of the **American Institute of Architects** (545-4242) concentrates on historic buildings. The **Chinese Chamber of Commerce** (533-3181) and the **Hawai'i Heritage Center** (521-2749) lead tours of Chinatown. Every Thursday, the **Mission Houses Museum** (531-0481) offers 3-hour tours of the historic capitol district. Reservations are necessary for any of these tours.

Reservations are not needed, however, for free Waikīkī tours, weekdays at 9 A.M. and Saturdays at 4:30 P.M. These tours are under the auspices of the **Native Hawaiian Hospitality Association** and focus on significant native sites and events. Meet at the beachside surfboard marker for "Beaches of Waikīkī," on Kalākaua Avenue across from the Honolulu Zoo. The 1.5-hour tour covers historic sites between Kapahulu Avenue and the International Market Place.

Waikīkī *and* Diamond Head

Waikīkī's newest attraction is the state's $350-million **Convention Center** (1801 Kalākaua Avenue; 943-3500), a stunning facility that opened in 1998. With 1.1 million square feet of total space and over 30,000 hotel rooms within a mile radius, the Convention Center aims to draw major events to Hawai'i. Designed to take advantage of Hawai'i's unique environment, the center incorporates native foliage and flowers, terracing, and water fountains in the landscaped courtyards. The work of nineteen of the state's premier artists was commissioned for the walls and courtyards, resulting in major artworks that complement the striking architecture. The building is open from 8 A.M. to 5 P.M. weekdays, unless an event precludes visitors; there is no admission fee. Docents give 1-hour tours of the artwork and building Wednesday and Thursday mornings; call to schedule a tour.

Opposite: Hawai'i Convention Center (built in 1998).

The monumental bronze sculpture in front of the Convention Center is *Gift of Water* by Shige Yamada (b. 1933), who was designated a Living Treasure of Hawai'i in 1993 for his achievements in art. An innovator in the art of ceramics, Yamada taught for thirty years in California, Japan, and Honolulu. In 1988, desiring to devote fulltime to his art, he moved back to his native Maui. Since then he has created several large-scale sculptures in addition to *Gift of Water*, including *Rainbows* on the University of Hawai'i campus and *Māui Releasing the Sun* for the Maui airport at Kahului.

Torch lighting on Kalākaua Avenue.

Right: International Market Place.

Fort DeRussy, established in 1909 as a military reservation at the 'ewa end of Waikīkī, is today primarily a vacation resort area for armed forces personnel (see Hale Koa Hotel, page 262), and the general public is not allowed to use its facilities. Only during World War II, however, was the beach (see Beaches) closed to the public.

The **U.S. Army Museum of Hawai'i** (corner of Kālia and Saratoga Roads; 955-9552), part of the military's Fort DeRussy reserve and recreation complex, is located next to the Hale Koa Hotel and *is* open to the public. The museum occupies the former Battery Randolph, built in 1911, from which a shot was never fired in battle. When the battery had outlived its potential usefulness, it proved almost impossible to destroy the solid structure with its 22-foot-thick walls; the blasts required to do so would have also damaged every other building in the Waikīkī district. Therefore, the Army turned it into a museum, displaying weapons and memorabilia from wars far and wide, from warfare in Hawai'i predating the arrival of Westerners up to the Vietnam War of the mid-20th century.

Also exhibited are some enemy artifacts, such as a Japanese mini-submarine captured at the Panama Canal. For those with an interest in the military history of the United States, this is one place to get an excellent overview. Open Tuesday–Sunday, 10 A.M.–4:15 P.M.; free.

Much of Waikīkī has become a magnet for shoppers. Little of historical or cultural interest remains in the area between Fort DeRussy and the Honolulu Zoo, though it's a great place to window shop and people watch. There are often hula performances in the **Royal Hawaiian Shopping Center** and in the **International Market Place**; at 6:30 each evening Hawaiian youths carrying flaming torches light the torches that line Kalākaua Avenue.

Two historic hotels are of note, the **Royal Hawaiian** (2259 Kalākaua Avenue) and the **Sheraton Moana Surfrider** (2365 Kalākaua Avenue), known as the

Moana. Both have lavish public areas and are well worth a visit. The Royal Hawaiian, the "pink palace" to its many loyal visitors, has been a Waikīkī landmark since its 1927 opening, billed at the time as Hawai'i's "greatest social event in years." It joined the Moana, an elegant four-story colonial-style building designed in 1901 by architect Oliver G. Traphagen, with two parallel wings added in 1918. The two hotels served as the home of well-heeled travelers in Waikīkī until World War II, when the U.S. Navy leased the Royal Hawaiian as a place for sailors and marines to spend their shore leaves. The Moana was the only large Waikīkī hotel to remain open to visitors during the war, though most of its guests were military personnel. The Royal Hawaiian reopened to the public in 1947, and the fiftieth anniversary of that event was celebrated in 1997. The Moana, greatly expanded but with the original building barely changed except for updating of facilities, celebrated its centennial in 2001. The banyan tree that shades the courtyard—scene of Webley Edwards's famous radio show "Hawai'i Calls," which was broadcast from 1935 to 1975—is more than a century old.

Waikiki Beach and hotels.

Below: The Royal Hawaiian Hotel (left) and the Sheraton Moana Surfrider (right).

The Moana from the beach at the old Outrigger Canoe Club, circa 1910.

Opposite: Guests arrive at the Royal Hawaiian, circa 1930s.

"Amid the sounding swash of the surf on the sands of Waikiki, the strains of music and . . . the clinking of glasses of bubbling wine, the beautiful Moana hotel at Waikiki was christened last night. Moana, known far and wide among the Polynesians and to every race in the Pacific ocean as the 'broad expanse of the ocean,' was a fit cognomen for the magnificent hostelry which was dedicated as a resting place for the tourists of the wide, wide world who visit the Paradise of the Pacific.

"Illuminated by the glow of thousands of electric, parti-hued globes, magnificent of exterior and interior and bearing in every detail the stately outlines of the old Colonial period, the new hostelry rivalled even the finest hotels which are to be seen in the most metropolitan cities on the mainland or on the continent. From the highest pinnacle of the observatory lanai, lighted by scores of red, white and blue globes to the basement where were stored amid arctic frosts edibles to pamper the most epicurean of tastes, there was nothing to criticize."

—*Pacific Commercial Advertiser,*
   March 12, 1901

"There was a blending of everything magnificent at the opening of the Royal Hawaiian hotel last night. . . .

"A great palace, thrumming with music. A great palace scintillating with brilliance. A great palace in which the myriad lights of myriad different hues blended into polychrome patterns. A great palace that was invaded by the most brilliant gathering that it has ever been the privilege of Honolulu to witness."

—*Honolulu Advertiser,*
February 2, 1927

Below: New landscaping and water features have "beautified" Waikiki.

Opposite: The Duke Kahanamoku statue, unveiled in 1990, has quickly become a Kūhiō Beach landmark. Located near the spot where beachboys continue to give surf lessons to tourists, the statue is often adorned with fresh lei.

The Waikīkī branch of the First Hawaiian Bank (2181 Kalākaua Avenue) has a 9-by-38-foot fresco by renowned artist **Jean Charlot** (see page 109) depicting *Early Contacts of Hawaii with the Outer World.* One historic building that has managed to avoid destruction is the **Waikīkī Theatre** (2284 Kalākaua Avenue), though its magnificent art deco facade is nearly hidden by the tacky shops constructed in front of it.

Saint Augustine's Catholic Church still sits on Kalākaua Avenue at the corner of 'Ōhua Street, dwarfed on either side by towering hotels. At the back of Saint Augustine's is the small but fascinating **Damien Museum and Archives** (130 'Ōhua Street; 923-2690). The museum chronicles the life of Joseph Damien de Veuster (1840–1889), the "martyr of Moloka'i." Included in the displays are some of Father Damien's possessions and correspondence, photographs of the priest and his charges at Kalaupapa, and a 20-minute video depicting the history of Kalaupapa settlement, where people with Hansen's disease, or leprosy, were sent until 1969, when the Hawai'i state government finally recognized that isolation was an obsolete treatment for the

disease. Open Monday–Friday, 9 A.M.–3 P.M., Saturday, 9 A.M.–noon; free.

Hawai'i's beloved surfer legend and acclaimed Olympic swimmer **Duke Pa'oa Kahanamoku** is memorialized in a bronze statue situated on Kūhiō Beach. At the erection of the statue, many local surfers were distraught at its placement. They felt that it should be facing the water, so that the Duke would be forever looking out to the ocean he so loved.

Nearby, serious chess players vie with one another at chess tables in a beachside pavilion across from the Pacific Beach Hotel. This section of Waikīkī has been "beautified" recently, with the addition of lots of water features and petunias in hanging baskets, a most incongruous touch. The four

Named Duke after his father, who in turn was named after the Duke of Edinburgh, Duke Kahanamoku (1890–1968) grew up with eight brothers and sisters in a home in central Honolulu. He learned to swim at his grandparents' Waikīkī home, where he spent much of his childhood. In 1910, when he was twenty years old, he swam a 50-yard sprint in 23 seconds, and in 1912, as a member of the U.S. swimming team, he brought home the gold at the Olympics and helped put Hawai'i on the international map.

Tall and handsome, the Duke caught the eye of Hollywood, where he lived off and on for twenty years, beginning in 1913. He played bit parts in the movies while he continued to surf in L.A., Australia, and Hawai'i. Once during the summer of 1917 he rode a Waikīkī wave for half a mile, a feat that Waikīkī beachboys still speak of with awe.

In 1933, back in Hawai'i, the Duke operated two Union Oil service stations for "something to do," and in 1936 he began a 26-year political career as sheriff of Honolulu. Named Hawai'i's "ambassador of aloha" in 1962, the Duke spent his last years entertaining visiting VIPs, such as the Queen of England and President John F. Kennedy. When he died at the age of seventy-eight, all of Hawai'i mourned its best-known citizen, and his ashes were scattered at sea.

A bronze statue of Princess Ka'iulani, installed in 1999 in a small park at Ka'iulani and Kūhiō Avenues, is another recent Waikiki addition.

Wizard Stones, previously an integral part of the landscape, are now surrounded by a wrought-iron fence.

On the edge of Waikīkī and bounded by Monsarrat and Pākī Avenues, Poni Mōʻī (Diamond Head) Road, and the Pacific Ocean, the green expanse of

Kapi'olani Park was established as a public recreation area by a group of influential citizens. It opened on Kamehameha Day, June 11, 1877. The 170-acre park, named for the queen-consort of King Kalākaua, was landscaped by Archibald S. Cleghorn,

Legend has it that in ancient times four large boulders were placed on Waikiki beach at the request of four powerful *kāhuna* who visited Hawai'i from the distant land of Kahiki (Tahiti). These learned men became famous for their powers of healing. Two of the boulders were placed at their favorite swimming places, waters fronting what are now the Moana and Royal Hawaiian hotels, and two were placed on the sands where the four *kāhuna* lived during their stay. Presumably they transferred their powers to the stones when they left. During the early 1900s the four stones were moved to sit near the sidewalk at Kūhiō Beach. Known as the Wizard Stones, they remain there to this day, next to the small police station.

father of Princess Kaʻiulani, and originally included a racetrack and, later, a polo field. The lands it occupies were formerly known as Kāneloa and Kapua, and the Waikīkī end of the park was once covered with picturesque waterways—ponds and canals with arched bridges and little islands—that disappeared when the land was drained by the Ala Wai Canal.

The largest of these islets, Makee Island, stood approximately in the place now occupied by the 42-acre **Honolulu Zoo** (151 Kapahulu Avenue; 926-3191), which opened in 1947 and today is the impressive home to about 1,200 specimens and 350 species. The zoo is a great place to visit, not too large and very low key. There are the usual zoo animals: elephants, tigers, giraffes, zebras, and

the like. Here you can also see the *nēnē,* Hawai'i's endangered state bird. Rather than being fenced in, most of the animals are permitted to roam in open fields that are bordered by moats (and electric fencing) to keep them in their areas. Where further barriers are needed, as in the case of a herd of African wild dogs, plexiglass panels are used. The Children's Zoo, Elephant Encounter, and Education Pavilion are *keiki* favorites. Several evenings a month, the zoo offers moonlight walks (reservations required). Open daily, 9 A.M.–4:30 P.M.; admission fee.

The new Kapi'olani Bandstand (built in 2000).

Kapi'olani Park is a popular center for jogging, kite flying, ballgames, picnicking, concerts, and many other family and community activities. It is the site of both the **Waikiki Shell** and the **Kapi'olani Bandstand**. The original 1890s bandstand has been torn down, and a new bandstand opened on July 4, 2000, a Victorian-style structure meant to recapture the glory of Hawai'i's monarchy at the end of the 19th century.

The **Kodak Hula Show**, now known as the **Pleasant Hawaiian Hula Show** (527-5666) is a Waikīkī institution. Started in 1937, when flash photography was not widespread or sophisticated, the show gave Honolulu visitors the opportunity to expose their Kodak film as well as themselves to performances of Hawaiian

Dancer in the Pleasant Hawaiian Hula show.

dance in an outdoor setting. Originally staged near the Natatorium, the show now takes place at the Waikīkī Shell in Kapi'olani Park. Performers include young and old, and they are happy to answer questions and pose for photographs after the performance. They also offer brief instruction to those who care to try their hand—or hips—at the hula. Tuesday, Wednesday, and Thursday, 10 A.M.; free.

The **Waikīkī Aquarium** (2777 Kalākaua Avenue; 923-9741), located along the seaward edge of Kapi'olani Park, was opened in 1904 as an end-of-the-line attraction for Honolulu Rapid Transit Company's new electric trams. Now associated with the University of Hawai'i and internationally recognized as a scientific research institution, the aquarium features numerous varieties of tropical Pacific fish and marine mammals. Exhibits include the endangered Hawaiian monk seal, rare corals, chambered nautilus, cuttlefish, giant clams, and more than 300 fish of 250 species, including the little one with the big name—Hawai'i's state fish, the *humuhumunukunukuāpua'a.* A museum display, Hawaiians and the Sea, explains the vital relationship between the ancient Hawaiians and their marine environment; another, Edge of the Reef, recreates rocky shorelines and reef environments for a close-up look at that habitat. An exhibition garden features Hawai'i's coastal vegetation. Excellent audio guides are available. The aquarium hosts occasional guided day and evening walks along shore and reef areas. Open daily, 9 A.M.–5 P.M.; admission fee.

In front of the Waikīkī Aquarium don't miss the three large and lyrical ceramic sculptures, titled *Tropical Sounds,* by Jun Kaneko, a Japanese-born artist who spends part of each year on Kaua'i. Installed in 2000, the sculptures are part of the state's Art in Public Places program.

The **War Memorial Natatorium**, on the beach next to the Aquarium, was opened in 1927 as a memorial to those who had lost their lives in World War I. Plaques at the entrance list the honor roll of local lads who died in World War I.

The very first swimmer in the Natatorium's 100-meter saltwater pool was Hawai'i's Olympic champion, Duke Kahanamoku. The Natatorium was for many years the scene of lively swimming contests featuring such Olympic greats as the Duke, Buster Crabbe, and Johnny Weismuller. The pool served residents and visitors until the early 1970s, when it was closed owing to great disrepair. In 2000 the facade of the building was restored, and the city hopes to renovate the swimming pool and open it once again to the public. Those opposed to the plan would prefer that the memorial be removed and the beachfront restored.

At the Diamond Head end of Kapi'olani Beach Park, next to the War Memorial Natatorium, lies **Sans Souci Beach**, named after the Sans Souci (French for "without care") Hotel that occupied the site where the New Otani Kaimana Beach Hotel now sits. Robert Louis Stevenson visited the hotel during an 1889 sojourn in Waikīkī and returned in 1893 to stay in a bungalow on the grounds. In the San Souci's guestbook he wrote: "If anyone desires such old-fashioned things as lovely scenery, quiet, pure air, clear sea water, good food, and heavenly sunsets hung out before his eyes over the Pacific and the distant hills of Waianae, I recommend him cordially to the Sans Souci."

Left: Entrance facade of the War Memorial Natatorium (built in 1927).

Below: Sans Souci Beach.

Robert Louis Stevenson with King David Kalākaua, 1889.

taking about half an hour. There are a few steep steps to climb and a couple of dark tunnels to pass through. The route leads to Diamond Head's 761-foot summit, where there are always crowds of people. The weather here is nearly always hot; a hat and sunscreen are recommended. To reach the trail, turn

Left: The view of Waikiki from Diamond Head.

The view from **Diamond Head**—an extinct volcanic crater previously known to Hawaiians as Laeʻahi—provides a 360° panorama of Waikīkī, downtown, Punchbowl (Pūowaina) crater, the Waiʻanae and Koʻolau mountain ranges, Koko Head, and, of course, the vast Pacific. The .8-mile trail to the top of the crater, undoubtedly the best-known landmark on the island, starts from inside the crater, where there is a parking lot. This easy hike is mostly a stroll, *mauka* off Diamond Head Road at the sign, between 18th and 22nd Avenues. There is ample parking at the information center. A fee of $1 per person is assessed in order to hike the trail.

Three lookout points along Diamond Head Road also afford views over the sea where you can watch surfers on the offshore breaks. This is a good spot too, in summer, to watch the ends of sailing races and long-distance outrigger canoe races (see Calendar of Events). A 147-foot lighthouse, built in 1899, stands sentinel on the *kiawe*-covered hillside, which once was the site of an ancient *heiau*.

Queen's Surf Beach, Kapi'olani Park, and Diamond Head

It is said that Hi'iaka, sister of the volcano goddess Pele, gave Lae'ahi (today Diamond Head) its name because the summit resembles the forehead *(lae)* of the *'ahi.* Hi'iaka was on O'ahu during her long journey to escort Pele's beloved Lohiau from his home on Kaua'i to Pele on the island of Hawai'i. A vivid chronicler of the landscape she passed through, Hi'iaka used Lae'ahi as a lookout spot from which her powerful vision allowed her to see as far as Hawai'i, where her sister Pele had covered the Puna region with fires. Furious at Pele for desolating the landscape, Hi'iaka determined to have vengeance on her sister by taking Lohiau as her own lover. Pele put many barriers in their way, but in the end Hi'iaka and Lohiau were united and celebrated in myth for their humanity, in contrast to the capricious destructiveness of Pele.

In the late 1700s Western explorers and traders visited Lae'ahi and mistook calcite crystals in the rocks on the slope of the crater for diamonds. Thus the name Diamond Head came into common usage.

Dietrich Varez, *Pele, Hi'iaka, and Lohiau,* linocut.

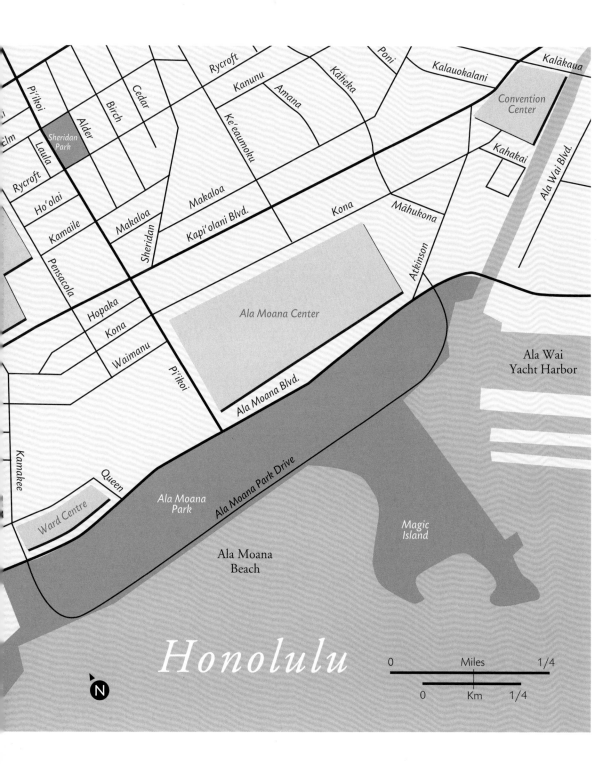

Pi'ikoi

Elm

Rycroft

Ho'olai

Kamaile

Pensacola

Laula

Alder

Birch

Cedar

Sheridan Park

Makaloa

Sheridan

Makaloa

Rycroft

Kanunu

Amana

Ke'eaumoku

Kāheka

Poni

Kalauokalani

Kalākaua

Convention Center

Kahakai

Ala Wai Blvd.

Makaloa

Kapi'olani Blvd.

Kona

Māhukona

Hopaka

Kona

Waimanu

Pi'ikoi

Atkinson

Ala Moana Center

Ala Moana Blvd.

Ala Wai Yacht Harbor

Kamakee

Queen

Ward Centre

Ala Moana Park

Ala Moana Park Drive

Magic Island

Ala Moana Beach

Honolulu

0   Miles   1/4

0   Km   1/4

N

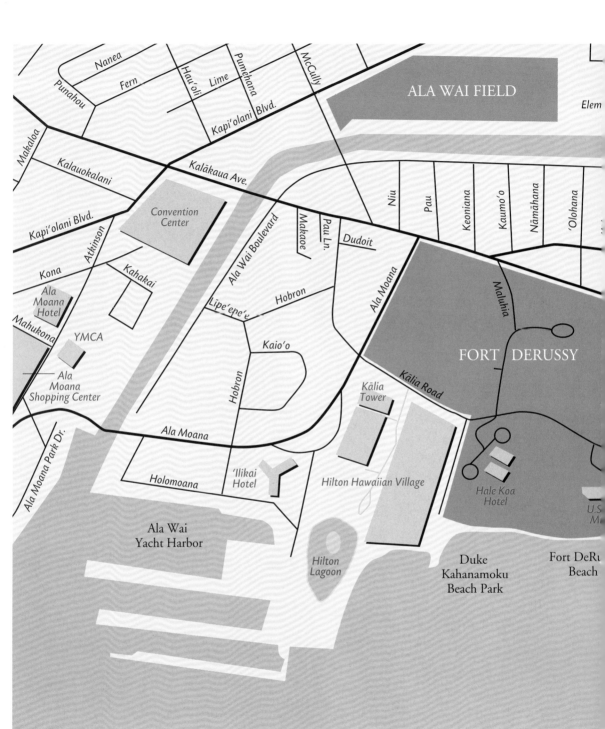

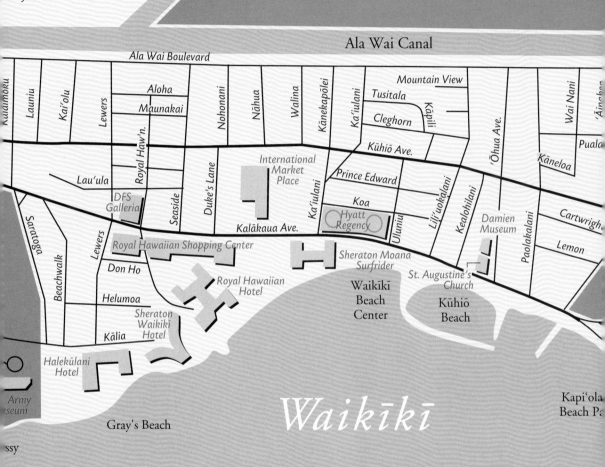

Hīhīwai

'Iolani School

ALA WAI GOLF COURSE

Ala Wai Elementary School

Ala Wai Canal

Ala Wai Boulevard

Kūalamoku

Launiu

Kaʻiolu

Lewers

Aloha

Maunakai

Royal Hawʻn.

Nohonani

Nāhua

Walina

Kānekapōlei

Kaʻiulani

Tusitala

Mountain View

Kāpili

Cleghorn

Wai Nani

ʻAinoka

Kūhiō Ave.

Puala

ʻŌhua Ave.

Kāneloa

Lauʻula

DFS Galleria

Seaside

Duke's Lane

International Market Place

Kaʻiulani

Prince Edward

Liliʻuokalani

Kealohilani

Cartwright

Saratoga

Lewers

Beachwalk

Don Ho

Helumoa

Kālia

Royal Hawaiian Shopping Center

Kalākaua Ave.

Koa

Hyatt Regency

Uluniu

Damien Museum

Paolakalani

Lemon

Royal Hawaiian Hotel

Sheraton Waikīkī Hotel

Sheraton Moana Surfrider

Waikīkī Beach Center

St. Augustine's Church

Kūhiō Beach

Halekūlani Hotel

Army Museum

Gray's Beach

Waikīkī

Kapiʻolani Beach Park

ssy

N

0

0

← To Airport

H1 Freeway

Kinalau

Kina'u

Beretania

Academy of Arts

Kaiser Permanente

Freeland

Victoria

Young

Alo

Miller

Lusitania

Alapa'i

Lunalilo

Queen's Medical Center

Thomas Square

S. King St.

yard St.

Emma Sq.

Lauhala

Lisbon

Hale-makai

S. Hotel

Straub Hospital

Concert Hall

McKinley High School

St. Andrew's Cathedral

Punchbowl

Alapa'i

Keala-maka

Ballrooms

Vashington Place

Beretania

Ticket Booths

Neal Blaisdell Center

Hawai'i State Capitol

Ward Ave.

Arena

CAPITOL DISTRICT

S. King St.

State Library

Honolulu Hale (City Hall)

Clayton

Kapi'olani Blvd.

'Iolani Palace

Likelike

Mission Houses Museum

Dreier

Waimanu

Ali'iōlani Hale (Judiciary)

Punchbowl

Kawaiaha'o Church

Mission

South

Kawaiaha'o

Emily

Kamani

Cummins

Kawaiahao

Queen

Queen

Mililani

Coral

Ilaniwai

Quinn

KAKA'AKO

Halekauwila

Kamani

Ward Entertainment Complex

Halekauwila

Reed

Mother Waldron Plgd.

Ward Ave.

Punchbowl

Pohukaina

Auahi

Ward Warehouse

Restaurant Row

South

Keawe

Coral

Cooke

'Ohe

Kō'ula

Ala Moana Blvd.

Auahi

92

Channel

Ala Moana Blvd.

'Āhui

Kewalo Basin

Kaka'ako Waterfront Park

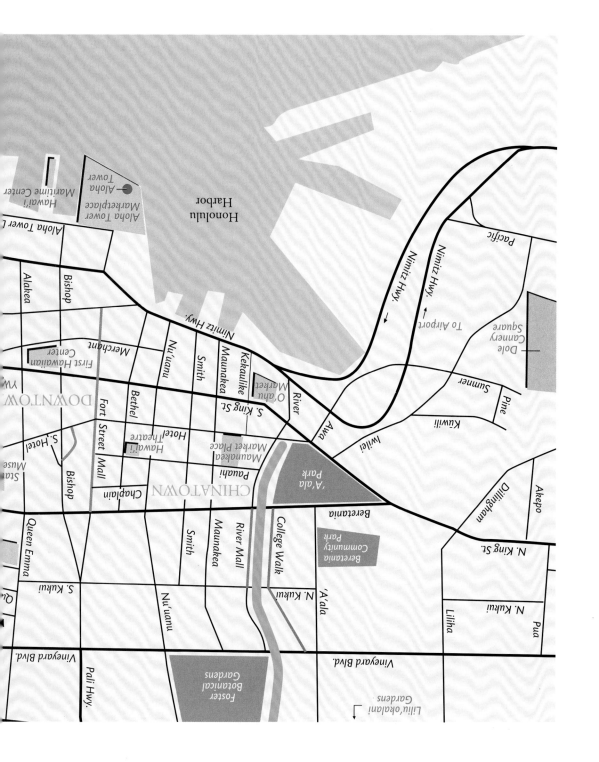

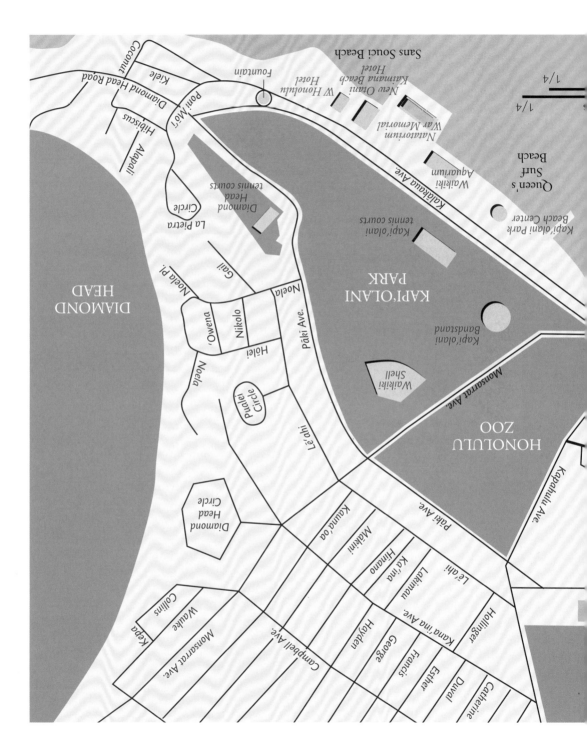

Capitol *district*

Many Honolulu buildings—old and new—played significant roles in the story of Hawai'i after European contact. The crown jewel and focal point of Honolulu's historic buildings is **'Iolani Palace** (522-0832) on South King Street. Inspired by his travels, King David Kalākaua commissioned the construction of this comparatively small European-style palace, which was completed in 1882 as the royal residence for him and his queen, Kapi'olani. It is said that he had stones brought to Honolulu from a *heiau* in Ki'i on the island of Hawai'i to use in the palace's foundations. After Kalākaua's death in 1891, 'Iolani Palace was occupied by his sister and successor, Queen Lili'uokalani, until the Hawaiian monarchy was overthrown in 1893.

The new government auctioned off the palace furnishings and converted the building for use as government head-quarters. It remained an office building for republican, territorial, and state governments until 1968. The state Senate met in the dining room and the House of Representatives in the throne room. The palace has since been restored and stands as a grand memorial to Hawai'i's days as a Polynesian nation. Newly opened downstairs galleries hold important royal artifacts, including a grand feather cape *('ahū'ula)* that Kamehameha won in a 1782 battle with Kīwala'o, ruling chief of Hawai'i. Open Tuesday–Saturday, 9 A.M.– 2:15 P.M., for 45-minute guided tours only; admission fee.

'Iolani Palace with the Royal Guard and the Royal Hawaiian Band.

Background: The palace as seen from the Judiciary Building, late 19th century.

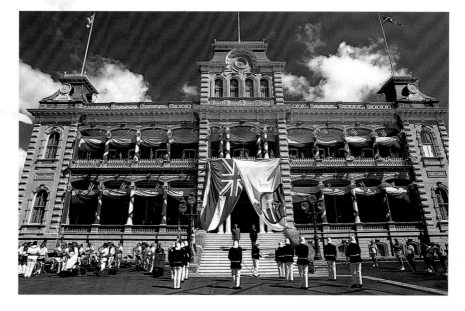

'Iolani Palace gates bear the coat-of-arms of the Kingdom of Hawai'i, designed in London in 1843–44, during the reign of Kamehameha III. The words, once the motto of the kingdom and now of the state, read *Ua mau ke ea o ka 'āina i ka pono* (The life of the land is perpetuated in righteousness).

Kamehameha III, during whose reign the British were for six months rulers of the land, uttered these words in a Restoration Day ceremony at Kawaiaha'o Church on July 31, 1843. Symbols on the coat-of-arms include the Crown of Hawai'i and the chiefly twins Kame'eiamoku and Kamana'awa, one holding a spear and the other a *kāhili.* Their feathered cloaks and helmets presumably were copied from specimens collected in 1778–79 by Captain Cook. Within the quartered shield, red, white, and blue stripes represent the eight inhabited islands. The two balls on poles represent *kapu* sticks, or *pūlo'ulo'u,* which were carried before a chief as insignia of royalty and warning of *kapu.* The triangular form and crossed spears in the center are ancient chiefly insignia.

Behind the palace stands a magnificent Indian banyan tree, which is over one hundred years old; the aerial roots eventually become new tree trunks. The small **Coronation Pavilion** on the palace lawn was originally built at the foot of the main stairs for Kalākaua's belated coronation ceremony in 1883 (he had then been king for eight years) and was surrounded by a temporary amphitheater that could seat 9,000 people.

Above: The Coronation Pavilion today.

Below: Kalākaua's Jubilee *lū'au* for his 50th birthday, November 16, 1886, was held at his Coronation Pavilion.

The pavilion was later moved to its present location, where it serves as a bandstand for the Royal Hawaiian Band. The roof is the original, but severe termite damage to the wooden structure necessitated its replication in concrete.

Behind the Coronation Pavilion is the coral block **'Iolani Barracks**, built by Kamehameha V near the site of the present state capitol. To make way for that construction, it was moved and reassembled—block by block, all 4,000 building blocks—on the palace grounds, where it now houses a small museum display and the palace's ticket office and gift shop. Originally the barracks housed the Royal Household Guard.

On the other side of the palace is the **State Archives** (586-0329), built in 1954. The small building in front of it, the original Archives Building, dates from 1906 and was constructed to prevent all important historical documents from being shipped to the National Archives in Washington, D.C. Open Monday–Friday, 9 A.M.–4 P.M.

Makai of the Archives is a fenced mound that marks the site of the original **Royal Mausoleum**, built for King Kamehameha II and his queen, Kamāmalu, who died of measles in England in 1824. Other members of the ruling family were also interred here until the present Royal Mausoleum in Nuʻuanu was built and all royal remains were ceremonially transferred there. The leaves of *ti* plants such as those surrounding the mound are traditionally used in Hawaiian spiritual and sacred ceremonies.

Leaves of a *ti* plant.

'Iolani Barracks once housed the Royal Household Guard.

This bronze statue of Queen Lili'uokalani stands between 'Iolani Palace and the capitol.

Opposite: The capitol district from the air, with 'Iolani Palace in the foreground and the capitol behind. Downtown high-rises are at the left.

Outside the *mauka* palace gate stands an 8-foot bronze statue of **Queen Lili'uokalani**, Hawai'i's only reigning queen and the last monarch of the Kingdom of Hawai'i. The statue, the work of Boston sculptress Marianna Pineda, was placed in 1982. In her left hand, the queen holds two documents: her new constitution of 1893, the planned declaration of which provoked her downfall, and her most famous musical composition, the melancholy farewell song "Aloha 'Oe." Though there is no official day set aside to honor Lili'uokalani, her extended right hand often bears a fresh flower lei.

The imposing structure *mauka* of the palace is the **Hawai'i State Capitol** (415 South Beretania Street; 586-0178). Designed with a great deal of attention to symbolic detail and speaking proudly of Hawai'i's island nature, it rises from reflecting pools as from the sea, supported by columns that symbolize stately

royal palms. The central court contains
a sealike mosaic floor mural designed
by **Tadashi Sato**, a renowned Japanese
American artist who lives on Maui and
has been named a Living Treasure
of Hawai'i. The central open court is
flanked by two conical towers, metaphors
for volcanoes, that house the legislative
chambers. The flared, craterlike roof
opens to the sky. The Senate and House

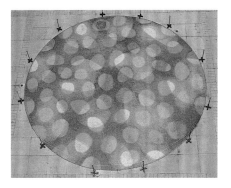

The Armed Forces
Memorial, a 1974
sculpture by Bumpei
Akaji with an eternal
flame (not seen),
is across the street
from the capitol.

Tadashi Sato's
Aquarius, 1969, a
mosaic floor mural,
decorates the capi-
tol's courtyard.

chambers hold light sculptures in the form of chandeliers by **Otto Piene** and woven tapestries by **Ruthadell Anderson**. The top level houses the offices of the governor and lieutenant governor. Their *koa*-paneled reception areas, with welcome signs in Hawaiian and English, display portraits of famous Hawaiians and works by island artists. Both entrances to the building are hung with huge bronze medallions bearing the state seal, an edited version of the Hawaiian royal coat-of-arms. The figure on the left represents Kamehameha I, and on the right Liberty holds the Hawaiian flag.

At the Beretania Street entrance to the capitol stands a bronze statue of **Father Damien** (1840–1889), the beloved leper priest of Moloka'i. Venezuelan sculptress **Marisol Escobar** wrought the likeness from a photograph of Damien made shortly before his death, when his features had become disfigured by the disease. Another cast of this statue stands in the Statuary Hall of the U.S. Capitol in Washington, D.C.

Across Beretania (the Hawaiian version of Britannia) Street from the capitol is a sculpture by another Living Treasure of Hawai'i, **Bumpei Akaji**, whose copper and bronze memorial with an eternal flame is dedicated to the men and women of the state who have served in the armed forces.

Washington Place, also on Beretania Street across from the capitol, has been the governor's residence since 1922. It was built in 1846 in the Greek Revival style by wealthy sea captain John Dominis, who soon thereafter disappeared at sea. His widow rented rooms to the American commissioner to Hawai'i, who hoisted his flag and presumed to name the building in honor of George Washington. Captain Dominis's son, also John Dominis, later married the future Queen Lili'uokalani and was governor of O'ahu. Upon his death, the queen inherited the house and, after her release from nine months' imprisonment in a room of the palace following an unsuccessful attempt to restore her to the throne, she lived at Washington Place until her death in 1917. In the main-floor rooms, which are open only for official receptions, a few of the queen's possessions are displayed, including her *koa* grand piano. The governor's private quarters are upstairs.

A bronze plaque in front of Washington Place contains the words of the lyrical love song "Aloha 'Oe," composed by Lili'uokalani in 1878. The song was inspired by a weekend trip that the princess made to a ranch in Maunawili, on the windward side of O'ahu, where

Above: Washington Place (built in 1846), has been used as the home of Hawai'i's governors since 1922.

Left: Marisol's 1969 sculpture of Father Damien bedecked with flower lei.

Aloha ʻOe

Aloha ʻoe, aloha ʻoe,
E Ke onaona no ho i ka lipo.
One fond embrace, a hoʻi aʻe au
A hui hou aku.

Farewell to thee, farewell to thee
Thou charming one who dwells
among the bowers.
One fond embrace
before I depart
Until we meet again.

—Princess Lydia Pākī
Liliʻuokalani
1878

Queen Liliʻuokalani attained the throne in 1891 and ruled until she was deposed in 1893.

Below left: Saint Andrew's Cathedral (built in 1867 and 1958), a blend of Gothic Revival and mid-20th-century modern.

she was touched by the tender farewell between one of her companions and a Hawaiian girl. She hummed the song on the long horseback ride home. "Aloha ʻOe" was published by the Boston firm of John Worley in the 1880s.

Saint Andrew's Cathedral (corner of Queen Emma and Beretania Streets; 524-2822) was begun in 1867 by Queen Emma, widow of King Kamehameha IV,

and his brother and successor, Kamehameha V. Kamehameha IV, an ardent Anglophile, made a special request to the English crown for the establishment of an Anglican diocese in Hawaiʻi and was married in an Anglican ceremony, though the bishop did not arrive from England in time to officiate. The king died in 1863 on the feast day of Saint Andrew, and the Gothic Revival church, built of stone from England, was named to commemorate this event. The first services were held in 1886, but the building was not completed until 1958, with the addition of the Great West Window, a stained glass mural by **John Wallis** depicting the history of Christianity (look for Christ on a surfboard). A statue of Saint Andrew and his fishes by **Ivan Mestrovic** from Yugoslavia fronts the church, flanked by olive trees. There is a service in Hawaiian on Sundays at 8 A.M. Open Monday–Friday, 8 A.M.–4 P.M.

Across the street from Saint Andrew's, the **Leiopapa A Kamehameha Building** (235 South Beretania Street), a state office building, has in its lobby a magnificent glass mosaic mural by Hawai'i artist **Yvonne Cheng**. In **Kauikeaouli Hale** (1111 Alakea Street) there are a number of works by local artists, including **Satoru Abe**, **John Barnett**, **Juliette May Fraser**, **Donald Harvey**, and **John Wisnosky**. Both of these state buildings are open weekdays during business hours.

On the other side of the palace is the neoclassical-style **State Library** (478 South King Street; 586-3500), built in 1913, courtesy of Andrew Carnegie and his architect brother-in-law, Henry Whitfield, with wings and an open courtyard added in 1929, designed by Hawai'i architect Charles W. Dickey. The original building has lost much to "modern"

improvements, but it is still quite elegant. The area around the courtyard provides a pleasant spot to read up on local history. The librarians in the Hawaiiana section are extremely knowledgeable and helpful. (If you want to check books out of this or any of the state libraries, it's very easy to get a library card, even for nonresidents.) *Ocean Current*, a 1996 tile floor mural in the courtyard by Hawai'i artist **Hiroki Morinoue**, echoes the 1969 mural by Tadashi Sato in the state capitol atrium. The children's reading room is painted on all four walls with murals

by **Juliette May Fraser** depicting legends of Hawai'i. The library has a large collection of illustrated Hawaiian and Pacific books that make for good browsing, as well as more informational tomes. Open Monday–Saturday.

Hawai'i State Library (built in 1913).

Hawai'i *kama'āina* Juliette May Fraser (1887–1983) attended Wellesley College and studied at the Art Students League in New York. Returning to Hawai'i at the advent of World War II, she established herself as a painter, with large-scale murals as her favored means of expression. Examples of her work, usually focused on Hawaiian legends, appear in many public buildings in Hawai'i.

Juliette May Fraser, *Lei Sellers* (*"Change, Please"*), circa 1941, oil on canvas. Honolulu Academy of Arts, purchase.

Below left: Barbara Hepworth, *Parent I and Young Girl*, 1973, bronze, on the grounds of the State Library.

Below right: Honolulu Hale (built in 1929).

On the State Library grounds, at the corner of King and Punchbowl Streets, are two bronze sculptures by British artist **Barbara Hepworth**, *Parent I* and *Young Girl*, both 1973.

The pretty Spanish colonial building across Punchbowl Street from the State Library is **Honolulu Hale** (Honolulu House—the Hawai'i equivalent of city hall), built in 1929 (530 South King

Street; 527-5666 or 523-4674). Its open-roofed interior courtyard, patterned after that of a 13th-century Florentine palace and often used for art shows and concerts, features a grand staircase, massive bronze chandeliers and doors, terracotta tiles, and cast stone sculptures. The building's coffered ceilings are decorated with *kapa*-patterned frescoes. Open Monday–Friday, 8 A.M.–5 P.M.

The cluster of colonial red brick buildings next to Honolulu Hale, known as the **Mission Memorial Buildings**, were erected in 1916 to honor the Congregational missionaries who wrought their handiworks in Hawai'i. They now house city and county offices. On the grounds next to these Georgian-style buildings is a monumental painted steel sculpture, *Sky Gate,* a 1977 commission from internationally famous artist **Isamu Noguchi**. Across the street, a waterfall and rock garden in the small park created by the triangle of King Street, South Street, and Kapi'olani Boulevard is the site of a bronze sculpture by **Charles Watson**, *Ka Mea Ku'i 'Upena*

("the person who stitches the net"). This little urban oasis with traffic on all sides, actually no more than a pedestrian walkway, was built in 1989 and is one of the city's nicer embellishments.

The **Mission Houses** (553 South King Street; 531-0481), diagonally opposite Honolulu Hale, are the original buildings (after the thatch houses) that served as both home and administrative center for the leaders of the American

Above: Charles Watson, *Ka Mea Ku'i 'Upena*, 1989, bronze.

Left: Mission Memorial Building (built in 1915–16). A replica of the Liberty Bell sits in front of the building.

Below: Mission Houses Museum (built in 1821 and 1831).

Protestant mission in Hawai'i during the early 19th century. Built on land granted to the missionaries by Kamehameha III, they are now a museum, run by the Hawaiian Mission Children's Society (whose members are descendants of the missionaries). The frame house, prefabricated in Boston and sent around Cape Horn in 1821, is the oldest European structure in the islands. The adjacent stone buildings are made of coral blocks quarried from the bedrock. The buildings are furnished much as they would have been at the time they were in domestic use, and some of the actual belongings of the early residents are on display. In the Mission Press building, where schoolbooks, newspapers, and the Bible were printed, docents demonstrate the printing process. A fascinating diorama in the entry hall depicts this area of Honolulu as it appeared in the early 19th century. The shop has a good selection of locally made crafts and items reflecting 19th-century styles. Call for information about guided tours. Open Tuesday–Saturday, 9 A.M.–4 P.M.; admission fee.

If you need a break for sustenance during your historical tour, **Winterbourne**, the parlor at the Mission Houses, is the perfect place for a reasonably priced and very delicious breakfast or lunch in a serene, pretty environment. Afternoon tea is served from 2:30 to 4:30 P.M. There is no entrance fee if you're just going to the café.

The mission's **Kawaiaha'o Church** (957 Punchbowl Street; 522-1333) was built in 1842, designed by the Reverend Hiram Bingham of Bennington, Vermont,

Above: Kawaiaha'o Church (built in 1842); below: water fountain at the site of Kawaiaha'o spring.

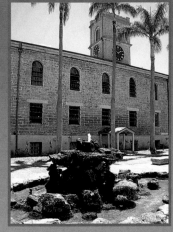

Kawaiaha'o Church bears the name of a plentiful spring that once stood on its ground. Named Kawaiaha'o, "the water of Ha'o," the spring was in ancient times the bathing place for a chiefess named Ha'o. The pool was edged with ferns and fragrant vines, and over it was built a house so that Ha'o could bathe in private, for she was a very sacred person, and it was *kapu* for the common people to look upon her. Her servants brought her to the spring in a *mānele,* or litter, curtained with fine *kapa.*

unofficial leader of the first group of fourteen missionaries to arrive in Hawai'i. The oldest Christian house of worship in Hawai'i, the church was constructed by the Protestant missionaries under the patronage of Kamehameha III. The simple coral block and wood structure, based on New England church architecture (the original wooden steeple is no longer there), was built of giant coral slabs that were quarried from under water, each weighing more than 1,000 pounds. The cost of construction was $20,000. The missionaries' church was a focal point for religious and state ceremonies involving Hawaiian royalty until the fall of the kingdom—indeed, King Lunalilo (see page 126) chose the grounds of Kawaiaha'o rather than the Royal Mausoleum as his final resting place. Sunday services are held at 8 A.M. and 10:30 A.M. in English and Hawaiian. Call for information about guided tours. Open Monday–Friday, 8:30 A.M.–4 P.M.

The church's cemetery is burial ground for many of the first missionaries and their descendants, with graves reading Bingham, Chamberlain, Dole, and Baldwin. On the other side of the church, toward the harbor, is the cemetery for the Hawaiian members of the congregation (though segregation didn't work very well since many Hawaiians married into missionary families and are buried with them, as names on the gravestones attest).

Directly opposite 'Iolani Palace on King Street is **Ali'iōlani Hale** (House of Heavenly Chiefs). Originally designed as a palace in the European style for King Kamehameha V and completed in 1874, it never became a residence. Though King Kalākaua used it occasionally at night for receptions and balls, it has always housed government offices: originally the Supreme Court, the legislature, and several ministries. It has been the home of the Judiciary since the change of government in 1893, when the other offices of the republican government were transferred to 'Iolani Palace. There's an excellent exhibit on the first floor detailing Hawai'i's judicial history with photos and artifacts. Two short

Ali'iōlani Hale (built in 1874) houses state government offices, including the Judiciary.

films document the unique evolution of law in Hawai'i. Open weekdays, 9 A.M.– 4 P.M.; free.

In front of Ali'iōlani Hale and facing 'Iolani Palace is a bronze and gilt statue of **King Kamehameha I**, a duplicate of the original work that was commissioned by the Hawaiian legislature in 1878 to honor the "discovery" of the Hawaiian Islands by Captain Cook. Carved by American artist Thomas Gould, whose studio was in Florence, the statue was cast in Paris and shipped from Bremen, but it was lost at sea when the ship carrying it sank off the Falkland Islands. The duplicate was unveiled in its present location during the coronation celebrations of King

Kalākaua in 1883. The gilt bronze figure is impressive, especially on Kamehameha Day (June 11) and for the next few days, when the neck and arms of the figure are draped with dozens of flower lei up to 30 feet long. Thomas Gould's original statue of Kamehameha I was recovered from the sea in 1882 and taken to the island of Hawai'i, where it now stands in front of the old Kapa'au courthouse on the Kohala Peninsula, near Kamehameha's birthplace.

Next to Ali'iōlani Hale, on Kamehameha's right, is the **Kekūanaō'a Hale** (465 South King Street), which houses state offices. Its facade still bears the inscription "Territorial Office Building," so named when it was built in 1926. The dome of its rotunda features a cut-glass rendition of the Hawaiian coat-of-arms surrounded by American flags. Between the two buildings are several noteworthy banyans. On the other side of Ali'iōlani Hale, on Kamehameha's left, is the beautiful Spanish colonial **Old Federal Courthouse Building** (335 Merchant Street), with its loggias, courtyard garden, towers, and red-tiled roofs. Built

Left: The statue of Kamehameha I in front of Ali'iōlani Hale is draped with lei in commemoration of Kamehameha Day, June 11.

Below: Old Federal Courthouse Building (built in 1922).

in 1922 to house the post office, courthouse, customhouse, and federal offices, it is now occupied by a small post office branch, customs offices, and a few state agencies. Development of this wonderful bit of gracious architecture into an upscale shopping and restaurant complex has been proposed, but so far all such plans have fallen through.

Diagonally opposite on Beretania Street is the 1927 **Hawaiian Electric Co. Building** (900 Richards Street), designed by the New York firm of York and Sawyer, the same architects as the Old Federal Building, and fronted by a pillared arcade with vaulted, hand-painted ceilings.

Facing the palace grounds on Richards Street is the 1927 **YWCA** (1040 Richards Street), also Spanish colonial, in keeping with the architectural mood of the neighborhood. The building was designed by San Francisco architect Julia Morgan

(1872–1957), famous for her design of the Hearst Castle in San Simeon, California. The building is open daily; ask at the front desk about tours. An attractive courtyard with lots of tables and chairs provides a good resting spot. Breakfast and lunch are served weekdays at the Café Laniakea, next to the courtyard. For lovers of ceramics, pieces made in the Y's classes run by famed potter **Toshiko Takaezu** are for sale at the front desk.

Completing the ring of historic buildings around the palace is another, even grander, Mediterranean structure, built in 1928, now named the **No. 1 Capitol District Building** (250 South Hotel Street), formerly the Armed Forces YMCA. The first building on this site was the original Royal Hawaiian Hotel (see pages 42–43), from which Hotel Street got its name. The current building was in recent years restored to its former grandeur by the Hemmeter Corporation before being purchased by the state. The state legislature has recently approved the development of a state art museum in this building, under the auspices of the State Foundation on Culture and the Arts. Artworks collected by the state that now hang in public buildings and state offices throughout the city or are in storage will finally have a home where they can be enjoyed by all. The museum, with a café and gift shop, is scheduled to open in the fall of 2002.

Downtown *business district*

A couple of blocks *'ewa* on Bishop Street is the **First Hawaiian Center** (999 Bishop Street), the newest building, and at thirty floors the highest, to join Honolulu's cityscape. This architecturally stunning building, designed in 1996 by the New York firm of Kohn Pederson Fox, houses the downtown gallery of the Contemporary Museum (see pages 149–50). Outside are significant bronze sculptures by Hawai'i artist **Satoru Abe** and by **Deborah Butterfield**, who hails from Montana but spends part of the year on the island of Hawai'i.

Across Bishop Street from the First Hawaiian Center, the Financial Plaza of the Pacific (111 South King Street) is the site of three immense columns by Italian modern artist **Arnaldo Pomodoro**. Constructed of stainless steel, bronze, and bronze and concrete, the three columns reflect the verticality of down-town architecture.

On Bishop Street between King and Hotel Streets, **Henry Moore**'s *Upright Motive No. 9,* a bronze sculpture from 1979, is set off from the sidewalk in a quiet reflecting pool. On the Hotel Street side of Pauahi Tower (1001 Bishop Street), native Hawaiian artist **Sean Browne**'s *Hui,* 1993, represents in bronze the concept of partnership.

Just *makai* of Hotel Street, where Bishop Street meets Union Mall, is the

Above: Deborah Butterfield, *Hōlualoa* and *Palani,* 1997, cast bronze.

Below: Satoru Abe, *Enchanting Garden,* 1997, bronze.

"**T**he further I traveled through the town [Honolulu] the better I liked it. Every step revealed a new contrast—disclosed some-thing I was unaccustomed to.... I saw luxurious banks and thickets of flowers, fresh as a meadow after a rain, and glowing with the richest dyes.... When the sun sunk down ... it was tranced luxury to sit in the perfumed air and forget that there was any world but these enchanted islands." —Mark Twain, 1866

Ali'i Bishop Building. Though the building is not in itself significant, the foyer displays an interesting series of historical wall murals. Executed in monochromatic tones suggesting old photographs, the murals' life-size figures and scenes portray downtown Honolulu as it might have appeared in November 1876. If historical perspective interests you, this is an excellent introduction to a walking tour of the downtown district.

The 1939 **Emerald Building** (1148 Bishop Street) was designed by Hawai'i architect Alfred Preis in a streamlined moderne style that reflects its period. The second oldest church and the oldest remaining building downtown is the 1843 **Cathedral of Our Lady of Peace** (1184 Bishop Street; 536-7036), a Roman Catholic church. Originally a coral block rectangle with a steeple, it has been embellished over the years with towers, lanai, vaulted ceilings, balconies, and other additions and, in 1893, a statue of Mary was placed in the courtyard near the stump of Hawai'i's parent *kiawe* tree, planted by a visiting priest in 1828. This church is where Father Damien, the leper priest of Moloka'i, was ordained in 1864. The current facade dates from 1929. Open daily, 6 A.M.–6 P.M.

The historic **Hawai'i Theatre** (Bethel and Pauahi Streets; 528-5535) was hailed as the "Pride of the Pacific" when it opened in 1922. In the neoclassical style, the ornate building has Byzantine and Corinthian ornamentation and Moorish grillwork. The building was recently refurbished and once again hosts performing arts events throughout the year.

Some of Hawai'i's finest old landmark buildings can be found along Merchant Street. The Renaissance Revival–style **Kamehameha V Post Office Building** (44 Merchant Street), built in 1871, is Hawai'i's first post office and the oldest reinforced-concrete public building in America. The first Japanese bank to be established in Hawai'i was the **Yokohama Specie Bank** (34 Merchant Street). The elegant 1909 structure is now used for business offices. Next door is the 1887 **Friend Building**, originally

Doug Young, *Hawaii Theatre*, 1998, digitally manipulated print from watercolor original.

Dillingham Transportation Building (built in 1929).

is a beautiful example of the Romanesque Revival style. The first passenger elevator in Hawai'i was in the 1899 **Judd Building** (851 Fort Street). When it was constructed in 1901, the **Stangenwald Building** (119 Merchant Street) was considered Hawai'i's first skyscraper. The towering height of this six-story masterpiece was not exceeded in Honolulu for half a century.

Heading *makai* from Merchant Street toward Queen Street, at the beginning of Fort Street Mall, stands the hacienda-like 1930 **C. Brewer Building**, once corporate headquarters of the smallest of the "Big Five" sugar companies and last to be built. This charming building was renovated in 1998. Occupying the block of Bishop between Merchant and Queen is the splendid **Alexander and Baldwin Building**, built in 1929 as corporate headquarters for this youngest of Hawai'i's "Big Five" (all now widely diversified). The building was designed by architect Charles W. Dickey, who was responsible for much of Honolulu's Mediterranean-style architecture during the territorial era. Diagonally opposite, running from Queen Street to Ala Moana Boulevard, is the elegant 1929 Italian Renaissance–style **Dillingham Transportation Building**, designed by San Diego architect Lincoln Rogers. Be sure to see the art deco lobby. The plaza at 737 Bishop Street has a sculpture by local artist **John Tanji Koga**

the offices of Hawai'i's first periodical, the *Friend of Temperance and Seamen,* a missionary publication.

The last corner here, indeed the entire block, is occupied by the grand 1931 Spanish colonial **Honolulu Police Station** (842 Bethel Street), later converted to a courthouse and now occupied by government offices. The building, renovated in 1987, is noted for its elaborate interior tilework. **Melcher's Store** (55 Merchant Street), constructed of coral block in 1853, is the oldest commercial structure in downtown Honolulu. The two-story **Bank of Bishop and Co. Building** (65 Merchant Street), dating from 1878, is in the Renaissance Revival style. The 1895 bluestone **Bishop Estate Building** (77 Merchant Street)

representing *mauka* (the land) with *kalo* plants and a *poi* pounder and *makai* (the sea) with a fishhook and fish forms.

The ten-story **Aloha Tower**, on the waterfront at the foot of Fort Street and the focal point of the attractive Aloha Tower Marketplace, once dominated the city skyline. This historic landmark was built in 1926 as the harbormaster's control tower, and, with its welcoming word "aloha" on all four faces, became a primary symbol of greeting for visitors arriving by ship.

Left: Aloha Tower (built in 1926) is today the site of a lively shopping center.

Below: Honolulu Harbor.

Right: *Falls of Clyde* (1878).

Far right: Hawai'i Maritime Center with a humpback whale skeleton hanging from the ceiling.

Below: The *Hōkūle'a's* arrival from Rapa Nui, 1999.

The tower houses on its ninth floor the **Hawai'i Maritime Center** (523-6151), a room in which photographs and other memorabilia of Honolulu Harbor history are displayed. There is a small reference library. Open daily, 8:30 A.M.– 5 P.M.; admission fee.

Showpiece of the Hawai'i Maritime Center is the ***Falls of Clyde*** (536-6373), moored at Pier 7, Diamond Head of

Aloha Tower Marketplace, at the foot of Bishop Street. This historic vessel, built in 1878, was active in Hawai'i waters during a significant portion of its career and is the world's only remaining fully rigged four-masted sailing ship and the world's only remaining sailing tanker. Open daily, 8:30 A.M.–5 P.M.; admission fee (included with admission to the Maritime Center).

Near the *Falls of Clyde* is berthed the 60-foot *Hōkūle'a,* a modern replica of an ancient Polynesian voyaging canoe. The *Hōkūle'a* has made world headlines by retracing legendary migration routes of the early Polynesians, using no navigational instruments, only the stars and ocean currents as guides. It has made several major voyages, its longest ending in May 1987, a two-and-one-half-year journey from Hawai'i to New Zealand and back, touching all the major island groups along the way and proving irrefutably that these voyages—even the difficult

west-to-east leg from Samoa to Tahiti against the prevailing winds—could have been deliberate and purposeful, rather than accidental, as some skeptics have held. Its most recent journey was to Rapa Nui (Easter Island), the most challenging destination in the Polynesian triangle. Navigator for the voyage was Nainoa Thompson, who has done much to share his knowledge of celestial navigation with the people of Hawai'i.

The launching site for the original journey and also the site for the canoe's triumphal return in 1987 was Kualoa Regional Park on the windward coast (see Beaches). In honor of this monumental achievement—one that provoked a powerful emotional and spiritual response among Polynesian people everywhere—the beach at this park is now called Hōkūle'a Beach.

Chinatown

The area bounded by King, Nuʻuanu, and Beretania Streets and Nuʻuanu Stream is Honolulu's historic **Chinatown**, though the ethnic origins of its residents have always been mixed. The district now has few residents, but the businesses are largely Chinese with a recent influx of Indochinese and art enterprises, such as the Pegge Hopper Gallery and Ramsay Galleries (see page 225). There are trendy restaurants, including Indigo and Duc's Bistro, as well as offices of architects and interior designers. The entire area was twice razed by fire, in 1886 and again in 1900—the first fire was accidental, but the second, which burned out of control for seventeen days, was set by government officials to contain an outbreak of bubonic plague. Many of the subsequent buildings are being restored and renovated, and several have been named to the Hawaiʻi Register of Historic Places. Chinatown comes alive on Saturdays, when the Chinese and everyone else come for weekly marketing, and the flowers and produce are as fresh as you'll ever find. Note that while Chinatown is perfectly safe during the day, it's advisable to drive or take a taxi if you plan to eat at one of the restaurants in the evening. Some pretty scummy characters have been known to wander the streets after dark.

The two marble **Lucky Lions** that flank the Hotel Street entrance to Chinatown (between Bethel Street and Nuʻuanu Avenue) were a 1989 gift from

the people of Taiwan in commemoration of the 200th anniversary of the arrival of Chinese in Hawaiʻi. Along the roofline at 1031 Nuʻuanu Avenue, note the twelve bronze medallions by artist **Jill Burkee**; they represent the animal signs of the Chinese zodiac and are placed north to south in the order each animal presented itself to Buddha.

The Merchant-Nuʻuanu intersection has been dubbed Merchant Square by the restaurateurs clustered at and near it. On the *mauka*–Diamond Head corner, the old **Waterhouse Warehouse** (901 Nuʻuanu Avenue) now houses Murphy's Bar and Grill, a friendly, popular restaurant and Irish tavern. Next door is the **Wing Wo Tai and Co. Building** (923 Nuʻuanu Avenue), built in 1916 by a Chinese export business.

Laura Ruby's site-specific sculpture *Site of Passage: Chinatown* (detail, below) refers to the history and physical structures of its neighborhood, including rooflines and shapes of door-ways, windows, and awnings.

Above right: The colorful lion dance marks a Chinese festival.

Right: An herb shop in Chinatown.

The corner **T. R. Foster Building** (902 Nuʻuanu Avenue), an ordinary office building when erected in 1891, is today considered quite decorative. Named for the founder of the Inter-Island Steamship Navigation Company, it is now home to O'Toole's, one of Honolulu's favorite Irish pubs.

Nearby Marin Tower Plaza (61 North Nimitz Highway) offers another entry into Chinatown by virtue of **Laura Ruby**'s *Site of Passage: Chinatown*, a 1994 sculp-ture that functions as an architectural space inviting viewer interaction. Design elements of the stainless steel, brass, porcelain, and tile sculpture are drawn from the immediate community— a trademark device of the artist.

Since 1904 the open-sided **Oʻahu Market** (King and Kekaulike Streets) has offered fresh fish, meat, and vegetables for thrifty shoppers. All along King and Hotel Streets are numerous small Chinese vendors, offering colorful window-

shopping opportunities. A Chinatown landmark is **Wo Fat** (115 North Hotel Street), established in 1882 and Hono-lulu's oldest Chinese café. Its present flamboyant building, at the corner of Hotel and Maunakea Streets, was erected in 1936. Today much of the grand exterior has been obliterated, and only the second floor is used as a restau-rant. The 1901 **Mendonca Building** (72 North Hotel Street), whose architect, Oliver G. Traphagen, designed the Judd Building on Fort Street (see above), was the first building to be erected in China-town following the great fire of 1900. It was renovated in 1979. (Another

Traphagen building, the abandoned **Kaka'ako Pumping Station**, located off Ala Moana Boulevard near South Street, is begging to be restored.)

Maunakea Marketplace (1120 Maunakea Street) holds a quirky collection of shops and is always good for an inexpensive souvenir or gift. Maunakea Street itself has more lei shops per linear foot than any other street on the island. Stop to watch the women at their work, stringing the colorful and fragrant lei.

A wonderful tradition in Hawai'i is to celebrate any event—birthdays, weddings, anniversaries, funerals—with the giving of a flower lei. Graduating students at the University of Hawai'i are heaped with lei given by relatives, friends, and neighbors. You can make your own lei, but these days most people opt for the inexpensive strands of flowers sold all over the island, in supermarkets, drugstores, and flower markets, where workers string them between customers. Locals shop for lei (the word is the same, singular or plural) at the many lei stands in Chinatown. Favorite flowers are plumeria, white tuberose, ginger, *pikake* (jasmine), and orchids. The rarer the flower, the more expensive the lei. In Hawai'i, May Day (May 1) is celebrated as Lei Day, and extravagant creations can be seen at the celebrations at Kapi'olani Park. This tradition was initiated in 1928 by island poet Don Blanding.

At the corner of Beretania and River Streets, beside the bridge, stands a bronze statue of **Sun Yat-son**, leader of the Chinese revolution that overthrew the Manchu Ch'ing Dynasty in 1911 and founder of the Republic of China. Dr. Sun lived and studied in Hawai'i during his youth and while leader-in-exile of the Kuomintang. The statue was given to Honolulu by people of the Republic of China (Taiwan) in 1976. Flanking the same bridge on the opposite side of the stream is a painted concrete statue of Philippine revolutionary leader **José Rizal**, erected in 1983 by the Filipino Society of Hawai'i. Many Filipino immigrants first settled in this area of Honolulu.

The triangle formed by King and Beretania Streets and Nu'uanu Stream is filled with the green haven of **'A'ala Park**. Here sprawling banyan and monkeypod trees shade the old residents of the area who come to play cards and "talk story." Just beyond Chinatown and 'A'ala Park, on King Street at Iwilei, is the **Old O'ahu Railway Station**, built in 1925 as a terminus for the narrow gauge railway that until 1947 ran around the island to Kahuku and its sugar mill. This grand Spanish mission–style building now houses the Kalihi-Pālama Community Center. A little farther 'ewa on King Street is the historic **Kaumakapili Church** (766 North King Street; 845-0908), which was built in 1911 by missionaries. It features unusual curved pews as well as Romanesque and Gothic architectural details. Located in the Kapālama area, which was once popular for "town" houses of the aristocracy and well-to-do, it, too, has been prominent in Hawai'i's public affairs. Open Monday–Friday, 8 A.M.–4 P.M.

Honolulu's eclectic history has given rise to a number of places of worship associated with Buddhism, Shintoism, and Taoism, several in Chinatown. Hawai'i's oldest Shinto shrine, **Izumo Taishakyo Mission** (215 North Kukui Street; 538-7778), was built in 1923 by a master carpenter from Japan using the traditional method of construction with no nails. It has the protruding horns and barrels atop the roof ridge traditional to Shinto shrines and the *torii* (gate) and handwashing basin at the entrance. Originally located in nearby Leleo Lane, this shrine was relocated to the McCully district after World War II, then moved to its present site beside the Nu'uanu

Stream in 1969. There is no schedule for services, the priest performing them at random; he is usually there on weekday mornings. Shinto is the ancient religion of Japan and involves acknowledging and honoring the spirits of nature.

The Taoist **Lum Sai Ho Tong** temple is across the street (1315 River Street; 536-6590), upstairs over a shop beside the Nu'uanu Stream. This temple is used mostly by members of the Lum clan and is dedicated to their illustrious ancestress. In addition to the altar, the temple contains a large and intricate gilded carving depicting important episodes in the family's long history. Open daily, 7 A.M.–5 P.M.

The **Chinatown Cultural Plaza** (100 North Beretania Street) houses ethnic shops and restaurants. At the *'ewa* end, next to the stream, is **Edward M. Brownlee**'s *T'Sung,* 1971, a monumental cast stone sculpture that references Chinese earth symbols.

Nu'uanu

Lionel Walden, *Luakaha: Evening,* ca. 1916, oil on canvas. Honolulu Academy of Arts, gift of Mrs. Philip E. Spalding, 1936. Luakaha was the site and name of the country home of Kamehameha III in upper Nu'uanu Valley. The name means "place for relaxation."

The Buddhist **Kuan Yin Temple** (170 North Vineyard Boulevard; 533-6361) is at the end of River Street, across Vineyard, next to the entrance to Foster Botanical Gardens. This colorful and typically Chinese temple is dedicated to Kuan Yin, the goddess of mercy. It is very popular with local adherents of the faith, some of whom are usually in the temple, leaving offerings and burning incense. The respectful presence of visitors is welcomed. Incense may be purchased. Open daily, 8:30 A.M.–2 P.M.

Foster Botanical Gardens (50 North Vineyard Boulevard; 522-7066), just *mauka* of Chinatown, holds the nation's largest collection of tropical plants. The twenty-acre garden, begun on a private estate in 1855, includes labeled plantings of varieties of palm, heliconia, ginger, and other fascinating plants. Of special interest are the orchid garden and the grouping of prehistoric plants. Foster Gardens also encompasses forty-three of O'ahu's designated "exceptional" trees, which are protected by law. The Foster Botanical Gardens Gift Shop has packaged plants and seeds cleared for entry into the U.S. mainland as well as plant-related clothing, crafts, and books. Open daily, 9 A.M.–4 P.M.; admission fee.

The five-acre oasis of **Lili'uokalani Gardens** (North Kuakini Street; 522-7060) is a sheltered glade on the banks

of Nuʻuanu Stream, *mauka* of the Lunalilo Freeway, near Foster Botanical Gardens. The small, natural park with its waterfall and swimming hole was a favorite recreation retreat for Queen Liliʻuokalani and was left to the public by her. Nestled in a quiet, shady neighborhood of "Polynesian modern"–style homes typical of the South Seas, the park is reached via a narrow lane called Waikahalulu (named after the Nuʻuanu Stream falls), off School Street. Open daily, 9 A.M.–4 P.M.; free.

Traveling up Nuʻuanu Valley above Vineyard, you will come to a number of churches and temples of all types and styles as well as cemeteries of interest.

The Japanese **Soto Mission of Hawaiʻi** (1708 Nuʻuanu; 537-9409) is a Buddhist temple that shows strong Indian influence in its external architecture, while its pew-filled sanctuary is reminiscent of churches (hours vary). The elegant, understated religious hall at the **Tenrikyo Mission** (2236 Nuʻuanu) sits in an exquisite Japanese garden that exudes tranquility. Here and at the **Tenrikyo Temple**, also known as the **Tenrikyo Hawaiʻi Dendocho** (2920 Pali Highway; 595-6523), Shinto and Buddhist practices are combined in an eclectic blend. Open daily, 6 A.M.–8 P.M.

The cross-shaped **Royal Mausoleum** (2261 Nuʻuanu; 537-1716) was built in 1865—designed by Honolulu's first professional architect, Theodore

Heuck—to house the remains of the ruling families and their retainers when the original Royal Mausoleum on the grounds of ʻIolani Palace became inadequate. The coral block Gothic building was converted to use as a chapel in 1922 after the royal remains had been buried in crypts around the grounds. Open Monday–Friday, 8 A.M.–4:30 P.M.

Nearby **Honolulu Memorial Park** (22 Craigside Place; 538-3925) is a beautifully kept cemetery with a diversity of

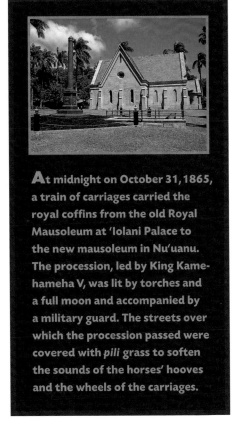

At midnight on October 31, 1865, a train of carriages carried the royal coffins from the old Royal Mausoleum at ʻIolani Palace to the new mausoleum in Nuʻuanu. The procession, led by King Kamehameha V, was lit by torches and a full moon and accompanied by a military guard. The streets over which the procession passed were covered with *pili* grass to soften the sounds of the horses' hooves and the wheels of the carriages.

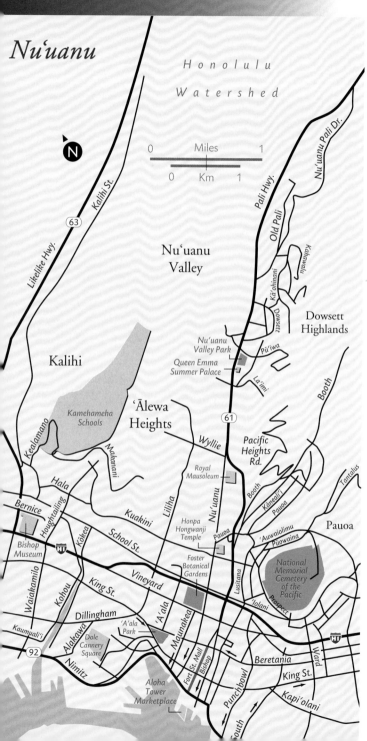

Nuʻuanu

Honolulu

Watershed

Nuʻuanu
Valley

Kalihi

Kamehameha
Schools

'Ālewa
Heights

Dowsett
Highlands

Nuʻuanu
Valley Park

Queen Emma
Summer Palace

Pauoa

Royal
Mausoleum

Honpa
Hongwanji
Temple

Foster
Botanical
Gardens

National
Memorial
Cemetery
of the
Pacific

Bishop
Museum

Dole
Cannery
Square

'A'ala
Park

Aloha
Tower
Marketplace

individual monuments and memorials.
It is most noted for its replicas of
Japan's treasures—the Sanju Pagoda
of Nara and the Golden Pavilion
(Kinkikaku-ji) of Kyoto. Open daily,
7:30 A.M.–3:30 P.M.

Near the *mauka* end of Nuʻuanu
Avenue, in a quiet lane across the road
from the Royal Mausoleum, is the
lovely red-lacquered and green-roofed
Hsu Yun Temple (42 Kawānanakoa
Place; 536-8458), operated by the
Chinese Buddhist Association of
Hawaiʻi. Open daily, 8 A.M.–3 P.M.

Impossible to miss is the vast **Honpa
Hongwanji Temple** (1727 Pali Highway;
536-7044), with its Indian-inspired
architecture, home of the Shinshu
Buddhist sect in Hawaiʻi. Dedicated to
the Amida Buddha of infinite wisdom
and compassion, the temple was constructed in 1918 of concrete and was
the first in Hawaiʻi to adopt features
of church sanctuaries, like pulpit, pews,
pipe organ, and choir. Sunday morning
services are in English. Open Monday–
Saturday, 8 A.M.–8 P.M.; Sunday, 8 A.M.–
4:30 P.M.

Hānaiakamalama, better known
as the **Queen Emma Summer Palace**
(595-3167), is located on the Pali Highway several miles *mauka* of downtown.
This gracious white frame home, built
in 1843, was purchased as a summer
retreat for Queen Emma, consort of
Kamehameha IV, and became her

Queen Emma Summer Palace (built in 1843).
Right: Nu'uanu Pali Lookout.

principal residence after the king's death in 1863. Furnished with Emma's possessions and displaying many of the royal *kāhili* and *lei hulu*, it is maintained as a historic house by the Daughters of Hawai'i. Guided tours are given daily, except major holidays. Open daily, 9 A.M.–4 P.M.; admission fee.

There are a couple of easily accessible and quite spectacular scenic outlooks on the mountains above downtown Honolulu. Most famous of these is the **Nu'uanu Pali Lookout**, off the Pali Highway, with unbeatable views of the windward side. The edge of this precipice undoubtedly wins honors for being the windiest place on the island. When people on O'ahu refer to the Pali, they mean Nu'uanu Pali (*pali* actually means "cliff" or "precipice," so there are lots of them). The old Pali Highway, now dilapidated and unused, can still be seen to the right of the scenic lookout. Until 1955 it was the main artery connecting the island's windward side with the thriving port of Honolulu.

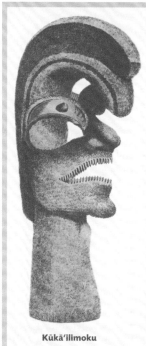

Kūkā'ilimoku

In 1795 Kamehameha I, chief of the island of Hawai'i and conqueror of Maui, invaded O'ahu. In the Battle of Nu'uanu, he and his men drove the defending forces of O'ahu's chief, Kalanikūpule, up this valley. At the *pali* many of the defenders jumped to their deaths rather than be captured and sacrificed by Kamehameha to his war god, Kūkā'ilimoku. (Another account has it that Kamehameha's forces pushed the O'ahu warriors over the *pali*.) Thus, the invader gained control of O'ahu and its modern history began. When the Pali road was constructed in 1897, workers found 800 skulls and other bones at the foot of the cliff.

Punchbowl *and* Tantalus

The **National Memorial Cemetery of the Pacific**, commonly known as Punchbowl (2177 Pūowaina Drive; 566-1430), is located Diamond Head of the Pali Highway, in the caldera of the ancient volcanic crater known to the Hawaiians as Pu'u o Waina (hill of sacrifice). Some *haole* saw in the shape of the hill a resemblance to a punch-bowl; the name stuck, and that is how it is now known. The vast, grassy floor of the caldera is filled with more than 40,000 graves of American war dead from World War I, World War II, the Korean War, and the Vietnam War, and those servicemen's families. Each year on Memorial Day every grave bears a flag and at least one lei. The monumental **Courts of the Missing** slabs list the names of 28,745 servicemen missing in action. The massive tablets lead to a

Above and right: National Memorial Cemetery of the Pacific (Punchbowl).

Opposite: View of Honolulu from Pu'u'Ualaka'a State Wayside Park.

30-foot marble statue called *Columbia*, representing a mother looking over her lost children. Punchbowl is the number two visitor attraction in all Hawai'i (the Arizona Memorial is first). Above the cemetery on the crater's rim is a lookout with sweeping panoramic views of the city below and the sea beyond. Open daily, 8 a.m.–6:30 p.m.

Below Punchbowl, at the corner of Ward and Beretania (on the Diamond Head side of the downtown area), is the wonderful 1927-vintage Honolulu Academy of Arts (see pages 144–49). **Thomas Square**, named for British Admiral Richard Thomas, is a soothing sward of green bounded by King, Beretania, Ward, and Victoria, between the Honolulu Academy of Arts and the Blaisdell Concert Hall. Its central feature is a fountain flanked by four large banyan trees. Admiral Thomas was thus honored for his role in restoring Hawai'i's

independence in 1843, a few months after an overly zealous junior officer had unofficially placed the islands under the protection of England to thwart what he saw as too-powerful American commercial interests. The park is regularly the site of local craft fairs and plant sales.

Spectacular vistas can be enjoyed by following the long, winding drive that leads past the National Memorial Cemetery and passes over the mountain called **Tantalus**, where the cool height and magnificent views enticed wealthy residents to build some of Hawai'i's finest homes. At the top, the street name changes from Tantalus Drive to Round Top Drive, and the road winds down the mountain.

About halfway down is a park called **Pu'u 'Ualaka'a**, which also offers sweeping views of the city and the Wai'anae Mountains in the distance. Seldom crowded, this park provides a great picnic setting. Well-marked hiking trails start

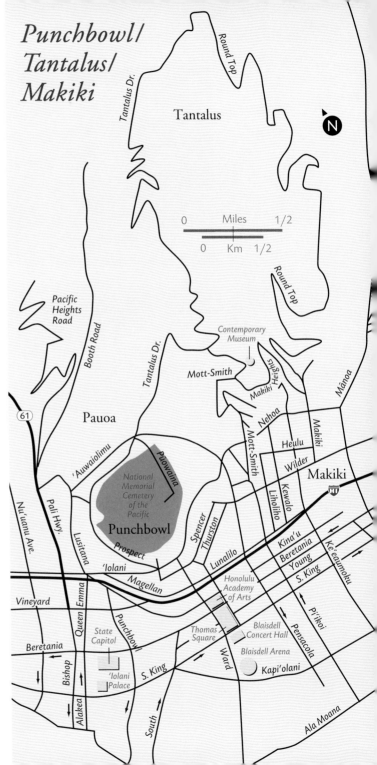

Punchbowl/ Tantalus/ Makiki

Tantalus Dr.

Round Top

Tantalus

N

0 — Miles — 1/2

0 — Km — 1/2

Round Top

Pacific Heights Road

Booth Road

Tantalus Dr.

Contemporary Museum

Mott-Smith

Makiki Heights

Mānoa

61

Pauoa

'Auwaiolimu

Puowaina

Mott-Smith

Nehoa

Heulu

Wilder

Makiki

Makiki

National Memorial Cemetery of the Pacific

Kewalo

Liholiho

Nu'uanu Ave.

Pali Hwy.

Lusitana

Spencer

Thurston

Kina'u

Beretania

Young

Ke'eaumoku

Punchbowl

Prospect

'Iolani

Magellan

Lunalilo

S. King

Vineyard

Queen Emma

Honolulu Academy of Arts

Pi'ikoi

Pensacola

Beretania

Bishop

State Capitol

Punchbowl

Thomas Square

Blaisdell Concert Hall

'Iolani Palace

S. King

Ward

Blaisdell Arena

Kapi'olani

Alakea

South

Ala Moana

The small hill named Round Top was once called ʻUalakaʻa, or "rolling sweet potato," referring to the sweet potatoes that Kamehameha I raised on the mountain. When they were ready for eating, the potatoes were rolled down the hill to workers who collected them and brought them to the royal cooks.

The top of Tantalus from one of the many trails on the mountain.

at the bottom of Tantalus and wind their way through here. A pleasant outing is to walk on one of these trails for a while, then turn back to the parking lot. The park can also be reached by driving 3 miles up Round Top Drive from Makiki.

Tantalus trails are in the Nā Ala Hele (Trails to Go On) program sponsored by the State Division of Forestry and Wildlife. The Hawaiʻi Nature Center (page 233) provides a map to the trails.

Makiki *and* Mō'ili'ili

The **Makiki Christian Church** and the associated building compound (829 Pensacola Street; 594-6446), on Pensacola near Kapi'olani, are modeled after a 16th-century Japanese castle. The only sign of its true function is the cross on the front of it. Open Monday–Friday, 8 A.M.–4 P.M.; Saturday, 8 A.M.–3 P.M.

Punahou School, a private grade and secondary-level school, is at the Diamond Head edge of Makiki, at the corner of Wilder Avenue and Punahou Street. Established as O'ahu College by the missionaries in 1841, led by the Reverend Hiram Bingham, the school is now a 75-acre campus with a number of striking buildings, both old and contemporary. The oldest building, Old School Hall, has been in constant use since 1852. Pauahi Hall, with its distinctive buff and blue dome, has been a landmark since 1894 (buff and blue, for Hawai'i's sand and sea, are the school's colors). Noteworthy among new buildings is the Thurston Memorial Chapel, a circular building designed by architect Vladimir Ossipoff, with stained glass by Erica Karawina and *koa* doors embellished with repoussé copper panels by artists Jean Charlot and Evelyn Giddings. The **Punahou School Carnival**, held in February to benefit the school, is a splendid event, with great ethnic

Dillingham Hall (built in 1929) at Punahou School.

"**B**eyond the reef and beyond the blue, nestling among cocoanut trees and bananas, umbrella trees and breadfruits, oranges, mangoes, hibiscus, algaroba, and passion-flowers, almost hidden in the deep, dense greenery, was Honolulu. Bright blossom of a summer sea! Fair Paradise of the Pacific!"
— Isabella Bird, *Six Months in the Sandwich Islands*, 1875

foods, an art sale to which all of the best local artists and craftspeople donate works, and thrilling rides for all ages.

In the section called Mō'ili'ili, the heart of which is where University Avenue comes down from Mānoa and meets Beretania and King Streets, there is a historical gallery at the **Japanese Cultural Center** (2454 South Beretania Street; 945-7633) devoted to the history of the Japanese in Hawai'i. The exhibits here are outstanding, telling the story of Japanese immigration from the 19th century, when they came as laborers for the sugar and pineapple industries, through the

postwar years, when Japanese Americans were responsible for major political and social changes in Hawai'i. Open Wednesday–Sunday, 10 A.M.–4 P.M.

Two museums in Makiki, the **Contemporary Museum** and the **Honolulu Academy of Arts** (pages 144–51), have elegant cafés for leisurely and delicious lunches. The Mō'ili'ili area, in particular South King Street, is home to a great many inexpensive restaurants favored by locals, including Maharani for Indian food and Mekong II and Montien Thai for the cuisine of Thailand (see Dining).

The lava rock walls that surround Punahou School are covered with a trailing cactus that looks ordinary enough most of the year. However, for a short period, especially in July and August, the cactus blooms, but only at night. Called night-blooming cereus (*Hylocereus undatus*), this prickly climber was brought from Acapulco in 1840 by a visiting ship's officer, Charles Brewer. He presented it to Mrs. Hiram Bingham, who planted it at the school. The large white and yellow blossoms emerge after dark and wilt by the next morning. If you're lucky enough to be driving by the campus in the evening when the cereus is in bloom, stop and take in this magical and fleeting sight.

Mānoa

The misty valley of Mānoa, site of the University of Hawai'i's main campus, was once lined with *kalo* and rice farms. The first pineapples in Hawai'i were planted in Mānoa on the farm of Captain John Kidwell in 1885. Earlier, in 1825, Hawai'i's first sugarcane and coffee plantation was at the site now occupied by the University of Hawai'i, established in 1907. Today Mānoa is home to many of the university's faculty members and students as well as business people who work downtown. Small homes may sell for as much as $1 million.

Free guided walking tours of the **University of Hawai'i** campus leave from the Campus Center, Monday, Wednesday, and Friday, at 2 P.M. (call 956-7235 for information). In addition, you may take a self-guided tour, picking up a brochure at Campus Center. There is no parking on the main campus itself. To park, take Lower Campus Road off Dole Street, close to the University Avenue intersection, to reach a parking garage. From there, walk *mauka;* just ask anyone where the Campus Center is.

"**W**hy did not Captain Cook have taste enough to call his great discovery the Rainbow Islands? These charming spectacles are present to you at every turn; they are common in all the islands; they are visible every day . . . barred with all bright and beautiful colors, like the children of the sun and rain." —Mark Twain, 1866

University of Hawai'i–
Mānoa campus.

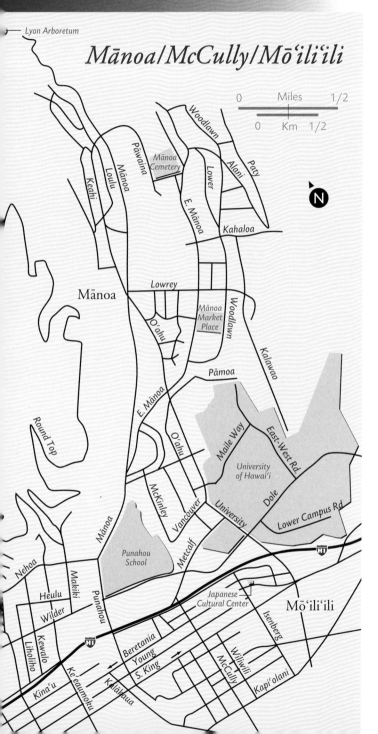

Lyon Arboretum

Mānoa/McCully/Mōʻiliʻili

0   Miles   1/2

0   Km   1/2

Woodlawn

Pāwaina

Mānoa Cemetery

Alani

Lower

Paty

Keahi

Loulu

Mānoa

E. Mānoa

Kahaloa

Lowrey

Mānoa

Manoa Market Place

Woodlawn

Oʻahu

Kalawao

Pāmoa

E. Mānoa

Round Top

Oʻahu

Maile Way

East-West Rd.

University of Hawaiʻi

McKinley

Vancouver

University

Dole

Lower Campus Rd

Mānoa

Nehoa

Makiki

Punahou School

Metcalf

Heulu

Punahou

Japanese Cultural Center

Isenberg

Mōʻiliʻili

Wilder

Kewalo

Liholiho

Beretania

Young

S. King

Wiliwili

McCully

Kapiʻolani

Kinaʻu

Keʻeaumoku

Kalākaua

Principal points of interest are **Bachman Hall**, with lobby frescoes by **Jean Charlot**; the **Art Building**, where first-class exhibitions are held in the gallery; **Hamilton Library**, with a magnificent mural created by **Juliette May Fraser** for the 1939 World's Fair in San Francisco; the **Center for Korean Studies**, modeled after the throne hall in Kyongbok Palace in Seoul; **Jefferson Hall**, with its Japanese tea house and garden; and the **East-West Center Gallery**, where exhibitions explore the arts of the Pacific. The **John Young Museum** has limited hours, but if it's open it's worth a stop to see the fine collection of ethnographic art from Asia, the Pacific, and Africa.

Outdoor sculptures on campus include **George Segal**'s *Chance Meeting* near the Law School (you'll pass it if you walk from the parking garage to Campus Center), **Tony Smith**'s *Fourth Sign,* near the Art Building; and

Above and opposite: Exhibitions at the University of Hawaiʻi Art Gallery.

Opposite top: Jean Charlot, *Commencement* (detail), 1953, fresco in Bachman Hall, University of Hawaiʻi.

Jean Charlot (1898–1979) was a Frenchman—and a leading figure in the Mexican mural movement—who came to Hawai'i in 1949, specifically to paint a mural for Bachman Hall at the University of Hawai'i. The painting, *The Relation of Man and Nature in Old Hawai'i*, was followed four years later by *Commencement*, a fresco on the second floor of Bachman Hall depicting the presentation of lei to graduates. Enamored of Hawai'i, Charlot took a position as professor of art at the university and lived here until his death thirty years later. He had a profound influence on the artists and arts of his adopted home.

Alexander Liberman's orange-painted *Gate of Hope,* near the East-West Road entrance to campus. You can pick up a guide to campus art at Campus Center or in any of the libraries.

More rainbows probably occur in Mānoa than anyplace else in Hawai'i, leading to the university's sports teams being named the Rainbows—until football coach June Jones decided that wasn't macho enough for his boys, and he renamed the football team the Warriors. Some of the other teams now call themselves the Rainbow Warriors. Tradition has it that if a rainbow appears on the day of a game, the Rainbows will win.

Among the several sites of interest in Mānoa is **Mānoa Cemetery**, a century-old Chinese cemetery founded by the Chinese farm workers who once populated the valley. It's interesting to walk among the headstones and look at the various offerings left by families of the deceased.

The well-watered upper reaches of Mānoa Valley offer ideal conditions for the University of Hawai'i's **Lyon Arboretum** (3860 Mānoa Road; 988-0464), a botanical research facility in a delightful tropical rainforest setting. These tranquil gardens, with a network of easily walked trails, are home to many tropical plants that are extinct in their native habitats. Visitors are welcome to tour portions of the 194-acre site, where they may view striking flowers, fascinating food plants, and both useful and ornamental trees. Locally made jams and jellies and island crafts, as well as a good selection of botanical and gardening books, are sold in the gift shop. Guided group tours are available by arrangement. Open Monday–Saturday, 9 A.M.–3 P.M.; free.

There are several notable Mānoa shops, including **Anne Namba Designs** (2964 East Mānoa Road; 988-9361), a boutique where traditional Japanese silks are made into elegant dresses; Hillary Rodham Clinton is only one of the famous who have shopped here. Stores in Mānoa Marketplace (the shopping center at 2752 Woodlawn Drive) include **Chelsea**, for fashionable women's wear, and **East of Java**, for home furnishings from Indonesia.

Mānoa has several popular local eateries, including Andy's (for the best smoothies in town), Beau Soleil, Donato's, Paesano, and the Wai'oli Tea Room (see Dining).

Alexander Liberman, *Gate of Hope,* 1972, on the Mānoa campus of the University of Hawai'i.

Kaimukī

For a taste of old Honolulu, head for the community of Kaimukī, a stretch of Waiʻalae Avenue at the head of Pālolo Valley. Here is an eclectic variety of shops, galleries, and eateries. You can get to Kaimukī via an open-air trolley that runs along Kūhiō Avenue in Waikīkī to Koko Head Avenue in Kaimukī. The trolley operates every half hour from 6 A.M. to 10 P.M. daily. The fare is $1. For information, call 566-7466. (We hope this fine service remains in business; originally funded by a HUD grant, the trolley has not become a profit-making venture.)

Our number one destination is always the gallery **Bibelot** on Koko Head Avenue (see pages 224–25), which is a great place to find locally made arts and crafts at reasonable prices. The **Crack Seed Store** (1156 Koko Head Avenue; 737-1022) is where to find the Chinese preserved and seasoned fruit called crack seed. Just ask the proprietor what he would recommend. Favorites include mango, plum, papaya, and coconut. Other shops on Koko Head are **Bead It** (1152 Koko Head Avenue; 734-1182), where jewelry-making

Looking down over Kaimuki to the back side of Diamond Head.

supplies are sold along with exquisite and affordable bead creations. **Montsuki** (1148 Koko Head Avenue; 734-3457) offers exquisite made-to-order women's clothing. Several racks of ready-to-wear include blouses and jackets that have been constructed from old kimono. Across Wai'alae Avenue on Koko Head, **Best of Friends**, upstairs in a green building, has a lot of cute locally made items.

There are two places to find great comic books and Japanese collectible toys: **Gecko Books and Comics** (3613 Wai'alae Avenue; 732-1292) and **Collector Maniacs** (3571 Wai'alae Avenue; 739-3912). The largest selection of fabrics on O'ahu is at **Kaimuki Dry Goods** (1144 10th Avenue; 734-2141. **Comme Ci Comme Ca** (3464 Wai'alae Avenue; 734-8869) is a consignment boutique with style.

Most of all, Kaimuki is the place to hone an adventuresome palate, tasting the foods of China, Japan, Vietnam, Thailand, Italy, France, Mexico, and Hawai'i. Some of the restaurants are listed in the Dining section (pages 278–301), but there are other food places of note.

Bakeries abound. Our favorite is **Scones** (1117 12th Avenue; 734-4024) for the most delectable scones we've ever tasted; go early, as they tend to sell out and close. **Kimuraya Bakery** (1048 Koko Head Avenue; 735-7875) has the best *haupia* donuts—rectangular pastries filled with *haupia* pudding. **JJ French Pastry** (3447 Wai'alae Avenue; 739-0993)

has rich and delicious pastries and chocolate creations. For a cup of joe with pastry and friendly service, there's **Coffee Talk** (3601 Wai'alae Avenue; 737-7444).

Several grocery stores are holdovers from the old markets that catered to the neighborhood, including **Kaimuki Produce** (3585 Wai'alae Avenue; 735-6778), known for its locally grown fruit and vegetables.

Fresh pasta is made daily at **C&C Pasta** (3605 Wai'alae Avenue; 732-5999), for eat-in or takeout. **Azteca** (3617 Wai'alae Avenue; 735-2492) has wonderful Mexican food. **Kaimuki Chop Suey** (3611 Wai'alae Avenue; 735-6779) looks like a hole in the wall, but the food is really tasty. **Hale Vietnam** (1140 12th Avenue; 735-7581) has excellent Vietnamese food. **Café Laufer** (3565 Wai'alae Avenue; 735-7717) offers salads, desserts, and one entrée a day in a European-style setting. **Big City Diner** (3569 Wai'alae Avenue; 738-8855) serves up a great breakfast and has economical and tasty meals the rest of the day. For fine Thai food, there's **Champa Thai** (3452 Wai'alae Avenue; 732-0054).

A bit off the beaten track (it's probably best if you ask a local for directions) is **Fort Ruger Market** (3585 Alohea Avenue; 737-4531), source of the best plate lunch in town, bar none. This combination deli/grocery store has lots of local delicacies, and once you've found it you'll want to go back.

Kapahulu/Kaimukī/Kāhala

Hanauma Bay *to* Hālona Blowhole

The parking area above **Hanauma Bay**, off Kalaniana'ole Highway, offers a splendid view of that broken, flooded crater with its reefs and palm-fringed beach. For those inclined to more active viewing, the underwater scenery is also spectacular (see pages 166–67, 185). On a clear day, the island of Moloka'i can be seen from this lookout.

The short, one-mile hike from Kalaniana'ole Highway to the 646-foot summit of **Koko Head** (Kuamo'okāne in Hawaiian) leads to fabulous views of Hanauma Bay and across the Kaiwi Channel to the islands of Moloka'i and Lāna'i. The hike starts at a closed-off paved road, on the *makai* side, before the parking lot. A little more than a mile up the road from Hanauma Bay, on the *mauka* side of Kalaniana'ole Highway, a trail from the Hawai'i Job Corps Training Center leads to **Koko Crater**

Hanauma Bay from Koko Head.

(Kohelepelepe), offering a hardy, one-mile climb to the 1,208-foot-high rim for a great 360° panorama. Park at the lot for Hālona Blowhole and walk back along the highway toward Hanauma Bay. The trail angles off the road where the guardrail on the right ends. Both of these short hikes are in areas unpro-

tected from the sun, which can be mighty hot. It's cooler during the winter months, also a time when you're likely to see migrating whales offshore in the Kaiwi Channel. The hike to Koko Head is easier than the one to Koko Crater, which passes along steep, narrow stretches.

A little more than a mile up the road from Hanauma Bay you'll come to **Hālona Blowhole**, a lava tube inside the cliff face that, when waves enter it with force, sends a spout of water shooting into the air. There are no official statistics on the upper limits of this event; locals variously report having

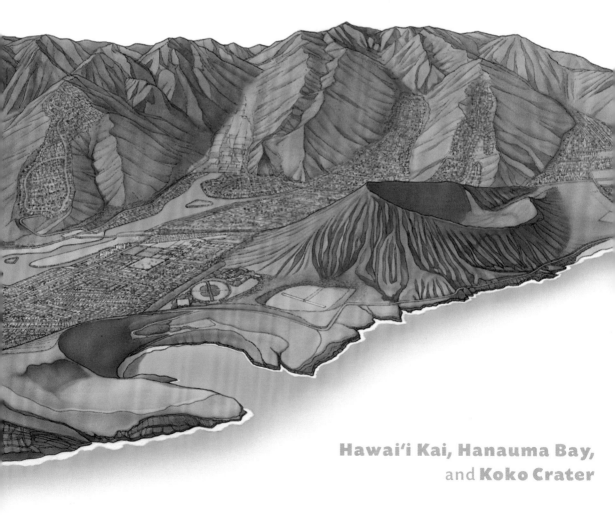

Hawai'i Kai, Hanauma Bay, and **Koko Crater**

short trail, is Hālona Cove, a popular scenic attraction, also known as From Here to Eternity Beach because it was here that Burt Lancaster and Deborah Kerr embraced in the 1950s movie by that name.

Koko Crater Botanical Garden (Kealahou Street; 522-7060) is reachable from Kamehameha Highway or from Hawai'i Kai Drive; follow the sign for Koko Crater Stables. This city-administered garden features dryland plants, including native *wiliwili* trees, cacti, plumeria, palms, bougainvillea, and African plants. There are no paved trails or facilities. Open daily, 9 A.M.– 4 P.M; free.

witnessed heights of 50 to 100 feet when the sea is rough. This scenic lookout also affords distant views of Lāna'i and Moloka'i on clear days.

To the left of the blowhole, hidden from the highway but accessible via a

Hālona Blowhole, above, and Hālona Cove, also known as From Here to Eternity Beach.

Windward Coast

The vista along the coastline when you round **Makapu'u Point** heading toward Waimānalo is stunning. Indeed, the drive along this stretch of coastline is the prettiest on the island. There is a lookout area at Makapu'u Point where the pleasure can be prolonged. The Makapu'u Lighthouse, built after a shipwreck off the coast of a luxury liner in 1909, had a keeper until 1974. **Makapu'u Beach** is below the lighthouse, on the left. The tide pools at Makapu'u are a nice place for a refreshing dip during the summer months, when the water is calm.

Makapu'u Lighthouse (above), and Makapu'u Beach (right and below). Rabbit Island is offshore.

Dolphins are among the spectacular sights at Sea Life Park.

frigatebirds. The Kaupō Falls area of the park nurtures a variety of indigenous plants and island waterfowl, and the Rocky Shores exhibit recreates the intertidal zone. Open daily, 9:30 A.M.–5 P.M.; admission fee.

The scenic country town of Waimānalo, about 2.5 miles up the road from Sea Life Park, offers a few holes-in-the-wall for good local-style plate lunch and shave ice. While here, stop by **Naturally Hawaiian Gallery and Gifts** (41-1025 Kalanianaʻole Highway; 259-5354) to see the nature-inspired artwork of Patrick Ching. As well as Ching's drawings and paintings, the gallery features stained glass by Joseph Dwight, *koa* bowls by Larry Deluz, and beach jewelry by Danielle Jerves. There is a good selection of Hawaiʻi-themed books here, including several children's books written and illustrated by Ching.

An easy *heiau* to get to, and one that is in fairly good condition, is **ʻUlupō** (off Kailua Road, a continuation of the Pali Highway, near the Kailua YMCA). Tucked away behind some houses and the Y's recreation yard, this stone platform is so ancient that Hawaiians believe it to have been built by Menehune, a legendary race of small people who lived in the islands before the known migrations from southern Polynesia. It was used by these later arrivals to honor and cajole the gods of agriculture. Though it can actually be seen

On the *mauka* side is **Sea Life Park** (41-202 Kalanianaʻole Highway; 259-7933), an outstanding example of an educational entertainment center, with a setting unmatched anywhere. Its 300,000-gallon glass tank is 18 feet deep, has seventeen viewing windows along a spiral ramp, and holds more than 2,000 species of marine life. Its Turtle Lagoon is a breeding facility for the endangered green sea turtle; its Seabird Sanctuary accommodates a nesting colony of boobies and is also home to other free-flying seabirds including albatrosses and

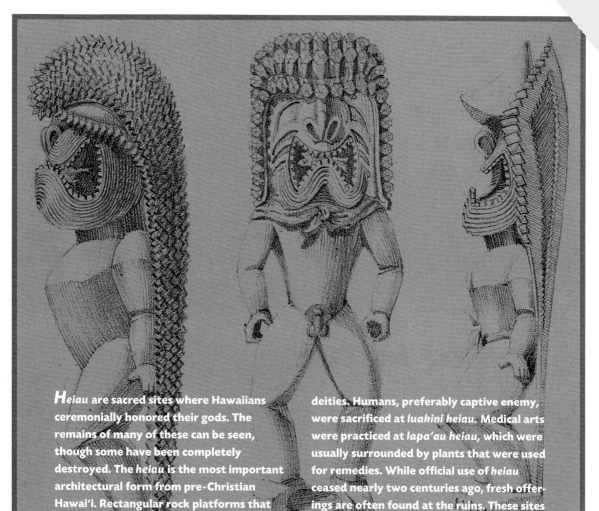

Heiau are sacred sites where Hawaiians ceremonially honored their gods. The remains of many of these can be seen, though some have been completely destroyed. The *heiau* is the most important architectural form from pre-Christian Hawai'i. Rectangular rock platforms that held grass huts, wickerwork towers, and wooden images, the *heiau* were where the ancient Hawaiians worshiped their gods of war (Kū), agriculture (Lono), fresh water (Kāne), the ocean (Kanaloa), and other lesser deities. Humans, preferably captive enemy, were sacrificed at *luakini heiau*. Medical arts were practiced at *lapa'au heiau*, which were usually surrounded by plants that were used for remedies. While official use of *heiau* ceased nearly two centuries ago, fresh offerings are often found at the ruins. These sites are considered sacred by many of Hawai'i's people, and they should be treated with respect. Though there are no extant *heiau* in the Honolulu urban area, there are several excellent sites to visit around the island.

Alphonse Pellion, *Studies of Carved Wood Images from a Heiau* (detail), 1819, graphite on paper. Honolulu Academy of Arts, gift of Frances Damon Holt and in memory of John Dominis Holt, 1995.

**Ho'omaluhia
Botanical Gardens.**

from the highway, it can't be reached directly from there. Turn down Manu'ō'o Road just *mauka* of the site, then take the first right, drive to the end, then turn right again. You'll be in the Y's parking lot. Walk down the path between the Y and the adjacent residences for a few hundred feet, and the *heiau* is there on your left.

Ho'omaluhia Botanical Gardens (45-680 Luluku Road, Kāne'ohe; 233-7323) is a gem missed by most visitors to our fair shores. Tucked away in a valley beneath the towering cliffs of windward O'ahu, this combination nature reserve and botanical garden is a hiker's and picnicker's delight—and it provides information and education in the bargain. The park's 400 acres are divided into sections devoted to different types of tropical plants. Guided hikes, scheduled for Saturdays at 10 A.M. and Sundays at 1 P.M., deal with such diverse subjects as local bird life, traditional food and medicinal plants, cloud watching, and ethnobotany. Or you can walk the trails on your own; be sure to pick up a trail map at the Visitor Center. Swimming is not allowed in the 32-acre lake. Tent camping is permitted weekends, from 9 A.M. Friday until 4 P.M. Monday (see page 276). To reach the gardens, turn onto Luluku Road off Kamehameha Highway (Route 83) in Kāneʻohe, near the H3 intersection. The turnoff is marked by a large state sign. Open daily, 9 A.M.–4 P.M.; free.

Haʻikū Gardens (46-336 Haʻikū Road, Kāneʻohe; 247-6671), about .2 of a mile off Kahekili Highway going in the *mauka* direction on Haʻikū Road, is open to the public without charge. This privately owned estate features lily ponds and exotic tropical flowers on six well-kept acres. On a hill overlooking the tranquil gardens is Haleʻiwa Joe's restaurant (see Dining; the restaurant used to be a Chart House), open for dinner only. A nice windward-side outing might include an early evening walk in the gardens followed by cocktails and dinner at the restaurant, which is in a picturesque South Seas–style building with the dining room open to the outdoors.

The beautifully kept expanses of **Heʻeia State Park** occupy a grassy knoll overlooking Kāneʻohe Bay and the ancient **Heʻeia Fishpond**, an 80-acre pond that was used as late as the 1950s. The lava rock walls are more than 12 feet wide. From the park there are lovely views of the bay and of the coast up to Kualoa Point and **Mokoliʻi Island**, also known as **Chinaman's Hat**. Mokoliʻi can be better seen from the shore along Hōkūleʻa Beach at Kualoa Regional Park.

Legend holds that the island of Mokoliʻi (known as Chinaman's Hat), offshore from Kualoa Regional Park, was created by Pele's sister Hiʻiaka, who slew a giant *moʻo* (dragon) and left his gigantic flukes in the water as a landmark.

Ancient Hawaiians built stone walls out into the sea to enclose a natural area or bay, creating ponds where fish could be raised. O'ahu's irregular shore once held more fishponds than any of the other islands. Eight fishponds can still be seen along the windward coast. The ponds usually had several *mākāhā* (wooden sluice gates), designed to let fish in to feed but prevent them from leaving once they were fattened. The He'eia fishpond originally had four watchtowers from which keepers could keep their eyes on the fish.

Kahalu'u fishpond
in Kāne'ohe Bay.

Kāne'ohe Bay and He'eia Fishpond

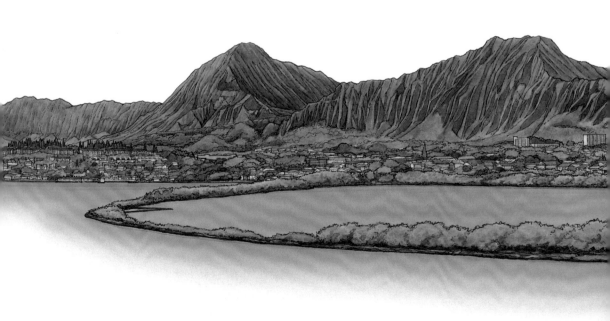

The **Valley of the Temples Memorial Park** (47-200 Kahekili Highway; 239-8811), with its tranquil gardens, pools, statues, and temple replica, is actually a cemetery for people of all faiths. Located in the enchanting 'Āhuimanu Valley, this park provides a peaceful and powerful setting for its main feature, a beautifully wrought concrete replica of Kyoto's classic Byōdō-in temple, mirrored in a

The turquoise waters of Kāne'ohe Bay, with Chinaman's Hat.

many varieties that have been hybridized on the property. The gallery is open only Saturdays, Sundays, and Mondays. To reach it from Kahekili Highway, turn *mauka* on Wailehua Road, and turn right on Lamaula Road. (Note that at this writing, the property is on the market, for a cool $1 million; you should call ahead to make sure it's still open.)

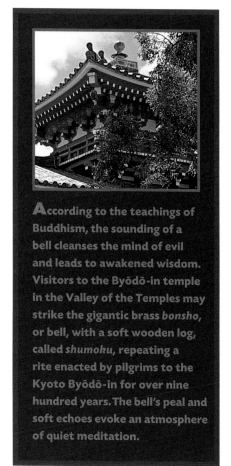

The Byōdō-in temple at Valley of the Temples. The temple's roofline is shown at the right.

two-acre reflecting pool filled with hundreds of *koi*. An immense, 9-foot golden Buddha, the largest wooden Buddha carved since the original was made for the Kyoto temple over nine hundred years ago, occupies the central building. Open daily, 8:30 A.M.–4 P.M.; admission fee.

Just beyond Valley of the Temples is the **Gallery and Gardens** (47-754 Lamaula Road; 239-8146), a beautifully maintained one-acre garden with an art gallery consisting of a series of rustic open-air rooms designed in the Japanese style. Paintings, jewelry, wooden bowls, pottery, and other artwork by local artists are sold at reasonable prices. The lush botanical gardens contain rare and unusual plants and trees, including

According to the teachings of Buddhism, the sounding of a bell cleanses the mind of evil and leads to awakened wisdom. Visitors to the Byōdō-in temple in the Valley of the Temples may strike the gigantic brass *bonsho*, or bell, with a soft wooden log, called *shumoku*, repeating a rite enacted by pilgrims to the Kyoto Byōdō-in for over nine hundred years. The bell's peal and soft echoes evoke an atmosphere of quiet meditation.

A little farther on in this lush area is **Senator Fong's Plantation and Gardens** (47-285 Pulama Road; 239-6775); follow signs from Kamehameha Highway. Hiram Fong, the first Asian American to serve in the U.S. Senate, retired in 1977 after a political career spanning thirty years. Senator Fong has turned his 725-acre plantation—comparable in size to all of Waikīkī—into an exotic garden for visitors to tour via guided tram rides. Much of the land is preserved in its natural state, just as it was when King

Lunalilo owned this acreage in the 19th century. The large **Ka'alaea Valley** *heiau* is in the upper valley and can be reached only by taking the tour. Open daily, 10 A.M.–4 P.M.; admission fee.

Kualoa Ranch (237-7321), about 4 miles up the road from Senator Fong's plantation, has turned its 4,000 acres into an adventure park where visitors can spend the day horseback and ATV

William Charles Lunalilo (1833–1874), a member of the royal family, owned large amounts of land, which he had attained by inheritance. Most of his holdings had been passed on to him by his grandmother Kaheiheimālie, a wife of Kamehameha I. At the time of the Great Mahele of 1848, when royal lands were divided, he was the second largest landowner in the islands. In the Mahele, Lunalilo had to relinquish three quarters of his land.

Beloved by the people of Hawai'i as "Prince Bill," Lunalilo became Hawai'i's sixth king in 1873 but died only thirteen months later from tuberculosis complicated by alcoholism. His remaining land passed to his father, Charles Kana'ina, with the stipulation that after Kana'ina's death the estate would be formed into a trust devoted to "poor, destitute and infirm people of Hawaiian blood." After Kana'ina's death in 1877, the Lunalilo Home for elderly Hawaiians was established in the Makiki area, on the site of the present Roosevelt High School. Today the home is in Hawai'i Kai.

Lunalilo and his father are entombed at Honolulu's Kawaiaha'o Church in an impressive Gothic Revival–style burial vault that bears the legend "Lunalilo ka Moi," or "Lunalilo the King."

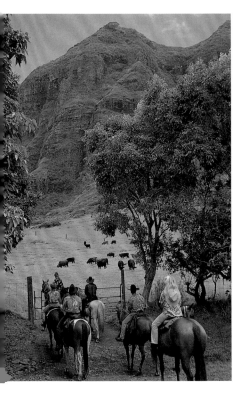

riding, fishing, shooting, snorkeling, kayaking, and more (see page 210).

Kahana Valley State Park, off Kamehameha Highway (Route 83), has been designated a "living park" by the state. This beautiful valley was once a thriving agricultural community of *ʻohana*—people related by blood, marriage, and *hānai*—that sustained itself by wetland agriculture and fishing in the nearby sea. A 1.25-mile hiking trail is situated nearby. The park is open during daylight hours only.

Top left: Kualoa
Ranch; top right:
Kahana Valley.

Opposite page:
Senator Hiram Fong
in his garden.

Pam Andelin,
Waiāhole, oil
on canvas.

O'ahu's northern coast extends all the way from Ka'a'awa in the east to Ka'ena Point in the west. There is still much agricultural land here. Military reserves, consisting of forests and open land, occupy a great deal of the landscape. Most of the beaches along the famous north shore—from Kawela to Hale'iwa—are near the road and, in winter when the surf is up, the enormous breaking waves provide some of the most spectacular ocean vistas anywhere.

To many, this ridge suggests a crouching lion.

The rock formation known as the **Crouching Lion** can be seen from the highway, above the Crouching Lion Inn. Ancient Hawaiians considered the form to be that of a large-headed dog, but some *haole* entrepreneur changed the name.

Along the coast to Lā'ie there are many lovely stretches of shoreline and beachfront that are beside or near the road. At Lā'ie is the famous **Polynesian Cultural Center** (Kamehameha Highway;

293-3333), one of O'ahu's most popular attractions. This 42-acre park features seven architecturally authentic village settings from ancient Hawai'i, Samoa, the Marquesas, Tahiti, Fiji, Tonga, and New Zealand, usually peopled with natives from those islands, some demonstrating their indigenous crafts. In the afternoons, the waterborne Pageant of the Long Canoes snakes its way along the canal that runs from village to village, and in the evenings a Polynesian stage spectacular featuring traditional and modernized dance forms from all the island groups represented is offered, at extra cost. The admission fee is high but well worth the price for an authentic view of Polynesia. Allow ample time, as a thorough viewing of all that's available here easily takes half a day. A film about Polynesian history and Hawai'i's earliest settlement and culture is shown on the three-story Imax theater screen. The evening Polynesian show, from 7:30 to 9 P.M., is entertaining and worth staying for. There are several dining options, including a Hawaiian *lū'au*. Traditional crafts of high quality and authenticity are for sale at the center's gift shop. Open Monday–Saturday, 12:30 P.M.– 9 P.M.; admission fee.

The **Mormon Temple** in Lā'ie (55-600 Naniloa Loop, off Kamehameha Highway; 293-2427) is the spiritual center for the 25,000 Mormons living in the area. They run the Polynesian Cultural

Maori dancers at the Polynesian Cultural Center.

A roadside shrimp stand (below right) has been a Kahuku fixture for years and a favorite stop for a tasty treat. Try the award-winning shrimp fresh from Kahuku's aquaculture ponds.

Center, and Mormon students come from around the world to attend the Hawai'i campus of Brigham Young University. The temple was erected by the Church of Jesus Christ of Latter Day Saints in 1919. Non-Mormon visitors are not generally allowed inside the temple but are welcome to stroll the beautifully landscaped grounds.

The road continues to **Kahuku**, where a sugar mill, established in 1890, once employed many north shore residents. The mill was a short-lived theme park after it stopped converting sugarcane to molasses in 1971, which is why the buildings and equipment are brightly painted. The mill is now closed to the public. The little plantation village of Kahuku is a reminder of plantation days.

Just north of Kahuku and after the Turtle Bay Resort is where the real north shore begins—the windswept beaches that are famous for their pounding winter surf. The names are magical, reminders of the romantic aura that surrounds the sport of surfing. You'll pass **Sunset Beach**, the **Banzai Pipeline** and **Pūpūkea** surf breaks, and **Shark's Cove**, a favorite summertime snorkeling spot but treacherous in winter. When the surf's up, this stretch of road is bumper-to-bumper cars; enjoy the views and pull over once in a while to watch the brave surfers ride the mighty waves.

The hike to Sacred Falls, off Kamehameha Highway, used to be a favorite of residents and visitors alike, until Mother's Day 1999, when six hikers were killed by an avalanche of boulders from mountain walls surrounding the valley. Since then the park has been closed to the public. The 80-foot cascade, known to Hawaiians of old as Kaliuwa'a, is at the end of an easy 2.2-mile trail alongside Kaluanui Stream. However, because of continuing threats of rockslides, the hike should not be attempted. The area, known as Kaluanui Valley, was indeed sacred to the ancients, having been the birthplace of the pig god Kamapua'a. There are many legends associated with the lush valley.

A reconstructed oracle tower at Pu'u o Mahuka Heiau. Such towers were originally enclosed with white *kapa*.

Above Waimea Bay stand the ruins of a *heiau* named **Pu'u o Mahuka**, which may have been built in the 1600s. The site, which offers a sweeping view of the northern shoreline, is reached by a bumpy dirt track off Pūpūkea Road,

on the hill behind Saint Peter and Paul's Church. The largest remaining *heiau* on O'ahu, it has three distinct enclosures. The two largest are about 150 feet wide and well over 500 feet long. Within the walls wooden and thatch structures would have sat on the rock floor. Atop the main terraced enclosure sits an altarlike stone structure. It is likely that this *heiau* was at one time a *luakini heiau*, or sacrificial temple, dedicated to the war god Kū. From 1795, when Kamehameha I conquered O'ahu, until the traditional religious practices were abolished in 1819, Kamehameha's high priest Hewahewa conducted religious ceremonies at this *heiau*.

Opposite **Waimea Bay** is the entrance to **Waimea Falls Park** (59-864 Kamehameha Highway; 638-8511), which occupies 1,800 acres of the picturesque valley above Waimea Bay. Waimea Valley was for centuries inhabited by a large population of Hawaiians who tilled its fertile soil and fished the nearby waters. There are some 6,000 plant species in the park, including plantings from other tropical regions and an especially interesting hibiscus garden that explains the evolution and eloquent hybridization of Hawai'i's state flower.

Numerous types of ground birds, including ducks, geese, and peacocks, wander freely; an aviary displays a variety of colorful and exotic non-native birds such as South American macaws; and lots of free-flying local birds hang around hoping for a handout. Open trams

In ancient times, *ti* leaves, which were believed to have spiritual power, were left as offerings at *heiau*. To prevent the leaves from being blown away, they were anchored with a stone. Today stones wrapped in *ti* leaves are often seen at *heiau* ruins, a modern take on an ancient practice. Native Hawaiians may frown on visitors leaving such relics, and out of respect for them nothing should be removed or changed by visitors.

Above: Waimea Bay.

Right: Hawaiians demonstrate digging with 'ō'ō (digging sticks) at Waimea Falls Park.

Far right: The reconstructed Hale o Lono Heiau at Waimea Falls Park.

provide transportation around the park, with narration by well-informed drivers, while short guided tours of particularly interesting areas are offered in frequent intervals throughout the day. There are also hiking trails through the lush forest that you may follow on your own (admission fee to the park required). At less frequent intervals are demonstrations of diving from the cliff beside the falls—which are pretty but not spectacular—and a very *hele wiki* version of ancient hula. The hula is followed by a short demonstration of ancient Hawaiian games.

The park's current owners have turned it into an adventure park. Horseback riding, kayaking, and mountain biking are offered for a fee in addition to the already steep admission fee of $24. The best deal is the Waimea Adventure Package for $59, which allows two of the adventure activities. In February 2002, the City and County of Honolulu entered into an agreement to purchase Waimea Falls Park—a major step in preserving this significant cultural site—so the nature of what will be offered in the future is unclear. Whatever may happen, it is the natural environment of the historic valley and the cultural significance it held for the native Hawaiians that are the main attractions of the park, and we hope visitors will always be able to experience an authentic view of Hawai'i's past here. Open daily, 10 A.M.–5:30 P.M.; admission fee.

Hale o Lono, a *heiau* dedicated to Lono, the peace-loving god of agriculture, is on the grounds of Waimea Falls Park, next to the parking lot (parking is permitted for half an hour without paying a fee). Carbon dating indicates that this *heiau* may have been in use as early as AD 1000. Other ancient Hawaiian sites can be seen within the precincts of the park.

Hale'iwa

No trip to the north shore would be complete without a stop at the funky, hippie/surfer town of Hale'iwa (pronounced Ha-leh-eva), perhaps most famous for its shave ice. There are several places to partake of this refreshing treat. The crowds are always lined up at **M. Matsumoto** (66-087 Kamehameha Highway), but equally good are **Aoki Shave Ice** and **Miura Store**, both just up the road from Matsumoto's.

Cooling off at Waimea Falls.

Opposite left: This graceful 1921 bridge crosses the Anahulu River at Hale'iwa.

Opposite right: Roadside sign for Hale'iwa.

The **North Shore Marketplace** (66-250 Kamehameha Highway) has some of the best shopping in Hale'iwa along with a quirky little museum, the **North Shore Surf and Cultural Museum** (637-8888), well worth a stop to check out a variety of old surfboards, surfer wear from the '60s, and an extensive collection of old bottles. Open daily except when the surf's up; free.

Also at the North Shore Marketplace are a **Patagonia** store (637-1245), great for outdoor wear, and the **Silver Moon Emporium** (637-7710), a decidedly high-fashion boutique with a unique collection of casual and evening wear for women. **Polynesian Treasures** (637-1288) has a large selection of authentic Polynesian and Hawaiian handicrafts. The locally made items include quilts and decorated gourds. In addition, there are fabrics printed in Polynesian patterns, wood products, baskets, hula supplies, and a good selection of books. Several fairly good art galleries plus a few surf-wear stores round out the shopping here.

The best coffee on the north shore is at the **Coffee Gallery** (637-5355) in the North Shore Marketplace, where you can also get excellent pastries, sandwiches, and salads. For tasty Mexican food, there's **Cholo's** (637-3059), serving up home-style breakfast, lunch, and dinner.

Café Hale'iwa (66-460 Kamehameha Highway; 637-5516), a surfer favorite, is

Shave ice, a unique Hawai'i concoction, is available from many roadside stands and refreshment vans parked near beaches. Finely shaved ice with flavored syrup poured over it, this cool thirst quencher closely resembles what are generally known on the mainland as snow cones, but it isn't the same. The texture of shave ice is much finer—more like actual snow—and the rainbow version is a delight to behold. On a hot summer afternoon this treat is ultra-refreshing. Some vendors add a scoop of ice cream and sweetened black azuki beans under the mound of delicate ice shavings for an extra treat.

A colorful surf shop in Hale'iwa.

Below: The Hale'iwa boat harbor.

Opposite bottom: A farm on the north shore where bird-of-paradise flowers are grown.

legendary for its breakfasts, especially the early bird special at the crack of dawn. Open for breakfast and lunch only, the café has a limited number of tables and closes at 2 o'clock. Finally, for fine dining we like the Pacific rim–inspired menu of **Hale'iwa Joe's** (see Dining).

If you're here in the middle of July, don't miss the annual bon dance and full-moon floating lanterns ceremony at the **Hale'iwa Jodo Mission**. Festivities begin with an evening of Japanese dance and traditional foods, ending after dark with the launching of hundreds of candle-lit lanterns into Kaiaka Bay.

It is possible to drive farther up the coast past Hale'iwa to **Mokulē'ia**, where you can watch gliders from Dillingham Airfield soaring in the trade winds, or even experience this thrill for yourself (see page 217). The rocky coastline between Hale'iwa and Dillingham is punctuated with patches of sandy shore, with calm water during the summer months. The road ends past Dillingham Airfield. From here you can hike or bike the 2.7 miles to Ka'ena Point (see Hiking).

From Hale'iwa, the drive across the island to the Pearl City interchange passes through the Leilehua Plateau, site of O'ahu's largest pineapple fields. First, where sugarcane used to be planted, you'll drive by fields of coffee trees, a new addition to O'ahu's economy. The pineapple fields, though not

Left: The North Shore Surf and Cultural Museum (see page 133) chronicles the history of the sport.

Above: A Hale'iwa street sign.

For ancient Hawaiians, virtually all natural features of the landscape had meaning. In a culture rich with oral tradition, the symbolic significance of every cave, crater, pinnacle, and headland was passed from generation to generation, giving life and immediacy to the historic and mythic legends of gods and heroes.

Ka'ena Point, considered the point from which the souls of the dead departed this world for the next, is associated with many legends and traditions. The large, flat boulder off the point is known as Pōhaku o Kaua'i (rock of Kaua'i). The demigod Māui once stood on this headland and,

in an attempt to draw together the islands of O'ahu and Kaua'i, threw across the intervening channel his special fishhook, called Mana i ka Lani (divine power of heaven), which he had already used to fish up islands all over the Pacific. Giving a mighty tug, he succeeded only in dislodging a boulder, which flew across the channel and landed in the water at his feet. It is still there. The hook flew far behind him and landed in Pālolo Valley where it gouged out Ka'au Crater. Mana i ka Lani was attached to a line made from the 'ie'ie vine; thus the channel separating the two islands has since been known as Ka'ie'ie.

Near Wahiawā, on the Leilehua Plateau of central Oʻahu, is a sacred site called Kūkaniloko, also known as the Royal Birthing Stones. *Aliʻi* women were brought to these large stones to give birth ceremonially in this consecrated setting, believed to have been so used since the 12th century. Use of the site declined and eventually stopped with the arrival of the Europeans in the islands. Surrounded by coconut palms and eucalyptus trees, it is reached by a dirt road off Kamehameha Avenue, just north of Wahiawā, opposite Whitmore Avenue.

Opposite: Kaʻena Point from Mokulēʻia Beach.

Below: Dole Pineapple Plantation.

spectacular sights, are usually of interest to those who have never seen them. The **Dole Pineapple Pavilion** (64-1550 Kamehameha Highway; 621-8408) is a refreshing stop on the long, cross-island drive. It's quite a commercial enterprise, selling everything related to the pineapple. There's a good food bar where you can sip juice and munch chunks of the fresh fruit. Outside, take a stroll over to the edge of the nearest field for a close-up view of the plants that produce this delightful delicacy. Here also is the world's largest maze, for which there is an entrance fee ($5; children $3). It takes 15 to 30 minutes to find your way from beginning to end, something that kids particularly enjoy. During the summer months you can purchase whole pineapples here for much less than in stores. Open daily, 9 A.M.–6 P.M.; free.

Immediately adjacent is **Helemano Plantation** (64-1510 Kamehameha Highway; 622-3929), where residents and day workers raise flowers, fruits, and vegetables and operate a bakery. Hand-made gift items are sold here, along with other local merchandise and jewelry. Helemano Plantation is run as a self-help center for people with developmental disabilities, helping them to become self-sufficient. This special place is worth a stop, though it's a bit too gussied up with cute displays to be of great interest. Open Monday–Saturday, 9 A.M.–3 P.M.; Sunday, 10 A.M.–2 P.M.; free.

To enhance your experience of the pineapple fields, stop at the **Del Monte Pineapple Variety Garden**, at the junction of Routes 99 and 80. Here are displayed living specimens of some thirty species of the South American bromeliad family, of which the pineapple plant is a member. Several varieties of the succulent fruit keep company here with their less productive cousins, and labels explain the life cycle of these plants and their cultivation. Pineapple plants grow from 2 to 4 feet high, and the fruit may weigh as much as four or five pounds, taking between eighteen and twenty months to reach maturity.

the **Leeward Coast**

From the Pearl City interchange, follow the signs marked Waiʻanae to drive along Oʻahu's leeward coast toward the other side of Kaʻena Point. There are lovely stretches of shoreline and some popular beach parks in this district, along with historic and sacred sites.

An interesting stop before reaching the coast is **Hawaiʻi Plantation Village** in Waipahu Cultural Garden Park (94-685 Waipahu Street; 677-0110). To reach the park, take exit 5 off H1 and head *makai* on Kunia Road (750) about .3 mile; turn left on Waipahu. The park is about a mile down this road, on the right. Here a reconstructed village tells the story of immigrant cane workers who came to Hawaiʻi from China, Portugal, Japan, Puerto Rico, Okinawa, Korea, and the Philippines to work the plantations. Camp houses have been faithfully restored and furnished to reflect their various ethnic heritages. Open Monday–Saturday, 10 A.M.– 3 P.M.; admission fee.

The *heiau* site with the most splendid setting is **Kūʻilioloa** at Kāneʻilio Point, at the edge of Pōkaʻī Bay in Waiʻanae, built in the 15th century. Nothing now remains but the several terraces of the former temple. When in use, and with its buildings, altars, oracle tower, and carved images of the gods intact, it must have been spectacular, jutting as it does out into the sea, with commanding views in all directions.

A most moving experience is a visit to **Kāneʻākī Heiau** in the Mākaha Valley. It is the only fully restored *heiau* on the island, rebuilt entirely by hand using only traditional materials and containing all the appropriate wood and thatch structures. Originally an agricultural

heiau dating from around 1545 and dedicated to Lono, it may have been converted by Kamehameha I to the worship of Kūkāʻilimoku, his war god. The altar is usually laden with fresh offerings of *ti*-wrapped stones and food. Over 3,000 wild peacocks live in Mākaha Valley, so don't be surprised if you see one wandering around the *heiau*. Kāneʻākī is located on private land. Though access is not limited, visitors should be respectful of this site so that it will remain open to all. To get there, drive 1.5 miles on Mākaha Valley Road between two golf courses to Maunaʻolu Estates, a gated community. You will need to show the guard your driver's license, registration, and automobile insurance papers. Open Tuesday–Sunday, 10 A.M.–2 P.M.; closed if it is raining (call 695-8174 if in doubt).

The road stops at **Yokohama Bay**, where a hot, 2-mile jeep trail continues to Kaʻena Point.

A reconstructed oracle tower and carved image of the war god Kū at Kāneʻākī Heiau.

Opposite top: Kaʻena Point with the Waiʻanae Mountains beyond.

Opposite bottom: The Chinese Society Hall at Hawaiʻi Plantation Village.

Dietrich Varez, *Māui Finding Fire*, oil on canvas.

It is said that when the Hawaiian demigod Māui was still a young boy he found the secret of fire making at Wai'anae on O'ahu. Here he observed mud hens (*'alae*) roasting bananas in a fire pit, but he did not know how they made the fire, which until then could be obtained only from lava flows. Māui captured the leader of the mud hens and threatened to harm her if she did not reveal the secret. But to put Māui off, the mud hen first told him that fire came from the *kalo* stalk, then that the *ti* leaf was the secret of fire. Māui rubbed these leaves hard to try to get fire, and that is why these leaves have hollows today. At last the mud hen told him that fire came from rubbing together pieces of dry *hau* wood, and so Māui learned to make fire. He was so angry at the mud hen for trying to trick him, however, that he burned a red streak on the mud hen's head with a blazing stick, a mark that appears to this day. For bringing the secret of fire making to the people, Māui was the hero of all of Hawai'i nei.

Central O'ahu

Most visitors choose to turn toward town at Pearl City. If instead you exit H1 at 'Aiea (exit 13), you can take an interesting side trip to **Keaīwa Heiau State Recreation Area**, at the end of 'Aiea Heights Drive. Near the remains of this *heiau hoʻola,* which was dedicated to the healing arts, is an exhibition garden of medicinal plants used by *kāhuna lapaʻau,* ancient Hawaiian medical practitioners. Said to date from the time of the great chief Kākuhihewa, around the 15th century, the *heiau* had been partly dismantled and its stones taken away by the time it was rededicated as part of the park in 1951. Open May–September, 7 A.M.–7:45 P.M.; October–April, 7 A.M.–6:30 P.M.

In the Moanalua Valley, only a few miles *'ewa* of Honolulu, are **Moanalua Gardens** (1350 Pineapple Place; 833-1944), part of the Damon Estate (a missionary-descended family). The 26-acre park is open to the public. Magnificent monkeypod trees shade the vast lawns, and two streams and a natural pool are bordered by ferns, vines, morning glories, and gardenias. White hibiscus trees soar three stories high. A cottage on the grounds, built in the 1850s to provide a card-playing haven for King Kamehameha V and his friends, was moved from a nearby site,

Kamehameha V's country cottage at Moanalua Gardens.

as was the Chinese Pavilion. The gardens also include a *kalo* patch, a *koi* pond, and a group of ancient petroglyphs. Each year in July, the Prince Lot Hula Festival is staged in the park (see Calendar of Events). To reach the gardens, take the Puʻuloa Road/Tripler exit off Moanalua Freeway (Route 78); they are located next to the freeway on the *mauka* side. Open Monday–Friday, 8 A.M.–4 P.M.; free.

Closer to town is the **Arizona Memorial** (Pearl Harbor; 422-0561 or 422-2771), the most highly visited attraction in the state, with attendance further spurred by the 2001 release of the movie *Pearl Harbor.* (To reach the memorial, take exit 15A from H1 and follow signs. City buses 20 and 47 run to the memorial.) A radiant white structure designed by Honolulu architect Alfred Preis, the

The Arizona Memorial.

Above right: The USS *Bowfin*.

Below: Aboard the USS *Missouri*.

memorial straddles the sunken hulk of the USS *Arizona* and marks the watery grave of the 1,102 men who went down with it and remain entombed there. The names of the 1,177 sailors and marines killed in the surprise attack, including the *Arizona*'s captain, are engraved on a marble wall. Before being shuttled by boat to the memorial, visitors are shown a film that recounts the Day of Infamy, December 7, 1941 (see page 39). A museum room in the Visitor Center displays two models of the *Arizona,* as it was in 1941 and as it is today, and other exhibits relate to Pearl Harbor and the attack. (A wait of up to 3 hours to get tickets for the Arizona Memorial is not uncommon during the summer months and over holidays; the best tactic is to be at the door before the information desk opens at 7:30 A.M.) Open daily except Thanksgiving, Christmas, and New Year's days, 8 A.M.–3 P.M.; free.

Near the Arizona Memorial Visitor Center is the **USS Bowfin** (11 Arizona Memorial Drive; 423-1341), a World War II submarine that is also open for self-guided tours. Visitors are provided a small radio receiver keyed to stops throughout the submarine that provides narration for the tour. In the adjacent **USS Bowfin Museum** there is a collection of historic submarine-related memorabilia and artifacts. Note: Children under age four are not permitted on the submarine. Open daily, 8A.M.–4:30 P.M.; admission fee.

A new addition to the Pearl Harbor experience is the battleship **USS Missouri** (423-1341), on whose decks the Japanese surrendered, bringing World War II to an end.

Museums

Several institutions that are considered museums, including 'Iolani Palace, Mission Houses Museum, the USS Arizona Memorial Museum, the U.S. Army Museum, and the Hawai'i Maritime Center, are discussed above, under sightseeing. Singled out here are the largest art and ethnographic museums. Local art galleries where works by Hawai'i artists can be seen and purchased are discussed on pages 224–25.

During the academic year, the **University of Hawai'i Art Gallery** (956-6888) hosts many superb exhibitions. Also on the Mānoa campus are the **East-West Center Gallery** (944-7111), which has a year-round exhibition program primarily relating to interactions between East and West; the ethnographic collection of the **John Young Museum of Art** (956-3634); and the **School of Architecture Gallery** (956-7225).

Bishop Museum

The Bernice Pauahi Bishop Museum and Planetarium (1525 Bernice Street; direct, 847-3511; recording, 848-4129), founded in 1889, is a world center for the study of Pacific island cultures and for marine research. In its magnificent Victorian-style galleries are displayed artifacts from throughout Polynesia, Micronesia, and Melanesia. Artifacts

The Bishop Museum is housed in a grand basalt stone building constructed in 1892 by Charles Reed Bishop in honor of his wife, Princess Bernice Pauahi Bishop.

relating to Hawai'i's culture and history are represented in depth. The collections include gourd utensils, ceremonial pieces carved from indigenous woods, and such rare items as Hawaiian featherwork and *kapa*—both crafts that several generations ago were on the verge of being lost but are today enjoying a revival—as well as more recent historical items. In addition, the museum boasts the largest natural history specimen collection in the world.

Exhibits are mounted along three *koa*-trimmed gallery levels in the Bishop Museum's Hawaiian Hall.

The Hawaiian Hall, the most spectacular of the museum's galleries, is dominated by a 55-foot sperm whale hanging from the rafters. A typical ancient Hawaiian house, thatched with *pili* grass, has been reconstructed in the great hall, using posts and rafters from an 18th-century dwelling. Also displayed is the royal carriage of Queen Lili'uokalani, Hawai'i's last ruling monarch.

The museum's collection of Hawaiian religious images carved from wood is unsurpassed. There are examples of stunning royal capes and standards made of thousands of feathers from the golden *'ō'ō* and red *'i'iwi* birds, both native to Hawai'i. Old surfboards, carved from native *koa*, serve as reminders that this sport of kings originated with the early Hawaiians.

Demonstrations of contemporary craftmaking and performances of music and dance are frequently scheduled and enliven the displays. A high-tech planetarium (847-8201) provides fascinating programs about the stars and planets, including the story of how the ancient Polynesians navigated by the stars. The Shop Pacifica has one of the most in-depth collections of Hawaiian-themed books, clothing, jewelry, music, and more.

The Bishop Museum is a treasure trove of the natural history of Hawai'i and its cultural artifacts, and it should be on the itinerary of every person who comes to Hawai'i. A new Bishop Museum branch in the Kālia Tower of Hilton Hawaiian Village makes it possible for visitors to get a sampling of the museum's amazing collections, but this should not be substituted for a visit to the main museum. Open daily, 9 A.M.– 5 P.M.; admission fee.

Honolulu Academy of Arts

The Honolulu Academy of Arts (900 South Beretania Street; 532-8700), noted for its fine collection of Asian art, holds a number of world-renowned American and European masterpieces as well. This wonderful midsize museum, a serene oasis in the Makiki area of Honolulu, 15 minutes from Waikīkī, should be on every art lover's list of places to visit. With outdoor courtyards at every turn, a splendid gift shop, and an excellent café for a leisurely lunch, the Academy is truly a delightful destination.

The graceful facade of the Honolulu Academy of Arts has remained unchanged since the museum opened in 1927.

The thirty-two galleries present superb exhibitions, further enhanced by the building itself, a 1927 design by New York architect Bertram Goodhue. The territorial-style building, perfectly suited to the tropics, has been enriched by later additions that have been seamlessly integrated with the original, tile-roofed structure.

The Asian collection is ranked among the top ten in the United States. Especially famous is the Japanese collection, with over 300 paintings, including

Above: Marguerite Blasingame, *Figure Composition,* ca. 1930s–40s, carved wood. Honolulu Academy of Arts, gift of Mrs. J. Garner Anthony, 1987.

A grassy courtyard at the Academy held a temporary exhibition of large ceramic sculptures by part-time Kaua'i resident Jun Kaneko.

Above: The Asian galleries at the Academy house one of the top ten collections of Asian art in the United States.

Left: The Academy's European galleries display masterpieces by such artists as Maillol, Matisse, de Chirico, Robert Delaunay, and Braque.

stellar examples of ink paintings from the Momoyama and Muromachi periods and 5,400 *ukiyo-e* prints that were given to the Academy by author James Michener. Chinese paintings, ceramics, and furniture include seminal works by artists of the Ming and Qing dynasties. An important collection of celadon ware, noted for its lustrous green glaze, highlights the varied Korean offerings. Asian textiles, too, are a major part of the Academy's holdings.

Art from the Western world spans the centuries from ancient to contemporary times. In 1961, when Samuel H. Kress distributed his collection to museums around the country, the Academy was the fortunate recipient of a number of fine Italian Renaissance paintings, including an exquisite Piero di Cosimo. Included in the permanent collection are works by, among the Europeans, Cézanne, Monet, Gauguin, van Gogh, Matisse, Léger, and Picasso, and Americans Copley, Stuart, Cropsey, Church, Whistler, Cassatt, Eakins, Sargent, and Hassam. Modern and contemporary art is represented by the likes of Dove, O'Keeffe, Calder, Nadelman, Frankenthaler, Rauschenberg, and Nam June Paik, among many others.

The Academy has the largest collection anywhere of art inspired by the tropical beauty of Hawai'i, and together the paintings, sculpture, prints, drawings, and artifacts represent a pictorial

history of Hawai'i. The Hawai'i collection has found a home in the new Luce Pavilion, a 2001 addition designed by Honolulu architect John M. Hara. Here are examples of fine *kapa*, featherwork, and *niho palaoa* (whale-tooth pendants worn by royalty), and views of Hawai'i by artists associated with early expeditions to Hawai'i or created by 19th- and early-20th-century painters like Enoch Wood Perry, Jules Tavernier, and John La Farge, who made the arduous journey to this Pacific paradise. Later works include premier examples by Hawai'i's finest modernist artists, such as Charles W. Bartlett, Shirley Russell, Juliette May Fraser, Cornelia Macintyre Foley, John Kelly, Madge Tennent, Isami Doi, and John Young.

The Academy offers changing exhibitions, lectures, films, and concerts on a

Cornelia Macintyre Foley, *Hawaiian Woman in White Holokū*, 1937, oil on canvas. Honolulu Academy of Arts, gift of the artist, 1997.

Alexander Samuel MacLeod, *Moonlight and Southern Cross*, ca. 1925, oil on canvas. Honolulu Academy of Arts, gift of the Wallace Alexander Gerbode Foundation.

Above right: John Kelly, *Hawaiiana*, 1937, color aquatint. Honolulu Academy of Arts, purchase, 1937.

regular basis (call 532-8768 for information). A new gift shop offers jewelry, glassware, ceramics, and other crafts by Hawai'i's finest artisans as well as books related to the collection, especially the arts of the Pacific and Asia. The lovely Pavilion Café, in airy new quarters in the Luce Pavilion's courtyard, serves a delicious assortment of homemade soups, pastas, healthy salads, and hearty sandwiches. Reservations are recommended (532-8734).

The Academy is open Tuesday–Saturday, 10 A.M.–4:30 P.M.; Sunday, 1 P.M.–5 P.M.; admission fee.

Across the street from the Academy, at 1111 Victoria Street, the Academy Art Center at Linekona offers artmaking classes for adults and children and sponsors changing exhibitions of a variety of exciting work by local artists, much of which can be purchased. Hours are the same as for the Academy, and admission is free.

The Contemporary Museum

Honolulu's **Contemporary Museum** (2411 Makiki Heights Drive; 526-0232; www.tcmhi.org) makes its home in the historic 1925 Spalding Estate overlooking the city skyline, Diamond Head, and the Pacific Ocean. Splendid galleries, a permanent David Hockney installation, exquisite gardens, a café, and a gift shop blend Hawai'i's gracious traditions with today's newest art forms. The

Pathways wind through the glorious gardens of the Contemporary Museum.

Opposite, bottom right: Theodore Wores, *The Lei Maker,* **1901, oil on canvas. Honolulu Academy of Arts, gift of Drs. Ben and A. Jess Shenson.**

The Contemporary Museum at First Hawaiian Center.

museum's permanent collection, which focuses on art since 1940, includes works by Josef Albers, Robert Motherwell, Louise Nevelson, Jasper Johns, George Rickey, Andy Warhol, and Deborah Butterfield among many others, but it is the regular program of temporary exhibitions that makes this museum a popular destination for art lovers. The museum's biennial of Hawaiʻi artists is perhaps Hawaiʻi's most prestigious exhibition, showcasing the work of emerging and established artists. Docent-led tours are held daily. The café is tucked away in a pleasant garden setting and offers an appealing selection of soups, salads, and entrées featuring Mediterranean and Pacific Rim cuisine. Reservations are recommended (523-3362). A shop specializes in unusual items related to the arts and offers many unique pieces by Hawai'i artists and artisans. Open Tuesday–Saturday, 10 A.M.–4 P.M.; Sunday, noon–4 P.M.; admission fee.

The Contemporary Museum has a downtown venue at **First Hawaiian Center** (999 Bishop Street; 526-0232), where changing exhibitions of work by Hawai'i's cutting-edge artists take place within the environs of a bank. The building is itself a masterpiece of modern architecture and makes a perfect setting for both large-scale and intimate artworks. Open Monday–Friday during banking hours; free.

Tennent Gallery

The Tennent Art Foundation Gallery (203 Prospect Street; 531-1987) is a private museum devoted entirely to the works of Madge Tennent (1889–1972; see also page 224), who is to Hawai'i what Gauguin was to Tahiti. Enamored of the Polynesian race, whom she considered as "having descended from gods," Tennent portrayed Hawaiians in heroic scale. Her primary subject was Hawaiian women, and she painted them large to evoke their innate beauty, power, and grace. Her audaciously bold, bright colors, applied to canvas in swirling masses,

bring her large paintings vibrantly alive. She depicted her beloved Hawaiians in a variety of media, including watercolors and drawings. About forty oils and drawings are displayed, along with a small selection of Tennent's early work, illustrating the evolution of her skills. The museum is in what was once Tennent's home and studio, designed in 1953 by noted Hawai'i architect Vladimir Ossipoff, who specialized in modern houses adapted to Hawai'i's environment. Open Tuesday–Saturday, 10 A.M.–noon; Sunday, 2 P.M.–4 P.M.; free.

Madge Tennent, *Portraits in Fort Street*, 1935, oil on burlap. Honolulu Academy of Arts, gift of Honolulu Art Society, 1935.

ʻoahu's beaches

O'ahu is wrapped in an almost unbroken ribbon of beaches, all of them beautiful and each special in its own way. When Stephen Leatherman, the famous Dr. Beach, issues his annual ratings of beaches, O'ahu sites are always among the topmost.

Ocean recreation was an important facet of life for the ancient Hawaiians and remains a major feature of island life for residents as well as visitors. We all have our favorite beaches. For people watching, Waikīkī is the place to be. Sandy's is great for bodysurfing. For soft, fine sand, no place is better than Kailua. And for surf, the north shore beaches of Sunset and Banzai are world renowned.

Beachboys

The professional beachboy is unique to Waikīkī. This phenomenon began in 1901, after the opening of the Moana Hotel, the first large tourist establishment in Waikīkī. As tourism grew, locals along the beach offered visitors various services.

Experienced and able watermen, they gave outrigger canoe rides and swimming and surfing lessons; they entertained their guests with songs and stories of old Hawai'i and acted as unofficial ambassadors for their homeland. They were colorful cultural characters who enriched the experience of Hawai'i for those who passed this way. Long-lasting friendships often developed between tourists and their beachboy hosts, who became confidants and, occasionally, lovers. The romantic reputation of early beachboys is not entirely mythical.

What began simply as a gesture of friendship and welcome gradually developed into a business of sorts. Tourists of the era when sea travel provided the only access to Hawai'i were necessarily wealthy and usually were generous to the beachboys who befriended them.

The golden era of beachboys was probably in the 1930s, when the Royal Hawaiian joined the Moana on the beachfront and movies began to be made here, throwing a national spotlight on the island—and particularly on Waikīkī.

After World War II, the advent of air travel brought an influx of tourists, and the beach scene became much livelier than in the preceding era. The profession of beachboy also evolved. Beachboys today must be licensed and hold lifesaving certificates; they provide information about parasailing, jet skiing, and canoe and catamaran rides, and all rent various types of surfboards and give lessons in this most Hawaiian of sports (see pages 187–91).

Page 152: A late-nineteenth/early-twentieth-century outrigger-canoe outing.

Page 153: Sailing off Waikīkī in the 21st century. The outlines of the landscape have remained unchanged.

Opposite: Pounders Beach on the north shore (see page 173) is placid during summer months but has a strong shorebreak in the winter, making for great bodysurfing.

Warnings

It's best not to leave anything in your car, even in a locked trunk, as thieves target rental cars. Some people suggest that the best way to avoid a break in is to leave the car unlocked.

Don't spoil your vacation with a sunburn. The sun in Hawai'i is much harsher than in northerly (or quite southerly) climes, primarily owing to the direct angle of the sun at this latitude. Always wear sunscreen.

The sea should be approached with caution. Never swim alone, and be respectful of the awesome power of the sea. The south and windward shores are mostly protected by long, fringing reefs. On O'ahu's north shore in winter, the sheer size of the surf is dangerous, with waves cresting up to 30 feet high. These are generated by seasonal storms

o'ahu's beaches

Kuilima Cove
Kaihalulu
Hana
Turtle Bay
Kawela Bay
Waiale'e
Kaunalā
Sunset
'Ehukai
Banzai
Pūpūkea
Shark's Cove
Waimea
Kapaeloa
Chun's Reef
Laniākea
Papa'iloa
Hale'iwa
Waialua
Ali'i
HALE'IWA

Kawailoa Beach

Kamehameha Hwy.

83

Ka'ena Point
Keālia
Mokulē'ia
Kaiaka Bay

930
Farrington Hwy.

Kaukonahua Road

803

99

803

80

WAHIA

Yokohama

Mākua

930

'Ōhikilolo
Kea'au
Mākaha
Laukīnui
Papaoneone
Mauna Lahilahi
Wai'anae
Pōka'ī Bay
Lualualei

93
WAI'ANAE

Kamehameha Hwy.

M

750

99

Farrington Hwy.

Mā'ili
Ulehawa

780

NĀNĀKULI

90

Pe
Ha

Nānākuli
Manner's
Hawaiian Electric
Kahe Point
Kō 'Olina

Kunia Road

76

93

Fort Weaver Road

'EW

KAPOLEI

'Ewa

Barbers Point

	Miles	
1		4

	Km	
1		4

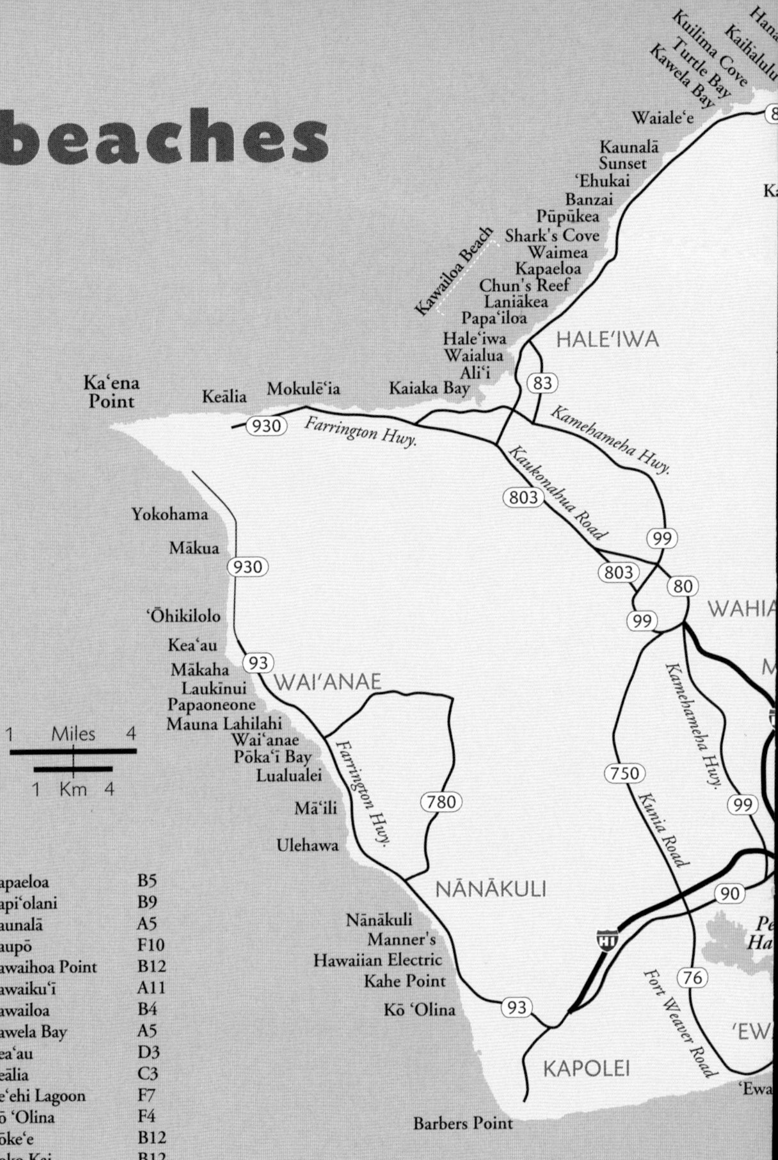

WAIKĪKĪ TO **KOKO HEAD**

in the north Pacific and travel unobstructed until they break on Hawai'i's shores. The leeward (west) shore surf is also high in winter, running as high as 20 feet. In summer, high seasonal surf of 10 to 15 feet—still potentially dangerous—can occur off the south shore.

Never venture out to the edge of rock ledges where surf is breaking. Freak waves can wash over the rocks without warning; many unsuspecting people have been knocked unconscious or swept away by such waves.

Most O'ahu beaches have lifeguards who are among the most well trained in the world. Rely on them for advice, and if the lifeguards request that swimmers leave the water, you can be certain that they have a valid reason.

Jellyfish

Box jellyfish visit many south and windward beaches once a month, eight to ten days after a full moon. They remain for up to three days. Particularly hard hit are Ala Moana Beach and Hanauma Bay. Kailua Beach and Bellows get influxes of Portuguese men-of-war, with long blue tentacles, when the trades are blowing inshore. There is no one antidote to jellyfish stings, though scientists at the University of Hawai'i are doing research in that area. The most common antidote, which seems to provide some relief from the sting, is to wash the sting with common kitchen vinegar.

Sharks

About eight species of sharks are commonly seen near Hawai'i's shores, most of them harmless to humans. The most dangerous is the tiger shark. Shark attacks in Hawai'i's waters are rare and usually occur in murky waters or at dawn or dusk.

Ratings

We have rated O'ahu's beaches according to our interpretation of the following criteria: water safety, bottom configuration (sand, rock, coral), cleanliness/maintenance of beach area, and type and quality of facilities (restrooms, showers, picnic tables, barbecue pits, parking). This is naturally arbitrary, and not everyone will agree with the ratings.

Our ratings are: Pure Paradise, Superb, Excellent, Good, Fair, and Poor. The descriptions of beaches are arranged beginning with those on the south shore, which is the central tourist area, then proceeding in geographical order around the island in a counterclockwise direction.

South shore *beaches*

Barbers Point *to* Sand Island
Poor to **Fair**

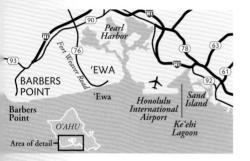

Most of the beach areas along this oceanfront are limited to military personnel, and those with public access afford poor shore conditions for water recreation. **'Ewa Beach Park** (Fair) is locally famous as the best place to collect several varieties of edible seaweed, attracting aficionados from all over the island. There are rideable waves in summer, and swimming is okay if you don't mind the seaweed.

The waters of Pearl Harbor, Ke'ehi Lagoon, and Honolulu Harbor are too polluted for swimming, though there is a public park on the shore of each. Outrigger canoe races are held at Ke'ehi Lagoon every summer and can be watched from the stony shore of the park there. **Sand Island State Beach Park** (Fair) occasionally has small rideable waves offshore and is a delightful place for picnics.

Ala Moana *and* Magic Island Lagoon
Superb

Across Ala Wai Yacht Harbor from Waikīkī's Kahanamoku Beach are **Magic Island Lagoon** and **Ala Moana Beach Park**, both manmade on reclaimed land. Once the Honolulu garbage dump, this area is now the most popular urban beach park for local residents. Though the quality of the beach sand is coarser and, in patches, rockier than that at Waikīkī, this slight shortcoming is offset by the large and well-kept park adjacent to it and by the availability of free parking, an amenity almost nonexistent in Waikīkī. In the summer there is excellent surfing beyond the reef, and the sandy-bottomed swimming area is calm and free of strong currents. However, the water becomes deep quickly, and nonswimmers and children should remain close to shore. There are lifeguards at Ala Moana, none at Magic Island.

Ala Moana Beach Park affords safe swimming and a splendid view of Diamond Head.

A favorite surfing spot for locals is outside the reef lining Ala Moana Beach.

159

Waikīkī Beaches Good to Superb
(depending on location)

Perhaps the most famous swatch of coastline in the world, Waikīkī Beach is actually an almost unbroken 2-mile stretch of a dozen beaches, stretching from the Ala Wai yacht basin to

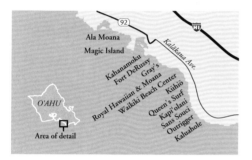

Diamond Head. Much of this shoreline fronts hotels, apartments, condominiums, and private facilities, and only a small portion is open parkland. There are great views of Diamond Head from nearly every part of the beach.

Some parts of the long stretch are better for swimming or for surfing than others; all are good for people-watching and for basking in the Hawaiian sun. Surfboard, windsurfer, sailboat, and outrigger canoe rentals are available at several locations along the beach. It's possible to walk on the sand from one end to the other, though little beach remains in front of the Halekūlani and Sheraton hotels, so you'll have to take the paved walkway that runs in front of those hotels.

It's impossible to rate these beaches as a single unit, as there are too many variances. Generally, the facilities of each section are meant only for guests of the nearest hotel, though there are some public facilities, and all beaches are open to public access.

It is interesting to note that the Waikīkī shoreline has changed significantly over the years through various developments. The beachfront was formerly cut by three streams— the ʻĀpuakēhau, Mānoa, and Pālolo— which were diverted by the Ala Wai Canal.

The individually named beaches along the Waikīkī shore are:

Duke Kahanamoku Beach and Lagoon (Superb) is a manmade beach created in 1955 for the guests of Henry J. Kaiser's Hawaiian Village, now the Hilton Hawaiian Village. This beach is named for Hawaiʻi's famous surfer and Olympic swimmer Duke Kahanamoku, who learned to swim in the waters nearby. Protected by a pier and breakwater, this is a very safe beach. There are lifeguards. Access is from Kālia Road, between the Hilton and Fort DeRussy.

Background: A sailboat at Gray's Beach.

Below: The beach and pier at the Hilton Hawaiian Village Resort and Spa.

Fort DeRussy Beach (Superb) fronts Fort DeRussy and its military hotel, Hale Koa, which are off limits to the public. This beautiful beach, shaded by *hau* trees, is a perfect spot for watersports of all kinds. Lifeguards watch the calm waters, and beachboys offer surfing lessons. Kayaks and surfboards may be rented at the beachboy stand. There are public rights-of-way on Kālia Road.

Fronting the Halekūlani, **Gray's Beach** (Excellent) is named for a former boardinghouse called Gray's-by-the-Sea. Surfing and windsurfing can be enjoyed here. At high tide there is little sand for sunning. There are public rights-of-way from Kālia Road on either side of the Halekūlani Hotel.

Royal Hawaiian Beach (Excellent) fronts the Royal Hawaiian Hotel. It is excellent for swimming as well as surfing, and the wide stretch of sand allows for lots of sunbathers. This beach was formerly called Kahaloa, or "the long place." Access is from Kalākaua Avenue, across from the International Marketplace.

Royal Hawaiian Beach fronts the famous Pink Palace of the Pacific.

Moana Beach is one of Waikīkī's most beautiful.

Opposite top: Waikīkī Beach Center has had a recent facelift, adding Victorian charm to this popular swimming area.

Opposite bottom: Kūhiō Beach is named for the prince who was Hawai'i's second delegate to the U.S. Congress.

Moana Beach (Excellent) fronts the Moana. Like the Royal Hawaiian, it is excellent for swimming and surfing. This beach has lifeguards and the best beachboy stand on Waikīkī, right next to Duke's. Here beachboys offer surfing lessons and outrigger canoe rides, or you can rent surfboards and other water equipment from them. The old name for this beach, before it took on the name of the hotel on the site, was Ulukou, or "the *kou* tree grove." As for the Royal Hawaiian Beach, the best means of access is the walkway off Kalākaua Avenue, across from the International Marketplace.

Waikīkī Beach Center (Superb) is a popular area fronting the section of Kalākaua Avenue opposite the Hyatt Regency and the Marriott hotels. Surfers take the waves farther out, while others enjoy the shallow, safe swimming area closer to shore.

Kūhiō Beach (Superb) is across Kalākaua Avenue from the entrance to the Honolulu Zoo. This beach is named for Prince Jonah Kūhiō Kalaniana'ole, whose house once stood here. It is a favorite spot for surfers. Swimmers should stay clear of the old offshore wall, erected many years ago as a sand-retaining structure; it is very slippery and accidents are common. Lifeguards are on duty daily. If there is a Brunch on the Beach while you are here, don't miss it. All the best restaurants set up food booths, and the event is lots of fun.

Queen's Surf (Excellent) is at the 'ewa end of Kapi'olani Beach Park. The popular Queen's Surf restaurant, famous for its Barefoot Bar, stood here from 1946 until 1970. This wide and sandy beach has been a local favorite for years and is also popular with the gay community.

Kapi'olani Beach Park (Good) is part of Kapi'olani Park, which lies opposite it. The beach isn't great for swimming, but it's fine for surfing. At one time, the city maintained what was called the "Public Baths" on this site, with showers, dressing rooms, and a dance pavilion. Today the only reminder of that era is the popular surfing spot called "Public's" that lies offshore. Lifeguards are on duty daily.

Sans Souci Beach (Superb), also known as **Kaimana Beach**, is adjacent to the New Otani Kaimana Beach Hotel, at the Diamond Head end of Kapi'olani

Beach Park. It is named for the Sans Souci hotel that once was here. Locals come to this beach, away from the crowds at the other end of Waikīkī. You may see swimmers wearing snorkel masks, but the snorkeling isn't very good. Parking is on the road or next to the Natatorium, and access is unlimited. There are shops for snacks in the hotel with easy access from the beach. There is a lifeguard.

Outrigger Beach (**Superb**) fronts the private Outrigger Canoe Club. There is no public access.

coral. During periods of high surf, there are dangerous currents, and there are no lifeguards. These beaches are most popular for basking or watching surfers or as access points to well-known surfing breaks. Windsurfing is also popular here. Good swimming can be found near the Black Point end at **Ka'alāwai** (better known locally as Duke's or Cromwell's), but the only parking near that beach is along nearby residential streets.

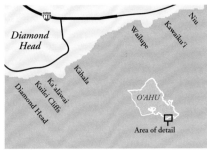

Kāhala *and* Wailupe   Good

This beautiful strip of coastline fronts exclusive residences and the equally highbrow Kāhala Mandarin Oriental. The calm waters protected by fringing reefs are very shallow except in front of the hotel where dredging has produced an excellent swimming spot. There are also occasional deeper holes on the flats. At low tide, you can continue walking past the Kāhala Mandarin to **Wailupe Beach Park**. The hotel provides lifeguards along its section of the beach; otherwise, there are none. This is a popular summer surfing area. Parking is quite limited; there is a pay garage at the hotel.

The beach at Diamond Head.

Diamond Head   Good

There are four beach areas around the curve of Diamond Head (Kaluahole, Diamond Head, Kuilei Cliffs, and Ka'alāwai); most afford poor swimming because of shallow inshore flats and

'Āina Haina *to* Portlock Fair

The small beach parks in this area are suited primarily to picnicking, the shoreline being mostly rock and mud and the bottom shallow. None of them have lifeguards. The turbulent water off **Kawaihoa Point** (commonly known as Portlock Point) can be extremely treacherous. Nonetheless, the point is popular with advanced surfers. Wave surges across the rock terraces below the park pose a danger even for spectators. Wave watching from above is exciting, especially during high surf. The deep waters offshore are often a dark purple color.

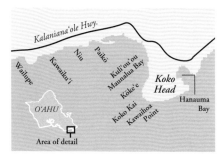

**Above and left:
The Kāhala Mandarin Hotel has a glamorous beach setting.**

south

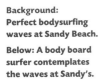

Kalanianaʻole Hwy. 72

Kaloko

Wāwāmalu

Sandy
Hālona

Koko
Head

Hanauma Bay

OʻAHU

Area of detail

Hanauma Bay   Pure Paradise

Hanauma Bay is a special place. Nestled in a breached crater, this almost circular bay, its inner curve lined with a long, narrow, palm-fringed beach, has always been one of the favored scenic and recreation spots on Oʻahu.

Now an underwater park and conservation district, it serves as a haven for the many varieties of marine life that dwell in Hawaiian waters. The large, diverse, and now quite tame fish population, along with the rich coral reef in the bay, make this the favorite spot on Oʻahu for snorkelers and divers. There are large holes in the reef near the beach that afford good swimming. On either side of the bay, near the entrance, are peculiar natural features known as Witches Brew (for the swirling, gurgling water) and the Toilet Bowl (for the way in which this bowl-shaped natural formation empties and refills). Lifeguards are kept busy just by the sheer number of visitors.

Unfortunately, Hanauma Bay's popularity has resulted in damage to its fragile ecosystem. In recent years,

**Background:
Perfect bodysurfing
waves at Sandy Beach.**

**Below: A body board
surfer contemplates
the waves at Sandy's.**

Hanauma Bay is one of the world's most beautiful beaches. Its wide sandy beach and grassy shoreline easily accommodate the crowds who come for the unforgettable snorkeling.

conservation measures have been taken by the City and County of Honolulu, closing the park Tuesdays and charging a user fee ($3) to nonresidents. Because of occasional closings for one reason or another, it's wise to call ahead (396-4229) before making the trek out to Hawai'i Kai. Locals, who remember when access was easy, hardly ever go there anymore, which is too bad, because it is a spectacular site—one of the world's top snorkeling spots (snorkeling gear may be rented at a beach concession).

No smoking is permitted at Hanauma Bay.

Hālona Cove *to* Kaloko   Good

Water conditions at the pretty beaches around this easternmost tip of O'ahu are dangerous, with treacherous currents and seasonal rough waters. Otherwise they'd get a higher rating. The little **Hālona Beach** below the blowhole look-out has no lifeguard and is dangerous for swimming except on very calm days. There are also no lifeguards at **Wāwā-malu Beach Park** and **Kaloko Beach** (also know as Queen's, and not to be confused with Queen's Surf on the south shore)—swimming is discouraged in both spots. There are lifeguards every day, year-round, at **Sandy Beach**, where more rescues occur than anywhere else in Hawai'i. Wave conditions at Sandy's are unequaled for experienced body-surfers, thus attracting throngs of local youth as well as tourists seeking the thrill of turbulent waters, despite the hazards. Another attraction at Sandy's are the brightly colored kites that are flown there.

Windward *beaches*

Mōkapu
Point

Kāne'ohe
Bay

O'AHU

Area of detail

Oneawa
Kalama
Kailua

KĀNE'OHE

83

KAILUA

Lanikai

Bellows

Waimānalo Bay

WAIMĀNALO

Waimānalo
Kaiona
Kaupō
Makapu'u

72

Kaloko
Wāwāmalu
Sandy
Hālona
Hanauma Bay

Kalaniana'ole

*Koko
Head*

Makapu'u   **Good**

The most famous beach for bodysurfing
in Hawai'i is **Makapu'u**. Visitors would
be wise to keep to the inshore waves, as
those farther out are best left to the local
youth who are experienced in these
treacherous waters. Board surfing is
prohibited here because of the density
of bodysurfers in the water. Makapu'u's
water is calm enough for reasonably
safe swimming in summer.

Waimānalo Bay **Pure Paradise**

Background: The Waimānalo coastline.

Opposite: Rabbit Island is just offshore of Makapu'u Beach. A farmer once decided to raise rabbits on the island, but they didn't live long in the inhospitable climate.

Top: The Waimānalo State Recreation Area is known as Sherwood Forest both for the towering ironwood trees and for the area's reputation as an enclave for petty crime.

This beautiful sweep of white sandy beach is the longest on the island at almost 4 miles. It encompasses five beach parks. Most of **Kaupō Beach**'s shore is fronted by reef and rock barriers; offshore areas provide good swimming and surfing. **Kaiona Beach** is shallower and also protected from strong currents by the outer reef; snorkeling is good here. **Waimānalo Beach Park** can develop a small shorebreak in rough weather, but its waters are typically calm and gentle, good for swimming, snorkeling, and windsurfing farther out. Lifeguards are on duty daily. **Waimānalo**

State Recreation Area, also known as Sherwood Forest, has a gently sloping sandy bottom and is sometimes washed by strong currents along the shore. It generally has the strongest shorebreak in the bay and is frequented by bodysurfers.

Lifeguards are stationed at **Bellows Field Beach Park** during the summers and on weekends and holidays. The beach area north of Waimānalo Stream is restricted to military personnel. This and the neighboring Kailua Bay are the best spots on the island for windsurfing owing to the almost constant presence of northeast trade winds.

Paradise

...us with the beaches of
...Bay is the equally lovely
...Bay with its beautiful 2-mile
stretch of white sand beach gently sloping outward to deeper water. At the
southern end is **Lanikai Beach**, which is
well protected from strong wave action
by outer fringing reefs. Lanikai is popular for surfing, windsurfing, and snorkeling. There are no lifeguards. The
adjacent **Kailua Beach Park** is cut by a
canal that forms a *muliwai* (estuarine
pond); the beach is protected from
strong wave action by the outer reef.
Onshore trade winds make this a
favorite spot for windsurfing. It is the
site of several local, national, and international competitions in this sport. Lifeguards are on duty at the beach park
side; the rest of Kailua Beach is relatively
safe, and lifeguards aren't essential. Both
Lanikai and Kailua beaches have been
number one on Dr. Beach's annual survey of the best beaches in the U.S.

Kalama Beach and **Oneawa Beach**
are the unofficial names of the next two
sections of Kailua Beach. Kalama has the
biggest shorebreaks in this bay and is
thus good for bodysurfing. Again, the
only lifeguards along the bay are at
Kailua Beach Park (see above).

Kailua Beach is
popular for sailing,
kayaking, and wind-
surfing. Walkers enjoy
the uninterrupted
2-mile stretch.

Mōkapu Point *and* Kāneʻohe Bay   Fair

Mōkapu Peninsula is occupied by Kāneʻohe Marine Corps Air Station, and access to its beaches is limited to military personnel. The entire shoreline of Kāneʻohe Bay is muddy with shallow flats fronted by rock and coral. There are four parks— **Kāneʻohe, Heʻeia, Laenani, Waiāhole**— none of which have beaches. They are, however, scenically lovely and ideal for picnicking and sunbathing.

Kualoa *to* Kaʻaʻawa   Good

The beaches and parks along this stretch of coastline all have shallow inshore waters, and most have rocky bottoms. **Kualoa Regional Park**, listed in the

Below left: There is a sandbar in Kāneʻohe Bay where volleyball can be played in the shallow waters.

Below right: Kaʻaʻawa Beach Park is protected by an offshore reef.

National Register of Historic Places, is traditionally one of the most sacred areas of Oʻahu and was very important in the life of the Hawaiian people of old. For this reason, it was chosen as the launching site for the original journey of the Polynesian voyaging canoe *Hōkūleʻa* in 1972 (see page 92), and the beach at this park is now called **Hōkūleʻa Beach**. A large grassy park adjoins the long, fairly narrow sand beach. Lifeguard service is provided daily from June through August and on weekends throughout the year.

Kualoa Sugar Mill Beach, Kanenelu Beach, and **Kalaeʻōʻio Beach Park** have no lifeguards. **Kaʻaʻawa Beach Park** has daily lifeguard service in June, July, and August. Snorkeling is good at all of these beaches. Only Kalaeʻōʻio Beach is good for swimming.

North shore *beaches*

Swanzy *and* Makaua   Fair

The unguarded beaches at these two popular parks disappear completely at high tide. **Makaua Beach** is overlooked by the rock formation resembling a crouching lion. Its waters are shallow, and the ocean floor consists of coral reefs, like the neighboring **Swanzy Beach** area.

Kahana Bay *to* Kaluanui   Excellent

Good swimming is a primary attraction along this stretch of shore. The beaches are relatively narrow, but the inshore waters are calm, and the bottom is sandy. Lifeguards are stationed at **Kahana Bay Beach Park** from June through August. The gentle shorebreak here makes it ideal for novice body-surfers. **Punalu'u Beach Park** and **Kaluanui Beach Park**, both unguarded, are good for swimming and snorkeling.

Mākao *to* Kaipapa'u   Fair

The beach areas here are mostly fronted by shallow water with rock and coral shelves extending right out to the reef, making for good snorkeling. Much of the beach sand is covered at high tide. The tiny **'Aukai Beach Park** borders a small bay with a sandy bottom. **Hau'ula Beach Park** has a deep, sand-bottomed channel at the northern end, but the strong currents there pose a hazard. Hau'ula has lifeguards on duty from June through August. **Kaipapa'u** is a rocky shoreline with a shallow, rocky bottom, no beach, and no convenient public access.

Kahana Bay Beach Park is a favorite among local fisherpeople.

Kokololio *to* Mālaekahana
Excellent

There are lovely, long stretches of reasonably wide sandy beach along this coast. **Kokololio Beach** and neighboring **Pounders Beach** are among Oʻahu's most popular bodysurfing spots. Both of these are subject to shorebreaks and strong currents during high winter surf from October to April. The mile-long sandy beach at **Laniloa** is fronted by shallow water over shelves of raised coral, except for two sandy pockets. The waters are protected and safe year-round, and snorkeling is especially good here. **Lāʻie Beach** has a protecting reef fronting the eastern end and a small shorebreak at the western end, where there can be dangerous currents from October through April. This is the best beach in the area for surfing.

Mokūʻauia Beach is on the leeward coast of Mokūʻauia (more commonly known as Goat Island); its waters are occasionally swept by strong currents in the winter months, but it is generally good for swimming and snorkeling. Access is by walking (wearing athletic shoes or Japanese tabis) across the shallows separating it from Kalanai Point (park at Mālaekahana Beach). The easiest and safest time to do this is in calm weather at low tide, when this is a great adventure.

Mālaekahana Beach, a long, sandy curve after Kalanai Point, has calm inshore waters that are safe all year and cover a gradually sloping sandy bottom with rock and coral patches. None of these beaches has lifeguards.

Pounders during the summer months, when the water is like a lake.

Background: Kalaeʻōʻio Beach Park (see page 171) is backed by a mountain ridge known as Kānehoalani.

Background: A north shore sunset.

Kahuku *to* Waiale'e   Good

Little of the coast in this scenic rural area provides good conditions for water activities, and only the beach area at the Turtle Bay Resort has lifeguards. **Kahuku Golf Course Beach, Hanaka-'ilio Beach, Kaihalulu Beach, Turtle Bay**, and **Waiale'e Beach Park** are subject to strong currents from October through April. Though waters are calmer in summer, they are poor for swimming because of the presence of rock and coral along most of the beachfront. The Turtle Bay Resort's little beach at **Kuilima Cove** is one of the nicest and safest in the area, and public access is allowed, with parking in the hotel's lot. The only access to **Kawela Bay**, another lovely, sheltered area, is by sea; however, its outer bay has hazardous currents during heavy surf.

Sunset *to* Hale'iwa   Excellent

Although the north shore technically runs from Swanzy on the windward side of the island all the way around to Ka'ena Point, this strip constitutes what people generally think of as O'ahu's north shore, famous for the dramatic and dangerous surf that pounds the coast each winter. Spectacularly beautiful and thrilling even to watch, the surf's deadly potential is such that these beaches are rated lower than they would be for their summer conditions, which sometimes approach placid. Running continuously for several miles—interrupted occasionally by rocky outcrops—this coast is almost entirely unprotected by reefs, and huge waves often crash directly on the shore. Winter erosion is severe; the ocean may remove as much as 40 feet of the foreshore in a season.

With the upsurge of interest in surfing during the past several decades, various areas of Sunset and Kawailoa have become popularly known by the names of the offshore surfing breaks that expert surfers from around the world come here to ride. Watching them perch precariously on the huge cresting swells is to witness performances that are often awesome, but even such experienced surfers sometimes come to grief in these waters. *Any surfing here is recommended for experts only.* Civil Defense authorities often close the beaches in winter.

The first in this line of famous surfing breaks is Velzyland, off **Kaunalā Beach**, which is fronted by beach rock and reef and has no lifeguards. **Sunset Beach Park** is safe in summer and in winter has some of the most spectacular waves on the island; it has lifeguards. **'Ehukai Beach Park** is small and not even visible from Kamehameha Highway, but it is one of the best places to watch surfers in the renowned Pūpūkea and Pipeline surfing breaks that lie to the east and west, respectively. It is staffed by lifeguards daily throughout the year. The Pipeline is sometimes also referred to as the Banzai Pipeline, a name consequently applied to the nearby shore area, known as **Banzai Beach**, which has some dangerous shore currents even in calm seasons. The large area of **Pūpūkea Beach Park** is fronted almost entirely by reefs, but the area

Above and below:
The Pipeline surfbreak
is at 'Ehukai Beach.

known as **Shark's Cove** provides excellent swimming and snorkeling in summer; in winter the water is too dangerous to go near, to say nothing of into.

The biggest rideable waves in the world roll into Waimea Bay in winter. Besides the towering, murderous breaks outside the point, the shorebreak often runs as high as 15 feet. In summer the bay looks like a lake, making **Waimea Bay Beach Park** a haven for casual and peaceful water recreation. The park has daily year-round lifeguard service. The unguarded areas known as **Kapaeloa Beach, Chun's Reef Beach, Laniākea Beach**, and **Pāpaʻiloa Beach** are fronted by rocks and broken reefs or are subject to strong currents even in calm seasons, making them ill-suited for swimming at any time.

The point outside Waialua Bay and the breaks opposite **Waialua Beach** offer the last of the great north shore surf. The protected cove of **Haleʻiwa Beach Park**, with its shallow, sandy bottom, offers safe swimming all year. Lifeguards are on duty in June, July, and August. **Aliʻi Beach Park**, on the opposite side of the bay (part of **Waialua Beach**) has lifeguards throughout the year.

Mokulēʻia Shoreline   Fair

The protected waters of **Kaiaka Bay** are usually muddy, and the bottom drops away abruptly, but swimming here is safe year-round; there are no lifeguards. Most of the beach areas between here and Kaʻena Point—the westernmost tip of the island—have little or no public access, except for **Mokulēʻia Beach Park** and **Keālia Beach**. In winter the inshore currents are dangerous; they can be strong even in summer.

Kaʻena Point   Poor
(but **Superb** for majestic surf)

Though there are no beaches near Kaʻena Point, on either side, this coast is worthy of note for the raw beauty of its rugged lava (see Hiking) and reef-bounded shoreline and its turbulent waters. Even on calm days, the nearshore currents are powerful, and when the high winter surf is running, the height of the waves here averages 30 to 40 feet, with freak waves even higher, making it the biggest surf in Hawaiʻi. No one has ever even attempted to ride these waves, though there is persistent speculation on the subject among the expert surfing fraternity. In the right season, there is no better place to pay homage to the might and majesty of the sea.

Haleʻiwa's protected cove is popular among outrigger canoers, especially during the summer months.

Opposite: Big Surf at Waimea Bay during the winter.

Opposite insets, left to right: summer snorkeling at Shark's Cove; winter surf at Shark's Cove; summer snorkeling at Waimea Bay.

Leeward *beaches*

Yokohama Bay *to* Mākaha   Good

Oʻahu's other world-famous surfing area is this far end of the leeward (west) coast. Though the winter waves on this side do not reach the monumental heights of those on the north shore, they are still spectacular—and dangerous. Surfing in these waters is again best left to the experts. The only lifeguards in the area year-round are at **Mākaha Beach Park**. The first beach area south of Kaʻena Point is **Yokohama Bay**. It

also marks the end of the paved road. The beach is narrow in winter, wide in summer. **Mākua Beach** has similar, only slightly less dangerous, conditions. **ʻŌhikilolo Beach** is accessible only by a trail from Kāneana Cave, and its rocky shoreline fronts deep and dangerous waters, but there is a small, secluded cove where a shallow inshore pond provides safe swimming. Most of the long stretch of **Keaʻau Beach Park** is fronted by coral and sharp lava rock that preclude swimming.

Mākaha Beach Park, site of the annual Mākaha International Surfing Contest since 1952, has some of Hawaiʻi's best surfing waves between October and

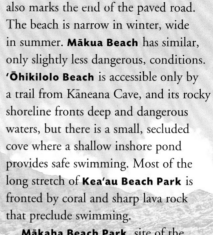

April. Swimmers during this season must beware not only of dangerous wave action but also of loose surfboards. The beach is narrow in winter with a steep foreshore; the sand returns in summer, and the beach is wide with a gentler slope. Mākaha has lifeguards. A tiny cove in the long rocky shoreline shelters a small beach called **Laukīnui**, and **Papaoneone Beach** lies in the crook of the point below Mauna Lahilahi ("thin mountain"). Both of these have inconvenient public access. **Mauna Lahilahi Beach Park** has fairly safe inshore waters even when the surf is up, but the water is often murky from runoff. The shoreline is mostly rock with a stretch of sandy beach that is seasonally wide or narrow; lifeguards are on duty daily during summer months.

Wai'anae to Ko'Olina   Fair to Good

Wai'anae Regional Park (**Fair**) is fronted by a low sea cliff that drops sharply to deep water, but across the bay at **Pōka'ī Bay Beach Park** (**Good**) is a lovely sheltered beach fronted by a sandy, gently sloping bottom, providing good, safe swimming all year. There are lifeguards at this beach. On the point at the edge of the park lie the ruins of a *heiau* known as Kū'ilioloa. The long strip of almost contiguous beach parks called **Lualualei, Mā'ili,** and **Ulehawa** (all **Fair**) comprises sandy beaches that are largely washed away in winter and are fronted with reef and rock, making swimming virtually impossible anytime and anywhere except in sandy pockets along the shore: in front of the lifeguard stands at Mā'ili and Ulehawa (staffed daily in summer and weekends all year) and at the western end of Ulehawa, where an enclosed lagoon provides safe swimming even when the surf is high.

Nānākuli Beach Park (**Good**), almost divided in half by a tract of homes, has areas of sandy beach at each end that are subject to heavy shorebreaks and rip currents in winter; lifeguards are on duty daily. **Manner's Beach** (**Fair**) and **Hawaiian Electric Beach Park** (**Fair**) have generally safe water conditions all year, though there are sometimes strong currents when the surf is high. **Kahe Point Beach Park** (**Fair**) has water access only at a small cove on the eastern edge where water conditions are unsafe from October through April.

At **Ko'Olina** (**Good**), site of the Ihilani Resort and Spa, a series of four manmade lagoons offers safe swimming and wading in waters that are calm year-round. Privately maintained, the beaches are beautifully landscaped. There is public parking, lifeguards are on duty daily, and access is easy, making this a favorite family destination. Currents can be strong outside the lagoons.

Background: The Wai'anae coastline.

Opposite top: Remote Yokohama Bay is usually uncrowded.

Opposite bottom: Kea'au's rocky waters are frequented by a few surfers.

Below: Manmade lagoons shelter swimmers at Ko'Olina.

activities

*A**ctivities on Oʻahu* are varied and many, most of them taking advantage of the crystal clear waters and the towering mountains. Among watersports are snorkeling, scuba diving, surfing, water skiing, parasailing, canoeing, kayaking, fishing, and sailing. Hiking, horseback riding, biking, running, golf, tennis, and volleyball round out land sports. In the air, you can take a glider ride or tour the island by helicopter. You can take a boat cruise, visit a spa, and shop till you drop. In the evenings, sunset cocktails are enhanced by enchanting performances of song and hula. Trendy nightclubs welcome the wee hours of morning. All of these activities and more are described in the pages that follow.

Note: In the months following the September 11, 2001, terrorist attacks on the United States and the subsequent decrease in the number of visitors coming to Hawaiʻi, many companies have curtailed operations, and several small businesses have closed. We have attempted to update information, though constant changes make that difficult.

Pages 180–81: A swirling tapestry of bon dancers, Jodo Mission, Haleʻiwa.	**Above: Hiking** in the Koʻolau Mountains, where there	are many moderately easy trails that offer splendid views.	**Right: Windsurfing** is a favorite activity off Diamond Head and at Kailua Beach.

On the Water

The island's beaches are described on pages 154–79. Nearly every watersport known can be indulged in on Oʻahu, from swimming and snorkeling to big-wave surfing, for which the island's north shore is justifiably famous.

Snorkeling

For swimmers curious about submarine scenery, snorkeling provides excellent and easy access to the underwater world. Snorkels, masks, and fins are available from all Waikīkī beach services pavilions, found on the beach and in hotel lobbies, as well as from the dive shops listed below, under Scuba Diving. There are many good inshore snorkeling areas around Oʻahu; the most spectacular is the protected reef community at **Hanauma Bay** (396-4229). Fish thrive in these waters, making it a favorite with visitors. A concession rents snorkel equipment for a reasonable fee. Open daily, 6 A.M.–7 P.M., except Tuesday; admission fee ($3); children and Hawaiʻi residents free.

Both the Circle Island and Trolley Island bus tours (see page 25) and other tour operators include Hanauma Bay on their itinerary, though they just stop for the view. Hanauma Bay snorkeling tours that include roundtrip transportation from Waikīkī, snorkeling equipment, and instruction include **Hanauma Bay Snorkeling** (373-5060) and **A Reef Adventure** (395-6133).

Other snorkeling areas are referred to in the Beaches section. Boat excursions to good snorkeling spots are described under Sailing (pages 194–95) and Boat Cruises (page 195). **Surf & Sea Hawaiʻi** (637-9887) offers snorkeling tours to north shore locations.

Scuba Diving

For an even deeper look at Oʻahu's undersea environment, take a tank dive. Certified divers may rent equipment and go out on their own or may arrange a chartered excursion. Those unfamiliar with local conditions are encouraged to take an escort. Introductory classes are readily available for those seeking certification. Dives take place wherever conditions are best at the time; this generally means the north shore in summer and the south shore in winter, as this is the prevailing pattern of calm waters. Depths range from 10 to

Opposite:
A snorkeling cruise in Kāneʻohe Bay.

A young snorkeler gives a shaka wave.

70 feet, with most areas falling into the middle of that spectrum.

In addition to the haven of **Hanauma Bay**, which is calm most of the time and is accessible from the shore as well as by boat, there are ten major dive spots around Oʻahu. Off the north shore, **Shark's Cove** affords the best and most popular cavern dives on the island, and the nearby **Three Tables** area offers caverns, ledges, and large rocky formations; both of these are accessible only from the shore and diveable only during summer. Lava formations, including caverns and arches, are also the principal attraction at leeward Oʻahu's **Mākaha Caves**, accessible from either boat or shore; the frequent presence in the area of large green sea turtles also draws many underwater wildlife enthusiasts. A sunken minesweeper named **Mahi** off Māʻili Point, also on the leeward coast, offers an interesting dive and lots of colorful marine life; it is accessible only by boat. A good site for beginners is **Rainbow Reef**, accessible by boat or from shore, off Ala Moana Park, where lovely tropical sea creatures are fond of being hand fed. Lava formations, small caverns, underwater canyons, a sunken barge, and an abundance of beautiful fish, eels, turtles, and crustaceans give the stretch of

Scuba diving in Shark's Cove on the north shore.

Opposite: Surf legend Gerry Lopez on a last wave at the end of a long pro-surfing career.

offshore waters from Diamond Head across Maunalua Bay the best concentration of fascinating diving on the island. Popularly known as Hundred Foot Hole, Fantasy Reef, Kāhala Barge, Big Eel Reef, and Turtle Canyon, these dive spots are accessible only by boat.

Dive rates usually include transportation to and from hotels in Waikīkī; the cost of equipment depends on what's required; some dive operators include equipment in the basic fee. **Aloha Dive Shop** (395-5922) in Hawaiʻi Kai is one of the older dive shops on the island and offers reasonable rates. **Aaron's Dive Shop** (261-1211) in Kailua has operated for more than thirty years in Hawaiʻi and has a good reputation for finding the best diving conditions. **Ocean Concepts Scuba** has two locations, in Kāneʻohe (254-7669) and in ʻAiea (677-7975), in addition to reservation desks in many hotels; call their hotline (677-7975) for information. **Reef Trekkers Hawaiʻi** (943-0588) operates in small groups and covers all the island, selecting sites based on what you have in mind. Another respected dive operator is **Dive Authority** (333 Ward Avenue; 596-7234).

Located near Shark's Cove and Three Tables, **Surf & Sea Hawaiʻi** (637-9887) in Haleʻiwa

offers an introductory dive that's designed for those without certification. They also take out groups of experienced divers. **A Reef Adventure** (395-6133) takes non-certified divers on a guided reef tour and also offers dives for more advanced participants.

Da Kine Scuba Repair (91-444 Komohana Street; 682-7372), near the Barbers Point Naval Air Station, specializes in the repair of all major brands of scuba equipment.

Surfing

While many Polynesians enjoyed riding the surf in their outrigger canoes, Hawaiians alone developed the art of riding boards specifically designed for play atop the rolling waves. The sport of surfing was perfectly suited to these strong, island-based people, who lived constantly within reach of the sea and its changing waves and who valued courage and agility.

In modern times, this ancient sport has been refined and extended beyond anything its inventors could ever have imagined. Its popularity has spread around the globe, and professional surfers demonstrate their skill and daring while vying for six-figure purses. The manufacture of surfing equipment has also developed, along with the emergence of new materials and technologies, and in recent years several new variants to surfing have been introduced, including windsurfing. The areas best suited to surfing and windsurfing are noted in the Beaches section (pages 154–79).

Many famous surfing exploits were passed down through the voluminous oral history of the ancient Hawaiians. Their name for what we call surfing was *he'e nalu,* which can be loosely translated as "wave sliding," but which, like everything else in the Hawaiian language, is rich with a range of subtlety and poetic nuance that says much more. The best surfing breaks were reserved for use by the ruling chiefs, and violators of this *kapu* could be punished by death.

Board Surfing

This is the original sport. No one knows how long ago it developed, but Hawaiian petroglyphs dating back to about the 8th or 9th century show people board surfing, and as early as the 15th century Hawaiians had so refined the sport that contests between champions were held for what even today would be considered high stakes. Ancient Hawaiians gambled with unbridled enthusiasm at every opportunity, wagering their property, their wives, even their lives on the outcome of a single competition.

Surfing, like all things Hawaiian, declined dramatically during the first century or so of European immigration to the islands. The missionaries frowned upon what they perceived to be idle pleasures, while Hawaiians for their part were busy adapting to Western lifestyles. In 1892 the anthropologist Nathaniel B. Emerson wrote that "today it is hard to find a surfboard outside of our museums and private collections." But surfing, both on boards and in canoes, began to be promoted again in Hawai'i early in the 20th century, when the islands first began to become a tourist destination. Surfing's international fame spread with demonstrations in Atlantic City, Southern California, and Australia by surfing champion and Olympic gold medal swimmer Duke Kahanamoku, whose performance at the 1912 Olympic games in Stockholm brought worldwide attention to Hawai'i.

By the 1960s a surfer culture had arrived in the islands, with long-haired "surf bums" populating favorite surf towns, especially on O'ahu's and Maui's north shores. Today, professional surfing is a highly regarded sport, and surfers travel the world to participate in big-wave competitions, including those in Hawai'i.

When the surf's up, Hawai'i school kids head for the beaches at first light, and workers bring their surfboards along for a lunchtime break. Waves are measured in feet, from trough to crest. However, Hawai'i custom doesn't measure wave faces objectively, but instead—in a sort of macho understatement, according to one local surf forecaster—measures them by about 50 to 70 percent of face height. So when you hear there is 15-foot surf, the waves may have a 30-foot drop as they come thundering to shore. The National Weather Service is trying to get Hawai'i surf fore-

Winter surfing at Waimea Bay.

Opposite: Long racks hold rental surfboards at Waikiki Beach.

Background: Dietrich Varez, *He'e Nalu* (Board Surfing) (detail), linocut.

casters to measure the wave face accurately from trough to peak, as the rest of the world does.

One of the activities you can do on O'ahu that's great fun is to take a surf lesson, available wherever surfboards are rented. Virtually all surf schools guarantee that you'll be standing by the end of your first lesson. The beachboys on Waikīkī Beach are friendly, experienced teachers, and their fees are reasonable. There are beachboy stands all along the beach, the largest being at Fort DeRussy Beach, Moana Beach, and Kūhiō Beach. Locals head for **Aloha Beach Service** (922-3111) at Moana Beach, between the Moana Hotel and Duke's seaside bar. No reservations are necessary.

Pro surfer **Hans Hedemann** operates a surf school out of the Park Shore Hotel (2586 Kalākaua Avenue; 924-7778), where his well-trained staff provides surfing and body-boarding lessons. Hans himself is somewhat of a movie star, having appeared in the surf flicks *North Shore* and *Back to the Beach*. **Hawaiian Fire Surf School** (384-8855) offers lessons from local firefighters, who are among Hawai'i's top surfers. They'll pick you up at your hotel and take you to a secluded beach for a day of fun-filled surfing.

On the north shore, Stan Van Voorhis III gives lessons for all skill levels through his **North Shore Eco Surf Tours** (638-9503). **Surf & Sea Hawai'i** (637-9887) offers surf lessons at 1 P.M. daily and also rents out boards.

Surfboards were treasured objects for the ancient Hawaiians. The original surfboards were 18-foot, 150-pound monoliths, often made of *koa* wood. After use, they were dried, oiled, wrapped in cloth, then suspended inside the house. Much ritual was associated with the making of surfboards. After a tree was selected for its wood, an offering of a red *hūmū* fish was made. The board was shaped in the *hālau*, or canoehouse, and dedicated with a special prayer before it was used.

Surfboard design didn't change much until the mid-1940s, which saw the introduction of hollow boards and ones built of such lightweight materials as balsa and redwood, then fiberglass and synthetic foam. The evolution of surfboards has also seen variations in length, width, and thickness. These innovations have resulted in boards that excel in varying conditions, so that today's top surfers keep collections of several boards from which to choose.

Bodysurfing

This cross between board surfing and swimming stems from the same principle as board riding, except that the body replaces the board as the vehicle. The ancient Hawaiians called this activity *kaha nalu* or *pae*. There are two basic techniques for accomplishing this feat: keeping the body straight with the arms pinned against the sides while riding the shoulder of the wave just ahead of the breaking water, or keeping one or both arms straight out in front for greater maneuverability. The former technique seems to work best in offshore breaks, such as those at Makapuʻu Beach. Most expert bodysurfers use both techniques, sometimes while riding the same wave.

Though purists decry the practice, virtually all bodysurfers use fins to increase propulsion and enhance their ability to catch a wave.

Body Boarding

The body board, developed from homemade short boards used by Hawaiians, was invented in Hawaiʻi in the early 1970s by Tom Morey. Made of flexible foam, the boards are a couple of feet wide, about 4 feet long, and about 3 inches thick. They are ridden prone. The latest development along this line is a high-performance body board (now termed "turbo board"), invented by Russ Brown in 1983. Considered the Porsche of body boards, it is stiffer and faster than the standard model. These inexpensive water toys have become ubiquitous in Hawaiʻi and are readily available for rent and for sale. **Sports Authority** (333 Ward Avenue; 596-0166) has a large selection of body boards, as does **Turbo Surf Hawaiʻi** (870 Kapahulu Avenue; 738-8726).

Sand Sliding

This too is an ancient pastime that has been given a modern twist. The original idea was to throw oneself onto the sand at the precise moment when a receding wave had left just a thin sheet of water on which the body would then slide. Precise timing was (and is) essential, as too early a leap results in a mere sinking into the sand, and too late a one ends in an abrupt, abrasive halt.

Bare-body sand sliding is seldom seen anymore, but body boards are also used in this fashion. Nowadays, the hot trend is the skimboard, a short foam board about three quarters of an inch thick that is thrown onto the receding wave then jumped upon.

Skilled standing riders have developed some fancy skateboard-like maneuvers on this type of board, and contests have been held at Sandy Beach and Waimea Bay. Skimboards can also be ridden as bellyboards in the waves.

Body boarding at Point Panic, near Honolulu Harbor.

Windsurfing

Windsurfing is a marriage of surfing and sailing that is even more complicated than it appears, requiring techniques and styles that are being improved on all the time. This modern variation of the ancient sport of surfing was conceived in 1970 by Californian Hoyle Schweitzer and developed by his friend Jim Drake (actually, the very first windsurfer was Hawai'i surfing pioneer Tom Blake, who in 1935 rigged his surfboard with a crude sail). The popularity of this new sport has spread like wildfire, and today a circuit of amateur and professional contests is well established. The sport is even included in the Olympic games.

Waikīkī is not a good place to windsurf because of the prevailing offshore winds and choppy water conditions; however, a lot of people do it here for convenience. If you're an expert, Diamond Head and the north shore afford the most challenging wave jumping. Otherwise, Kailua Bay on the windward coast is O'ahu's best windsurfing spot; its waters are protected by a fringing reef, and the prevailing northeast trade winds blow fairly steadily onshore (see Beaches). These conditions also make it one of the easiest places to learn. Most

Parasailing is family fun.

shops that rent sailboards also offer lessons.

Topping the list for having been around the longest, Kailua's **Naish Hawai'i** (262-6068) runs a professional operation. Rates for standard equipment are quite modest, and custom equipment costs only slightly more. Instruction is reasonably priced and geared for all skill levels. Another established company, **Kailua Sailboards & Kayaks** (262-2555), offers beginner lessons as classes—one on land and two at sea—and as private instruction; they offer transportation from Waikīkī. On the north shore, **North Shore Windsurfing School** (638-8198) and **Surf & Sea Hawai'i** (637-9887) give lessons.

Water Skiing

The most popular areas around the island for water skiing are Ke'ehi Lagoon, Maunalua Bay, and Kāne'ohe Bay. Another good site for water skiing is Koko Marina Lagoon, located near Hanauma Bay. **Hawai'i Sports Wakeboard & Water Ski** (395-3773) at Koko Marina Shopping Center offers half-day excursions and instruction for all skill levels, with free pickup from Waikīkī hotels. The store is stocked with a full line of equipment and accessories, and rentals are available.

Parasailing

Some people prefer to rise above it all—up to 800 feet—in a parasail. Powerboats tow the parasails, and the wind does the rest. You don't have to do anything but sit and enjoy the stunning and everchanging views. Since you launch and land directly from a boat, you don't even have to get wet. Rides last 8 to 10 minutes, and tandem as well as single rides are available. This is an activity the physically challenged can enjoy; those who use a wheelchair must have another person with them. **Sea Breeze Parasailing** (396-0100), **Aloha Parasail/Jet Ski** (521-2446), and **Hawaiian Parasail**

(591-1280) all provide free Waikīkī pickup and return. All offer comparable rates for this not inexpensive joy ride in the sky.

Outrigger Canoeing

Waikīkī is one of the few places in the Hawaiian islands where visitors can take an outrigger canoe ride. Most beach activity centers in Waikīkī offer canoe rides, and those that don't can steer you in the right direction. Most of the Waikīkī outriggers seat four to eight people. Two beachboys ride along, the stroker who sets the pace in the front and the steersman, who rides in the back and guides the course. You'll be expected to paddle, though the hard work is done by the beachboys. This is an exhilarating experience that shouldn't be missed. Prices vary greatly, so shop around.

Locals engage in canoe paddling races in Waikīkī and elsewhere, and a number of fun races in the Waikīkī surf—usually fundraisers—are held throughout the year by various canoe clubs and other organizations. On the windward side, **Outrigger Connection** (261-8424) in Kailua offers one-, two-, and six-person outrigger canoes for rental.

Kayaking

This ancient Eskimo pastime translates well to the tropics. In addition to the waters around Waikīkī, two of Oʻahu's most scenic bays, Kailua and Kāneʻohe, are frequented by the regulars. **Go Banana Kayaks** (737-9514), near Waikīkī, has a good reputation and offers kayak rentals, lessons, and tours. **Bob Twogood Kayaks Hawaiʻi** (262-5656) rents kayaks and gives free introductory lessons in Kailua, the location also of **Kailua Sailboards & Kayaks** (262-2555), which provides transportation from Waikīkī for a great day of water fun that includes a hot lunch.

Fishing

Shore fishing is popular at Ala Moana, Waikīkī, Sandy Beach, Waimānalo Beach, Kāneʻohe Bay, Waimea Bay, ʻEwa Beach, and Pōkaʻi Bay. Deep-sea fishing lures a lot of enthusiasts to Hawaiian waters to catch

Dietrich Varez, *Waʻa Kaulua*, linocut.

Brought to Hawaiʻi by the Polynesians, the outrigger canoe (*waʻa* in Hawaiian) is a unique design with an outrigger float, called an *ama,* that stabilizes the vessel in heavy surf. Today's outrigger canoes differ very little from those that Captain Cook saw by the thousands when he arrived at the island of Hawaiʻi in 1778.

For travel across the vast Pacific, double-hulled canoes (*waʻa kaulua*) that could carry over a hundred voyagers were used by ancient Hawaiians, powered by a *pandanus* mainsail mounted on a central platform. The port hull of the dou␣ noe is called an *ama* because it replaces the float. The *Hōkū␣ uilt* in 1976, is an authentic re-creation of an ancient sailing canoe (see page 92)

Sportfishing for *mahimahi* (left) and *aku* (right).

Below: Pole fishing in Waimānalo Bay on the windward coast.

mahimahi (dolphinfish), *ono* (wahoo), *'ahi* (yellowfin tuna), *aku* (skipjack tuna), and, if lucky, *a'u* (marlin). Most fishing charters operate out of Kewalo Basin, which is just past Ala Moana Beach, heading in the airport direction.

Island Charters (593-9455) and the ***Maggie Joe*** (591-8888) have been reeling them in for a long time. The boats of **Tradewind Charters** (973-0311) are staffed by an experienced and able crew. They offer a range of excursions daily, taking out no more than six fisherpeople at a time. Other well-known boats worth investigating are the ***Kamome*** (593-8931), ***Meagan II*** (696-3474), and ***Sea Verse III*** (591-8840). On the north shore, **Surf & Sea Hawai'i** (637-9887) sets up big-game fishing charters.

Reservations should be made in advance for these excursions; most trips are 8 hours in duration. Aficionados know this is not an inexpensive pastime. On some fishing boats in Hawai'i, it is customary for the boat captain and crew to keep the catch; oth-

ers allow visitors to retain any fish they catch. Ask ahead of time which practice the boat you choose subscribes to in order to prevent any misunderstanding. It is customary to tip the skipper

and crew after a successful voyage (roughly 10 to 15 percent is a good tip). Unless stated otherwise, you bring your own food and beverages on fishing trips (coolers and ice are provided).

Sunset cruises off Waikīkī Beach.

Sailing

Hawaiian waters offer exquisite sailing, on whatever scale you choose—from 14-foot catamarans to 60-foot yachts. Small boats, such as Hobies, are available for anywhere from half an hour to all day.

To participate in a 4-hour sail on a 43- or 54-foot yacht from Honolulu Harbor, contact **Honolulu Sailing Company** (239-3900). Their excursions are uncrowded, and, for a small additional charge, lunch with an open bar is available. Passengers bring their own snorkeling gear. This outfit also gives sailing lessons.

Tradewind Charters (973-0311) offers sailing, snorkeling, sport fishing, whale watching (seasonal), and sunset excursions. The friendly and helpful Tradewind crews encourage hands-on participation by passengers in sailing the vessel. Boats leave from Keʻehi Marine Center at Keʻehi Lagoon (15 minutes from Waikīkī, near the airport) and sail to Diamond Head, stopping on the way back in the waters off Magic Island and Ala Moana Beach Park. Snacks, beverages, and equipment are included in the prices. Private overnight and interisland cruises are also available, as are private sailing lessons, giving visitors the opportunity to develop basic sailing skills.

Located in Waikīkī between the Sheraton Waikīkī and the Halekūlani, the *Maitaʻi* (922-5665) makes frequent 1.5-hour sails during the day as well as a sunset mai tai sail at 5 P.M.

Captain Bob's (942-5077) offers a snorkeling tour in beautiful Kāneʻohe Bay aboard the *Barefoot I;* the price includes a picnic lunch and transportation to the windward side from Waikīkī.

The boat is glass-bottomed, for those who would prefer to see exotic sea creatures without getting wet.

Boat Cruises

All the boat tour companies provide transportation from Waikīkī, sometimes for an extra fee, sometimes included in the basic price.

Snorkeling and other water fun off Waikīkī can be had aboard the **Starlet II** (983-7827). There are a water slide and a trampoline; snorkeling gear is provided, as is an all-you-can-eat lunch prepared on the boat's own BBQ grill. **Dream Cruises** (592-5200) also operates a "barefoot fun cruise" off Waikīkī that includes snorkeling, a water slide and trampoline, and a lunch of burgers, hot dogs, corn on the cob, etc.

Two big sightseeing boats depart from Aloha Tower, the **Navatek I** (848-6360), which offers a variety of cruises aboard a vessel so well stabilized that even the most ardent landlubber will feel comfortable on it, and the state-of-the-art **Star of Honolulu** (983-7827), which cruises from Diamond Head to Pearl Harbor. The catamaran **Ali'i Kai** (539-9495) makes Pearl Harbor coastal cruises several times a week.

See also Dinner Cruises (page 240).

Submarine Rides

Atlantis Submarines (973-9811) allows you to tour the ocean's reef and see its exotic creatures from the window of a spacious passenger submarine; tours leave from the dock at Hilton Hawaiian Village, starting at 8 A.M. No passengers under 30 inches tall are allowed on submarines, following U.S. Coast Guard regulations.

Dolphin- *and* Whale-Watching Tours

Safe and fun dolphin-watching tours are run by **Hawaiian Parasail** (597-8643), operating out of Kō 'Olina Harbor on the leeward side. Their 21-passenger aluminum hull inflatable boat travels past Mākaha Beach and Yokohama Bay, through prime dolphin-feeding grounds. In season, December through April, whale watching is added to the mix. Tours include transportation from Waikīkī hotels and an excellent lunch.

Dream Cruises (592-5200) offers dolphin and whale watches aboard boats leaving Wai'anae Harbor, on the leeward coast, with transportation from Waikīkī. Dolphin sightings are guaranteed, as are whale sightings in season. Visitors can hear the songs of dolphins and whales via a hydrophone that is dipped in the water.

Some of the tours include a meal; others offer meals at an additional cost.

Interisland Cruises

Norwegian Cruise Lines

(800-327-7030; www.ncl.com) offers one-week cruises of the Hawaiian islands aboard the 2,200-passenger *Norwegian Star,* whose homeport is Honolulu. Ports of call include Hilo, Hawai'i; Lahaina, Maui; Nāwiliwili, Kaua'i; and the Fanning Islands in the Republic of Kiribati, 1,000 miles south of Hawai'i.

The *Star,* Norwegian Cruise Line's newest and largest vessel, has ten restaurants and 24-hour room service. The sports deck has a golf driving range and volleyball and basketball courts, while the two-deck fitness center boasts state-of-the-art equipment. Hawai'i-based Mandara Spa offers the ultimate in spa treatments.

There is a huge children's center complete with outdoor pool, movie theater, and computer rooms.

This fast-sailing ship provides visitors with excellent service and exquisite vistas by sea. Travelers can choose from a selection of land tours at island stopovers, including golf outings. This is a wonderful, romantic way to see the islands.

On Land

Hiking

Most of the bookstores in Honolulu have a good selection of Hawai'i hiking guides. The place with the most information is the **Hawai'i Geographic Society** (49 South Hotel Street; 538-3952), which has a full range of hiking and camping books as well as topographic maps for the experienced outdoorsperson. They carry the University of Hawai'i Press maps of the islands, which are excellent for locating historic sites. They also fill mail orders for books; from the mainland call 800-538-3950 to request their latest listing.

Another good source for hiking information is the website for the Nā Ala Hele (Trails to Go On) program sponsored by the State Division of Forestry and Wildlife (www.hawaiitrails.org).

Our hikes are rated easy and moderate. The estimated times we have given allow plenty of time for stops to admire the views or examine plants; however, many people will take less time, many more time.

Opposite: Hiking on the Maunawili Falls Trail (page 200).

Right: Mānoa Falls.

Mānoa Falls

Easy; estimated time: 2 hours

Just 15 minutes away from Waikīkī is Mānoa Falls, where you can explore a lush tropical rainforest. Leave the towering concrete hotels and hot pavement behind for banyan trees that stretch into a green jungle canopy and a trickling stream that flows over cool, mossy rocks. Mānoa Falls is probably one of the most popular hikes on O'ahu. At 1.6 miles roundtrip, it covers easy terrain and is simple to accomplish.

Mānoa Falls is just one of many waterfalls in Mānoa Valley. The word *mānoa*, which means "vast" in Hawaiian, aptly describes the valley's large size. Cattle once grazed in Mānoa, but today the valley is filled with homes and

a busy shopping center. Only the back of Mānoa, which has been designated as part of O'ahu's vital watershed, has been protected from development.

To get to Mānoa Falls, follow Mānoa Road *mauka* to the very end, past the sign for Paradise Park (see map, page 108). The road becomes a single lane leading to a shaded gravel parking area and the trailhead. To the left of the parking area is a winding road that leads to the Lyon Arboretum. If the few parking spaces at the trailhead are taken, overflow parking is available at Paradise Park for a fee.

Shortly after the trail begins, a cement bridge crosses 'Aihualama Stream. There is no bridge at the next stream crossing, but the water is relatively shallow during normal flow conditions.

The trail stays close to the water. Occasional shafts of sunlight penetrate the shade and flicker on the gurgling stream. Most of the vegetation along the trail is introduced, but there are some fine examples of the tangled *hau* bush along the way.

Near the falls the trail enters a bamboo thicket, then ascends a steep series of steps to the waterfall, where mossy black rocks surround a shallow pool. On the final approach to the falls, the 'Aihualama Trail appears to the

left. You can return to the parking area the way you came in or follow the 1.4-mile 'Aihualama Trail to Pauoa Flats—a moderate climb that ends in a rewarding view across Nu'uanu Valley (see the Pu'u 'Ōhi'a Trail, below).

Pu'u 'Ōhi'a Trail to Nu'uanu Lookout

Moderate; estimated time: 4 hours

Whether you want sweeping views of the city or of O'ahu's lush interior Ko'olau range, Pu'u 'Ōhi'a Trail has them both. This trail is one of eighteen that make up the Honolulu *mauka,* or mountain, trail network. Part of this network connects Mānoa, Makiki, Pauoa, and Nu'uanu valleys together. The Pu'u 'Ōhi'a Trail is a direct route to where many of these trails converge. It is also the quickest way to the Nu'uanu Valley overlook (2 miles one way).

To get there, drive up Tantalus Drive to the very top of the mountain (see map, page 103). Before the road descends and is renamed Round Top Drive, look for a large parking area on the right. The marked trailhead is directly across the road from the parking area.

The trail begins as a series of switchbacks that ascend a steep hill. Guava trees are plentiful along this section. Near the top of the hill is a small bamboo thicket. A spur trail leading down to the right goes to a small crater that is a remnant of O'ahu's last volcanic eruption. Staying on the main trail brings you to a concrete road. To the left is a short sidetrip by which you can walk uphill to the very top of the mountain where there is a communications substation. From here you can catch a fantastic view of Honolulu (see photo, pages 2–3). Turn around and you will see the Ko'olau Mountains.

Turning right on the concrete road takes you downhill, then up again as the road leads to another communications substation. Bear to the left of the fenced facility and find Pu'u 'Ōhi'a Trail again as it descends into a bamboo thicket. Here Pu'u 'Ōhi'a Trail meets with the Mānoa Cliffs Trail. Memorize this junction

Pu'u 'ōhi'a means "'ōhi'a tree mountain" in Hawaiian. The 'ōhi'a is a beautiful hardwood tree with small, waxy leaves and delicate blossoms, called lehua, which are usually red, though yellow and orange varieties exist. These trees once dominated the Hawaiian landscape, ranging from shrubs to tall trees, depending on the environment. However, the introduction of foreign plants and insect pests that began in the 18th century has caused a huge decline in their numbers.

for the return trip. Turn left onto Mānoa Cliffs Trail and continue until you reach another signed junction. Memorize this junction as well for the return trip. At this junction, there is an excellent map that displays all the different trails that come together at Pauoa Flats.

To get to the flats, turn right at the junction as Puʻu ʻŌhiʻa Trail resumes and drops down a steep section. Once at the bottom, you'll come to a heavily rooted area where several trails come together. The first trail on the left is a shortcut trail called Kalawahine that leads to the Mānoa Cliffs Trail and eventually back to Tantalus Drive. Continue walking past the next trail junction marked Nuʻuanu that also appears on the left. (The 2-mile Nuʻuanu Trail leads back down into Nuʻuanu Valley where it eventually meets the Judd Memorial Trail.)

Stay on Puʻu ʻŌhiʻa past these junctions and over more roots, into a dense bamboo forest that clicks and clatters in the wind. Past the bamboo forest the Puʻu ʻŌhiʻa Trail forks. To the right is a trail marked ʻAihualama. (This 1.4-mile trail leads down into Mānoa Valley to the Mānoa Falls Trail.) To the left is the Nuʻuanu Valley Viewpoint Trail that leads to our destination.

Bear left and continue to the Nuʻuanu overlook through a grove of cinnamon trees that shade the muddy trail. At the overlook be ready for a blast of cool air (a reminder that Nuʻuanu means "cool heights") and a spectacular view of upper Nuʻuanu, the scene, in 1795, of Kamehameha's successful battle to bring the eight major Hawaiian islands under his rule (see page 101). To the right of the Nuʻuanu Pali are the twin peaks of Kōnāhuanui, the highest in the Koʻolau chain.

Retrace your steps back to the Puʻu ʻŌhiʻa Trail, or add on to this hike by combining it with one of the many other side trails with which it connects.

Judd Memorial Trail (Jackass Ginger)

Easy; estimated time: 1 hour

Despite its modern surroundings, Nuʻuanu Valley has strong ties to old Hawaiʻi. Its modern houses and highways cover ancient Hawaiian paths and ways. Kamehameha's troops marched through this valley, and today the street names describing his last battle—such as Pūʻiwa ("startled")—bear witness to his struggle to unite the Hawaiian islands under one rule. In the forest, lichen-covered rock walls lie deep within the under-growth, and trees are surrounded by thick carpets of moss laid down by thousands of years of rainfall.

Judd Memorial Trail in Nuʻuanu is a quick one-mile loop through a forest of Norfolk Island pine trees. It is a good trek for families, easily walked by young children. The area was named in 1953 after forester Charles S. Judd, who planted the pine trees here in the 1930s. The trail crosses one wide stream, but otherwise it covers fairly easy terrain. The biggest attraction is the Jackass Ginger swimming pond, also known as Kahuailanawai ("site of tranquil water"). The name Jackass Ginger came from a donkey that was tied up among the prolific yellow ginger plants that grow nearby.

To get to the trail, take the Pali Highway (see map, page 100) north to Nuʻuanu Valley. At the Waokanaka Street intersection, turn right onto Nuʻuanu Pali Drive. Bear to the right again when the road forks, and continue on Nuʻuanu Pali Drive into a tunnel of trees. The road winds its way along a steep ravine with a stream below. Continue through a tight S-turn, and pass the Ilanawai condominiums on the right. Find street parking just before you cross a bridge dated 1931. A small reservoir and concrete spillway are across the road on the left.

The trailhead is to the right, just beyond a flat gravel parking lot area, the gravel for which was originally laid down by a crew filming a television series in the late 1980s. Since then the parking area has been periodically closed to the public because it is a favorite place for people to dump their ōpala (rubbish).

Follow the trail downhill to a stream, then use the large boulders to hop over the water and into a small bamboo forest. Ignore the side paths and head straight to the edge of the bamboo forest, where the trail turns uphill to the right and away from the stream.

Moving uphill, the trail goes through eucalyptus trees to a clearing. The trail from the clearing is unmarked, which makes it easy to lose. Bear left toward the Norfolk Island pine trees and into a small gully. The cut trail resumes on the other side of the gully, where it leads into the grove of pines. The trail winds through the trees, then turns left and crosses two small runoff streams. Shortly after is the Nuʻuanu Trail junction on the left, which ascends the valley wall and eventually leads to Pauoa Flats. Venturing farther on this trail will connect you with several other trails within the Honolulu mauka trail system (see the Puʻu ʻŌhiʻa Trail, above).

To reach the cool waters of Jackass Ginger, continue on the memorial trail as it passes nearby houses then starts downhill and circles back toward the stream. Along the way the trail passes through a thicket of waiawī, or strawberry guava trees. The tart red fruits of these trees are a favorite of wild pigs. The trail also cuts through a twisted thicket of hau. In the past Nuʻuanu was known for its dense hau bushes, where thieves would lurk hoping to steal from unsuspecting travelers making the trek across the Koʻolaus. Hau trees grow exceptionally quickly in Nuʻuanu, and they often are slippery with moss. If it weren't for the well-established trail, traversing just a short distance through the hau would be an exhausting, slippery exercise.

The trail emerges from the pine forest just above Jackass Ginger pond. Here the trail gets a bit difficult to follow again. You can descend to the pond for a swim and hop the rocks upstream until you reach the original crossing point; or you can follow the edge of the ridge above the stream until it eventually drops down and brings you back to the bamboo thicket and original stream crossing. Watch out for broken glass in the area, mostly next to the stream.

Maunawili Falls

Easy; estimated time: 2.5 hours

Maunawili is on the windward side of Oʻahu, where the Koʻolau Mountains first meet the northeasterly trade winds. The warm trade-wind air is pushed up the 3,000-foot Koʻolau slopes after traveling over miles of flat, open ocean. As it moves up the mountains the moist air cools, condenses, and relinquishes its precious cargo, fresh water. Maunawili Valley drains a large volcanic crater that has been softened by years of natural weathering and covered by dense jungle.

The falls trail is a popular 2.6-mile hike. To get there drive mauka on Maunawili Road to the end, where it reduces into a single-lane road (see map, page 125). Street parking is available to the right on Kelewina Street. The trail begins on the left behind a gate that restricts vehicular traffic.

About 100 yards past the gate, the Maunawili Falls Trail branches off from the right-hand side of the access road. This part of the trail, which crosses Maunawili Stream three times and passes through hau bushes, is flat. There are several large mango trees on the trail, and

The trail to Maunawili Falls crosses the stream three times.

Moderate; estimated time: 6 hours

The Koʻolau Mountains are best experienced on the windward side of Oʻahu in the early morning, when the rising sun reaches deep into the sleepy folds of the mountains and fills them with shimmering golden light. The eastern Koʻolaus near Makapuʻu have exposed faces of gray rock and sparse vegetation. But on the Maunawili Trail the Koʻolaus take on a different character. Here they are emerald green, heavily vegetated, and pulsing with life.

The Maunawili Trail is long—nearly 10 miles one way—but it gains only 600 feet elevation. It passes over the undulating terrain in the back of Maunawili Valley to reach Waimānalo. The best way to hike it is to be dropped off at one end and have a parked car waiting on the other end in Waimānalo, or better yet, arrange to be picked up. Some choose to hike the trail halfway, then turn around and come back to the trailhead. There is also the option of using the Maunawili Falls junction trail and finishing the hike in Maunawili Valley.

The description of this hike is from the Pali Highway trailhead

mountain apple, guava, and a few stands of wild banana trees are also nearby. Maunawili has always been widely used for agriculture because of its fertile soil and abundant rainfall. Hawaiians used Maunawili for the extensive cultivation of *kalo*. Today farmers who tend fields deeper within the crater grow commercial crops of bananas, flowers, and papayas here. Recently *kalo* is making a comeback in Maunawili—farmers have been discovering and reusing ancient rock terraces where *kalo* was cultivated hundreds of years ago.

After following the stream closely, the trail ascends a ridge with panoramic views of Mauna-

wili. On this ridge there is a fork in the trail. The trail that continues straight uphill is the Maunawili-to-Waimānalo trail, while the trail to the left descends back into the valley to Maunawili Falls. The waterfall itself is less than 30-feet high, but there is a deep pond below that invites a swim on a hot day. The volume of water flowing through Maunawili has been reduced by a system of dikes that transports the water to farmers in nearby Waimānalo ("potable water").

From the ridge, you can either follow the same trail back to the parking area or explore farther on the Maunawili-to-Waimānalo trail (see below).

to Waimānalo, the most popular route, but no matter which way you choose to do this hike you will not be disappointed.

To get to the Pali trailhead, take the Pali Highway toward Kailua. After passing through

On the Maunawili Trail heading toward Waimānalo, below the Pali Lookout.

two tunnels at the top of the Nu'uanu pass you will drive downhill to a sharp left-hand hairpin turn. Parking for the trailhead is on the right just past the hairpin turn, next to a low rock wall.

To reach the Waimānalo trailhead at the other end of the hike, continue on the Pali Highway past the hairpin turn. Go straight through three traffic lights. At the fourth light, by Castle Memorial Hospital, turn

right onto Kalaniana'ole Highway (see map, page 125). Follow the highway for about 5 miles into Waimānalo and turn right onto Kumuhau Street, heading *mauka*. At the end of the road, turn right onto Waikupanaha Street, which crosses over a small bridge. After you pass the intersection with Mahiku Place look for street parking. The marked trailhead is on the right.

Starting from the Pali Highway trailhead, Maunawili Trail contours the base of the tallest Ko'olau peak, Kōnāhuanui, which stands just over 3,000 feet above sea level.

If you're interested in identifying different Hawaiian plant species, definitely bring a good picture guide on this hike. Along the trail are *'ōhi'a lehua, lama, koa, 'ōhi'a 'ai, hau,* and *kukui* trees. The *kukui,* Hawai'i's state tree, is most frequently found growing in gullies and ravines. *Kukui* means light in Hawaiian, and the tree is identified by its silvery, light-green leaves. The Polynesians brought it to the islands and had many uses for it. They used its lumber for canoe gunwales, its sap and flowers for medicinal purposes. The tree also produces an oily nut that can be burned as a candle, polished and worn on a lei, or chopped fine and mixed with other ingredients to produce a relish.

The trail winds in and out of the folds of the mountains, which stand almost vertical in some places, like the pleats of a huge green ribbon standing on its edge. Intermittent streams trickle through the inner curves of the trail. On the outer curves, the brush has been carefully trimmed low to create lookouts. Views sweep across Maunawili to Olomana, Paku'i, Ahiki, and the Anianinui Ridge, all remnants of a huge volcanic crater that stretches nearly 7 miles from Waimānalo to Kāne'ohe.

Much of the trail has been cut through *uluhe* ferns. These

According to Hawaiian legend, the twin peaks of Kōnāhuanui come from the genitals of a giant that once stood guard at the Nu'uanu ("cool heights") pass, preventing people from traveling between the windward and leeward sides of the island. One day an old woman slipped by while he was sleeping. As she descended the trail into Nu'uanu Valley, she laughed and awakened the giant. When he realized what had happened, he tore off his genitals and threw them down in disgust, creating the twin peaks.

native ferns are green and supple on top but have a dry and brutally sharp under story. Fortunately, the trail is very well maintained and there is little need to break through the ferns. *Uluhe* play a vital role in this ecosystem. Usually they are the first plants to move in and stabilize sheer cliffs where landslides have occurred.

Along the trail keep an eye out for the Maunawili Falls junction, which is marked on the left-hand side. Following this trail takes you straight downhill along a ridge that connects with the falls trail (see above).

Continue following the main trail as it flows across the back of Maunawili onto the Anianinui Ridge and under electric power lines. Stay on the trail the first time it junctions with Old Government Road.

On your final descent from the ridge into Waimānalo, look for *'ilima,* a native shrub with small orange flowers. Today lei are made with thousands of these flowers and presented to people to mark special occasions, just as they were used to honor people long ago.

Where the trail meets up with Old Government Road for the second time, turn right onto the road and follow two switchbacks to the trailhead at Waikupanaha Street in Waimānalo.

'Aiea Loop

Moderate; estimated time: 3 hours

The 'Aiea Loop Trail provides a good opportunity to combine a hike with a tour of a Hawaiian archaeological site. The trail begins at Keaīwa Heiau State Park, where there are beautiful places to picnic and relax even if hiking is not on your agenda.

This popular 5-mile trail is well maintained and allows you to experience the lower sections of the Ko'olau Mountains without having to scamper up steep ridges. The trail is wide, well graded, and shady for most of its length.

To get there from Honolulu, follow H1 west. Continue west onto Route 78 and move into the far left lane. Take the 'Aiea exit and bear right onto Moanalua Road. From Moanalua Road, turn right onto 'Aiea Heights Drive. The road switchbacks up the mountain until it reaches Keaīwa Heiau State Park.

Keaīwa Heiau is located near the entrance of the park. Keaīwa means "mysterious" in Hawaiian and well describes this place where students were believed to have learned the art of Hawaiian medicine. The area surrounding the *heiau* was likely cultivated with various plants and herbs that were used in the practice of traditional Hawaiian healing.

Today, Norfolk Island pines planted during a 1928 reforestation program dominate the landscape.

At first glance the 100-by-160-foot enclosure could be mistaken for a pile of rocks. But take time to inspect the care in which the stones were laid. The Hawaiians did not use mortar in their construction. Instead, the stones were carefully placed to lock into one another. Modern rock walls are constructed in such a way that the rocks are arranged with their flat edges facing outward, creating a smooth exterior face. Ancient builders seemed less concerned about this, choosing instead to fit the rocks together for strength and stability. Hundreds of years later these rock walls remain as a testament to the skill of ancient Hawaiian builders.

The hike begins at the upper parking area of the park. Follow the one-lane road to the top, where you will find a pavilion and restrooms. The first part of the trail is littered with exposed roots, but the roots melt away as the trail follows a ridge and gradually makes its way uphill to the back of 'Aiea Valley. Look for the scratchy *uluhe* ferns and *'ōhi'a* trees along the way.

The trail turns gradually downhill and makes a loop back to the state park. Views of Hālawa Valley and the controversial (because it crosses land sacred to Hawaiians)

H3 Freeway are possible on the left. On the right, a strip of aircraft aluminum is visible from the trail, part of a World War II–era plane that crashed in the valley in 1944. Just before the trail reaches its end, it descends into, then climbs out of, a deep gulch. A runoff stream that flows through here makes the trail muddy most of the time. Save your energy climbing, as you still have to walk up the one-lane road back to your car parked at the top of the park.

Hau'ula Loop

Easy; estimated time: 2 hours

This lightly used trail on the windward side of the north shore is a good option for those who want an easy hike without the crowds that frequent many trails closer to town. It is a good family hike, offering fine views and sightings of native vegetation, including *'ōhi'a, lama, hala,* and *ti.* The well-maintained loop trail is 2.5 miles.

To reach the trailhead, take the Likilike Highway to the windward side, exiting at Kahekili Highway (Route 83 west), which leads to Kamehameha Highway (still 83). From here it is roughly 14.5 miles to Hau'ula, passing through Ka'a'awa and Punalu'u. After a fire station and a small bridge, you'll come to

Hau'ula Beach Park. Turn *mauka* on Hau'ula Homestead Road. After .2 miles the road makes a sharp curve to the left; continue straight ahead here onto the access road (Ma'akua Road). At the end of the road, park near the access gate and walk past the hunter/hiker check-in station. The trail begins on the right just past the check-in station.

After about 200 yards the trail comes to a fork; for the Hau'ula loop, take the trail to the right. Stay to the right for a short, steep climb (the trail coming in on the left is the return portion of the loop). A gentle climb up long, leisurely switchbacks climbs two ridges and provides rewarding views of the village of Hau'ula and the Pacific, with the highest elevation at 700 feet. This northern section of the Ko'olau range is drier and sunnier than areas where there are steep *pali.*

Keālia Trail

Moderate; estimated time: 5 hours

Hiking in the Wai'anae Mountains above Mokulē'ia is a stark contrast to hiking in the Ko'olau Mountains. Gone are the constant misting rains and overhead canopies of lush green foliage. They are replaced by the merciless sun, which makes you thirst for water just two steps from the

car, and by hardy, drought-adapted trees and shrubs.

Keālia Trail is 7 miles round-trip and ascends about 2,000 feet in elevation to the Mākua Valley lookout. The trail covers rocky terrain and graded dirt roads. Parts of the trail are steep, but the most overwhelming factor is the heat. Take at least 2 liters of water per person.

To get there, take H2 north toward Wahiawā. At the end of the freeway continue straight on Wilikina Drive around Wahiawā town. After passing Schofield Barracks on the left, the road narrows and drops into a gulch. Stay to the left when the road forks as it ascends out of the gulch. Wilikina Drive becomes Kaukonahua Road (Route 803). Follow Kaukonahua downhill and straight past the yellow blinking light. Bear left and drive under the overpass, continuing on Farrington Highway (Route 930). Drive until you see the main entrance to Dillingham Airfield and Glider Port on your left. Pass this entrance and continue on until you reach the airfield's back entrance. Turn left and pass the signs warning of low-flying aircraft and around the end of the landing strip. Driving parallel to the landing strip, you will pass a concrete building. Park in the parking lot on the left near the airfield control tower.

Walk toward the mountains following the broken pavement. Bear left when the road forks, passing a concrete structure on the right. The road narrows and is lined on either side with *koa haole* (a common roadside shrub related to the *koa;* literally, foreign *koa*). Keep following the road to the right until it reaches an opening in a low green fence.

The trail starts off behind the fence and to the left. A series of rocky switchbacks quickly takes you above Dillingham Airfield, with views of O'ahu's north shore and a huge rock quarry.

At the top of the switchbacks there is a picnic area. Gliders from the nearby airfield float by silently above, using updrafts from the cliffs to push them higher into the sky.

From the picnic area the trail joins a dirt road that continues up the mountain. Continue uphill past an intersection with another dirt road that appears on your right. The road continues uphill and passes a junction with a foot trail on the right. Keep following the main road (ignoring side roads) uphill until it bends and passes a water tank on the left. Soon after is the Mākua Valley lookout.

From a distance Mākua takes on a beautiful green hue. The word *mākua* means "parents" in Hawaiian. Because it is almost totally undeveloped, the valley looks unblemished. However, since 1941 the U.S. military has used Mākua for live fire exercises. The dangers of unexploded ordnance and environmental damage have caused area residents to challenge the military's practices, and many would like to see the area used for other purposes. Long ago Hawaiians used the valley as a training area for *lua,* a form of Hawaiian martial arts. Whatever happens with Mākua Valley, one cannot deny its remarkable beauty.

Retrace your steps on the dirt road to return to the trailhead. As the road rejoins the trail, look for native *a'ali'i* plants. This native Hawaiian plant species, with shiny green leaves and dry tissue-paper seed packs, is being used to reforest drought-stricken areas like the island of Kaho'olawe.

Exercise caution as you descend the switchbacks. The consequences of inattention or a misstep are severe.

Ka'ena Point Trail

Easy; estimated time: 2 hours

It used to be that you could drive a car around the coastal perimeter of O'ahu. Over the years, however, the road going around Ka'ena Point, the island's westernmost tip, has eroded away, and now cars are forced to stop. This inconvenience to motorists has become a boon to hikers and environmentalists interested in preserving the area's unique sand dune ecosystem.

Although the terrain along the Ka'ena Point Trail is rocky and sandy, the gradient is easy and flat. It's about 5 miles back and forth to the point from the Moku-lē'ia, or north shore side of the island. In Hawaiian the word Ka'ena means "the heat," which is a very accurate description of what you will feel if you get a late start on this hike. The entire length of the trail is exposed to the sun, so make sure to bring plenty of water, sunscreen, a hat, and a good pair of sunglasses. Ka'ena is the name of a cousin of the volcano goddess Pele who, according to legend, dwelled at this place.

To get there, take H2 north toward Wahiawā. At the end of the freeway continue straight on Wilikina Drive around Wahiawā

Looking toward Ka'ena Point.

town. After passing Schofield Barracks on the left, the road narrows and drops into a gulch. Stay to your left when the road forks as it ascends out of the gulch. Wilikina Drive becomes Kaukonahua Road (Route 803). Follow Kaukonahua downhill and straight past the yellow blinking light. Turn left and drive under the overpass, contin-

uing on Farrington Highway (Route 930). Continue on the highway, passing Dillingham Airfield on the left and Mokulēʻia Beach Park on the right. Roughly one mile after Camp Erdman, the paved road ends and a dirt road begins.

Begin your hike along the dirt road as it follows the coastline. The road will gradually bend to

the left as it contours the base of the Waiʻanae range. Break off from the road here and head for the tip of the point, following your interests but making sure to stay on the established trails that criss-cross through the sand dunes.

Stabilizing the sand dunes are a variety of fantastic Hawaiian plants. *Pāʻū o Hiʻiaka* is a vine-like plant that stretches out

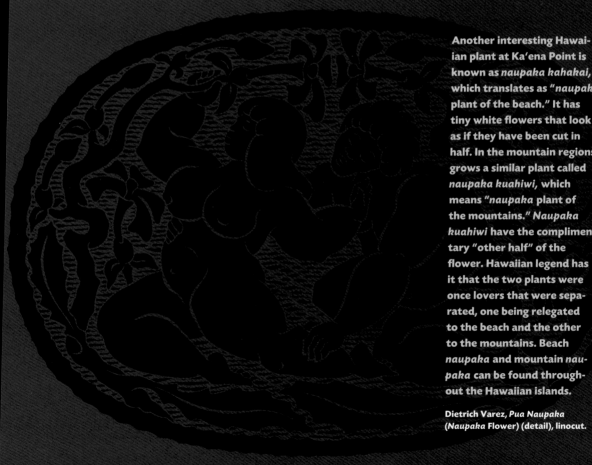

Another interesting Hawaiian plant at Kaʻena Point is known as *naupaka kahakai,* which translates as "*naupaka* plant of the beach." It has tiny white flowers that look as if they have been cut in half. In the mountain regions grows a similar plant called *naupaka kuahiwi,* which means "*naupaka* plant of the mountains." *Naupaka kuahiwi* have the complimentary "other half" of the flower. Hawaiian legend has it that the two plants were once lovers that were separated, one being relegated to the beach and the other to the mountains. Beach *naupaka* and mountain *naupaka* can be found throughout the Hawaiian islands.

Dietrich Varez, *Pua Naupaka (Naupaka Flower) (detail)*, linocut.

across the sand. It has pale blue, bell-shaped flowers. Legend has it that Pele left her infant sister, Hi'iaka, on the beach while she went fishing. While Pele was away, this vine with its pale blue flowers crept over her baby sister, creating a thick *pā'ū*, or skirt, that protected Hi'iaka from the harsh rays of the sun. To this day the vine is known as "the skirt of Hi'iaka."

More difficult to find among the black boulders is the plant called *ma'o*. This plant has yellow flowers, but it receives its name from the Hawaiian word for the color green, which is the color of the bright green fabric dye that Hawaiians were able to extract from the plant. *Ma'o* used to be more abundant on O'ahu, but its natural habitat has steadily disappeared as shoreline ecosystems have been modified to suit the needs of hotels and beachfront homes.

Even more endangered is the Ka'ena *'akoko,* found only among the boulder slopes at Ka'ena Point. During the summer months it is easy to mistakenly trample over this vinelike plant, as it loses all its pale green leaves. It is rare plants such as this that caused the establishment of Ka'ena Point as a natural area reserve in 1983.

A plant called *'ilima papa* also grows at Ka'ena Point. *Papa* means "flat" in Hawaiian and aptly describes the way this plant grows to the ground. The growing strategy is ideal for Ka'ena where there is no protection from the wind and blowing sand. *'Ilima papa* have yellow-orange flowers that are the traditional symbol of O'ahu. Lei made from the delicate flowers are highly regarded and require thousands of blossoms to make a single strand.

The ocean at Ka'ena Point is rough and dangerous, especially during the winter months. On calm days during low tide you may be able to see tiny fish called *manini* stranded in pools among the black rocks. From the tip of the point it's possible to see down both the north and south shores of O'ahu.

Hawaiian oral traditions indicate that on each island there was a place where souls of the dead would transition, or leap, into the spirit world. Ka'ena Point is such a place on O'ahu. Such a place is called *leina a ka'uhane,* or "leaping place of the souls."

Guided Hikes

Several outfits specialize in providing guided hikes to various areas of the island. The best of them emphasize cultural and archaeological aspects of the land. Most guided hike operators will pick visitors up at Waikīkī hotels.

Mauka Makai Excursions (593-3525) offers hikes to archaeological sites and short walks through tropical rain-forests. They have full- and half-day excursions, with hotel pickup. One hike on the windward side visits *heiau,* petroglyphs, an ancient house complex, and waterfalls and includes a swim on a secluded beach. Another takes visitors to Ka'ena Point as well as north shore *heiau.*

Nature walks are led by **O'ahu Nature Tours** (924-2473). The emphasis is on viewing native bird and plant species. The company is run by environmentalist Michael Walther, the author of two books about Hawai'i's native flora and fauna. Tours explore waterfalls, rain-forests, and volcanic craters. A nature photographer, Walther will help you find excellent photographic opportunities.

Hawaiian Islands Eco-Tours (236-7766) offers half- and full-day waterfall and rainforest adventures. Groups are small (no more than ten), and cultural history is imparted by the knowledgeable guides. Hikes are novice level, though custom tours can be arranged, including neighbor island camping.

Horseback riding at Kualoa Ranch.

Horseback Riding

Horseback riding on ranches where *paniolo,* or Hawaiian cowboys, lead a quiet life away from the glitter and bustle of Honolulu provides a unique view of the island's mountain terrain. Experienced equestrians should note, however, that few of the stables will allow you to do much more than walk, with an occasional short trot; be sure to ask beforehand so you won't be disappointed.

Happy Trails Hawai'i (59-231 Pūpūkea Road, Waimea; 638-7433), on the north shore near Waimea Falls, has quality, well-cared-for horses and offers small, personal riding groups for all skill levels. Managed by polo player Mark Becker, the stables are home to many still active and retired polo ponies, making for a unique riding experience. These

smart and gentle creatures respond quickly to their riders' commands and seem to enjoy their lives more than many horses in such facilities. First-time riders feel comfortable at once, while others delight in their brief encounter with a horse trained for playing polo. With a large part of their business coming from the local community, Happy Trails welcomes children as young as six years of age. In fact, it is the only such outfit on O'ahu to take people this young, allowing children to become acquainted with horses at an early age. The well-maintained trail hugs the rim of Waimea Valley and provides spectacular mountain and ocean views.

Also on the north shore, the **Stables at the Turtle Bay Resort** (57-091 Kamehameha Highway, Kahuku; 293-8811) welcome nonguests for their rides, either along the beach or through a pretty wooded area. This is the only beach on O'ahu where horseback riding is allowed. **Correa Trails Hawai'i** (41-050 Kalaniana'ole Highway, Waimānalo; 259-9005) provides transportation from Waikīkī for their one-hour trail rides in the lush Ko'olau Mountains, with wonderful views of Rabbit Island and the coast. Inexperienced riders will be comfortable on their gentle horses.

Among the adventure activities at **Kualoa Ranch** (page 210) and **Waimea Falls Park** (pages 130–32) is horseback riding. At Kualoa, we suggest you select the longer trail ride, which goes deep into a valley and past the movie sets for *Godzilla* and *Jurassic Park.* At Waimea Falls, 30-minute rides bring you to picturesque views of the falls. The rides at Waimea Falls are conducted by Happy Trails Hawai'i (see above).

Biking

Pedaling along under your own steam provides an excellent means of experiencing the natural beauty of O'ahu's tropical environment. The loop trip (135 miles) around the island mostly hugs the coastline and is the easiest island loop in the state. In fact, aside from walking, this is the only way you can go all the way around the perimeter of O'ahu, as the 9 miles of rough, unpaved track around Ka'ena Point are impassable by car; it's really a bit rough for cycling, too, but still popular with avid cyclists. Virtually the entire route around the island is peppered with beautiful and accessible beaches, so it's easy to stop for a refreshing ocean plunge.

A slightly shorter loop (108 miles) circles only the Ko'olau Mountain range, cutting across the Leilehua Plateau, through fields of pineapple and coffee, and eliminating the rough Ka'ena segment as well as the entire leeward coast. To avoid headwinds, it is best to travel counterclockwise, and, in any case, much of the journey is more scenic when taken in this direction.

Traffic in rural areas varies from light to heavy, but traffic in Honolulu is very heavy indeed, and cycling in the downtown area and in Waikīkī is not recommended, particularly during rush hours. TheBus (see page 251) provides bicycle racks, so you can take the bus to the outskirts of the city to begin your tour on more hospitable roads.

Bicyclists at Pu'u 'Ualaka'a State Wayside Park, off Round Top Drive.

This said, the in-city Tantalus roadway should be noted as a favorite of hardcore bicyclists. The 10.5-mile circuit from Makiki Heights Drive to Tantalus Drive and down the mountain via Round Top Drive is best taken in this (clockwise) direction.

For bicycle rentals, see page 253. An excellent resource is *Short Bike Rides Hawaii* by William Walters (Globe Pequot Press), available in most O'ahu bookstores. Information is also available from the Hawai'i Bicycling League (www.hbl.org).

Bicycle tours are offered by **Bike Hawai'i** (734-4214), which has two great bike rides on its agenda, one a mountain biking tour of the windward Ka'a'awa Valley, with sheer cliffs and the ocean providing scenic views, and the other a bike/hike trip to a waterfall in the Ko'olau Mountains. The cost of both trips includes transportation from Waikīkī, bike and helmet, and breakfast or lunch, depending on the time of day.

Jogging *and* Running

Honolulu is a runner's paradise, with an almost unending procession of bodies hurrying along such byways as Kapi'olani Park, Ala Moana Park, and the Ala Wai Canal, especially in the early morning and late afternoon "rush hours."

If you're indefatiga[...] km run around Diam[...] just follow the road (co[...] clockwise is the easier dire[...] The circuit around Kapi'olani Park is 1.8 miles; around the Ala Wai Golf Course is 3.6 miles.

For the competitive of spirit, there are about one hundred running events in Honolulu each year, including the well-known Honolulu Marathon, held in December. More than 30,000 runners from all over the world take part in this race. The marathon begins at Ala Moana Beach Park and ends at Kapi'olani Park. If you are interested in participating in the Honolulu Marathon, send a stamped, self-addressed envelope to the Honolulu Marathon Association, 3435 Wai'alae Avenue, #208, Honolulu, HI 96816, or call the association at 808-734-7200 for information.

Volleyball

A great seaside pastime is beach volleyball. There is a net at Fort DeRussy Beach, where anyone with a volleyball can play. One major professional tournament takes place there during the summertime, drawing all the hot Southern California players. Tournaments are also frequently held at Queen's Surf Beach at the other end of Waikīkī.

ualoa Ranch

Not fitting into any one category because it offers nearly every outdoor activity possible on O'ahu is **Kualoa Ranch** (237-8515) on the windward coast. Nestled at the base of stunning cliffs, this working ranch provides a full day of fun, both on land and in the water. Activities include horseback riding, a gun range, ATV trails, tours of sets for the films *Godzilla* and *Jurassic Park,* volleyball, tennis—you name it, they've got it. You can snorkel, scuba dive, kayak, jet ski, or just relax in the sun at their secret island. Transportation from Waikīkī is included in the admission fee, which ranges from $69 to $139 (children $35 to $89), depending on the activities one selects.

Spas

Spas are the latest trend to sweep the islands, and on O'ahu there are a number of such places to soothe the body and soul, from small spas located in shopping centers to elaborate hotel facilities. It seems that the busier Honolulu gets, the more of these oases of tranquility appear on the scene.

The Hilton Hawaiian Village's new **Mandara Spa** (2005 Kālia Road; 923-7721), in the elegant Kālia Tower, is Hawai'i's newest. With 42,000 square feet, it is also the largest in Waikīkī. Mandara is known worldwide for its day spas in luxury hotels and cruise ships. Featuring such treatments as a chocolate macadamia nut scrub and a vanilla and *pīkake* facial, Mandara Spa incorporates local flowers, fresh fruits, Kona coffee, and Hawaiian sea salt into several of its island specialties, while also offering traditional Eastern and Western massages, facials, and body treatments. There are twenty-five treatment rooms, including spa suites for couples to share their experience, as well as a full-service salon, sauna and steam rooms, an outdoor area with hot spa and pool, and a cardiovascular fitness center. The Ola Pono Spa Café offers healthy meals and snacks for Mandara Spa guests.

Mālama Spa (Ala Moana Center; 988-0101), located next to Neiman Marcus, offers complete beauty services as well as body care in a remarkably serene environment. The entire salon is tastefully decorated, with special attention to detailing in the spa area, where hand-painted walls and *koa* wood accents create spaces that invite relaxation. A warm complimentary footbath is offered before any treatment, and you may use the eucalyptus steam room before or after your session. Hydrotherapies, massage treatments, and reflexology are some of the pampering services. Hot stone massage is a heavenly treat, as is a pressure-point massage while you are bathing in their luxurious 180-jet hydro tub filled with botanical essences. Several spa day packages are available, which include a lunch of healthy spa cuisine from chef Douglas Lum at Neiman Marcus as well as hair and makeup sessions in the salon. Only Aveda products are used.

At the Hyatt Regency, **Nā Hō'ola Spa** (2424 Kalākaua Avenue; 921-6097) is a two-story, 10,000-square-foot luxury facility, including a fitness and exercise area. In addition to massage in all the traditional styles, they offer Polynesian body scrubs and body wraps. Native Hawaiian healing practices are emphasized.

The **Ihilani Spa** (92-1001 Olani Street; 679-0079), at the J.W. Marriott Ihilani Resort and Spa, ranks among the foremost spas in the world and has been the recipient of numerous awards. The spa offers authentic Thalasso therapy, an underwater massage treatment with warm seawater pulsating out of 180 jets. A full range of massage therapies is offered, along with special body services. A green tea wrap, for example, is intended to detoxify and revitalize the body, and a milk and honey body mask will sooth sunburned skin. The spa even sets up visits with holistic health practitioners, including a psychologist to help deal with such issues as your weight and your relationships with others.

At the regal Royal Hawaiian, the **Abhasa Resort Spa** (922-8200) offers salon services and spa treatments, including facials, body wraps, and massage. Treatments use Japanese herbs, tropical Hawaiian herbs and flowers, Moroccan spices, seaweed, and aromatherapy for the ultimate in pampering pleasure.

Serenity Spa Hawai'i in the Outrigger Reef Hotel (2169 Kālia Road; 926-2882) offers a complete array of traditional Hawaiian methods and European day spa services. Exotic treatments include aromatherapy facials, body polish with Hawaiian sugar and salt, and an after-sun *ti* leaf body wrap using aloe,

kukui, and other essential oils. Manicure and makeup services are available.

Paul Brown Salon & Day Spa (Ward Centre, 1200 Ala Moana Boulevard; 591-1881), though essentially a full-service beauty salon, also offers a variety of spa treatments, including massage and body care. Mud packs, seaweed wraps, and loofah polishes are among the body treatments. Make-up specialists provide application and lessons. Prices are reasonable for the spa services.

Health Clubs

Most Honolulu gyms offer special arrangements and rates for out-of-town guests. **24-Hour Fitness**, with locations at 1680 Kapi'olani Boulevard (951-7677) and in Waikīkī in the Pacific Beach Hotel at 2490 Kalākaua Avenue (923-9090), offers the most complete fitness facilities close to Waikīkī hotels. The

latter location has a bank of treadmills up against a plate-glass window facing the ocean, making it extremely appealing.

Gold's Gym, 768 South Street (533-7111), is a large facility with a juice bar and is not as crowded as the 24-Hour Fitness locations.

The **Honolulu Club** at 932 Ward Avenue (543-3900) is not just a fitness center but a private club with amenities that include, among other things, basketball, racquetball, and squash courts; therapeutic massage; childcare; and fine dining. They have nonresident memberships for the frequent or long-term visitor to O'ahu.

Yoga

Whether you're new to yoga and just feel like doing something unusual for yourself during an extended holiday, or an ardent practitioner of the art, you are welcome to join the classes at the Silent Dance Center (2535 South King Street; 526-9642) in the Mō'ili'ili Community Center. Classes are given daily, during the day and in the evening, for beginners and experienced students. All of the center's instructors are trained in the Iyengar method of teaching Hatha Yoga, and some hold senior teaching certificates from the Iyengar Institute in India.

Massage on a guestroom lanai at the J. W. Marriott Ihilani Resort and Spa.

Golf

Oʻahu has an abundance of golf courses, and, as golf is a favored sport among the locals, most are crowded. Green fees for nonresidents range from $42 at municipal courses (less for seniors) to $100 and more at a resort course. According to author George Fuller (*Discover Hawaiʻi's Best Golf,* Island Heritage Publishing), the top Oʻahu courses are Koʻolau Golf Club, Ko ʻOlina Golf Club, the Links at Kuilima (now Palmer Golf Course), Luana Hills Country Club, Hawaiʻi Prince Golf Club, New ʻEwa Beach Golf Club, and Makāha Golf Club.

Koʻolau Golf Club on Oʻahu's windward side.

Waikiki-area Golf Courses

Ala Wai Golf Course (404 Kapahulu Avenue, Honolulu; 296-2000), an easy course adjacent to Waikīkī, is especially crowded. Tee times are booked a week in advance. The very low rates at this municipal facility and its proximity to Waikīkī make it one of the busiest courses in the nation; it hosts 170,000 rounds of golf each year. Par 70; 5,817 yards.

South Shore Golf Courses

Hawaiʻi Kai Golf Course (8902 Kalanianaʻole Highway, Hawaiʻi Kai; 395-2358), near Koko Head, has two 18-hole courses that are often windy and difficult. Amenities include a pro shop, driving range, and restaurant. Championship course: par 72; 6,350 yards. Executive course: par 55; 2,433 yards.

Windward Coast Golf Courses

Bayview Golf Park (45-285 Kāneʻohe Bay Drive, Kāneʻohe; 247-0451) has moderate rates. Par 60; 2,231 yards.

Koʻolau Golf Club (45-550 Kiʻonaʻole Road, Kāneʻohe; 236-4653) is next to the Pali Golf Course. This 18-hole course, designed by Dick Nugent and Jack Tuthill, consistently receives top ratings, and playing it is a must for all serious golfers. With extreme elevation changes and breathtaking views, this rainforest course is one of the world's most challenging from the back tees, but from the forward tees all skill levels are comfortable. In addition to a driving range and practice facility, there is a restaurant. Shuttle service is available from Waikīkī. Par 72; 7,310 yards.

Luana Hills Country Club (770 ʻAuloa Road, Kailua; 262-2139), in lush Maunawili Valley, offers 18 holes of championship golf amid an incredible tropical forest setting. Designed by Peter Dye and Perry Dye, the course has provided challenges for golfers at all levels, including President Bill Clinton. The views of the surrounding mountain range are spectacular. It has a restaurant, and the clubhouse features a Jacuzzi and a Japanese furo. Par 72; 6,164 yards.

Olomana Golf Links (41-1801 Kalaniana'ole Highway, Waimānalo; 259-7926) is an 18-hole course with a driving range that's open until 10 P.M. Par 71; 5,820 yards.

Pali Golf Course (45-050 Kamehameha Highway, Kāne-'ohe; 296-2000) is a popular course; players are strongly urged to reserve a starting time, thus avoiding the standard wait of about 3 hours. Rates are very low at this municipal course. Par 72; 6,494 yards.

North Shore Golf Courses

Fazio Golf Course (57-049 Kuilima Drive, Kahuku; 293-8574) is at the Turtle Bay Resort, along with the Palmer Course, and guests at the hotel receive lower rates. It was formerly called the Turtle Bay Golf Course. Par 36; 3,204 yards.

Kahuku Golf Course (Kahuku; 296-2000) is very low key. Open Monday through Friday, this municipal course has the lowest rates in town for 9 holes ($20 for nonresidents), which is all they have. Par 35; 2,699 yards.

Palmer Golf Course (57-049 Kuilima Drive, Kahuku; 293-8574) is an Arnold Palmer/ Ed Seay design located at the Turtle Bay Country Club (formerly called the Links at Kuilima). A tough course, and a favorite among serious golfers, it offers 27 holes of championship golf. Be prepared to battle the winds. Par 72; 6,366 yards.

Leeward Coast Golf Courses

Coral Creek Golf Course (91-1111 Geiger Road, 'Ewa Beach; 441-4653), opened in March 1999, is the newest and most heralded addition to O'ahu golfing. The landscape is beautiful, and this luxury facility caters to every need. Par 72; 6,808 yards.

The 13th hole at Luana Hills Country Club.

'Ewa Villages Golf Course (91-1760 Park Row Street, 'Ewa Beach; 296-2000) is an 18-hole municipal course. Par 72; 6,430 yards.

Hawai'i Prince Golf Club (91-1200 Fort Weaver Road, 'Ewa Beach; 944-4567) is an Arnold Palmer–designed 27-hole championship course. Located on former sugarcane fields, the course is relatively flat and enjoys brisk winds. PGA instruction is available through the pro shop. There is a restaurant. Guests of the Hawai'i Prince Hotel get lower rates. Par 72; 7,255 yards.

Kapolei Golf Course (91-701 Farrington Highway, Kapolei; 674-2227) has 18 holes, a pro shop, and a restaurant. Host to the LPGA's Hawaiian

Ladies Open Tournament since 1996, Kapolei is one of Ted Robinson's finest creations. Par 72; 6,600 yards.

Ko 'Olina Golf Club (92-1220 Ali'inui, Kapolei; 676-5300) is situated on the southwestern side of O'ahu in the newly developed Ko 'Olina resort. This beautifully landscaped course with appealing water features was designed by Ted Robinson and wins many accolades. It is a very popular course. There is a restaurant. Par 72; 6,324 yards.

Makāha Golf Club (84-626 Makāha Valley Road, Wai'anae; 695-9544) is a long, tough, and beautiful 18-hole course. It has a pro shop, driving range, and snack bar. Shuttle transportation is available from Waikīkī. Par 72; 6,414 yards.

The 18th hole at Ko 'Olina Golf Club, Ihilani Resort.

Makāha Valley Country Club (84-627 Makāha Valley Road, Wai'anae; 695-9578) has a course that is shorter and easier than the neighboring Makāha Golf Club, and green fees are lower. A pro shop, driving range, and restaurant round out the offerings. Par 71; 6,091 yards.

New 'Ewa Beach Golf Club (91-050 Fort Weaver Road, 'Ewa Beach; 689-8351), designed by Robin Nelson, is interesting for the several archaeological sites on the course, including an ancient Hawaiian fishing shelter. Par 72; 5,992 yards.

West Loch Golf Course (91-1126 Okupe Street, 'Ewa Beach; 296-2000) is a popular course. A Nelson-Wright design, this municipal course is quite a challenge owing to its many water hazards, strong winds, and narrow fairways. Green fees are inexpensive here, contributing to the course's popularity. Par 72; 5,849 yards.

Central O'ahu Golf Courses

Hawai'i Country Club (94-1211 Kunia Road, Wahiawā; 621-5654) is a short course with very low rates and scenic mountain and ocean views. There are 18 holes, a driving range, a pro shop, and a restaurant. Par 72; 5,761 yards.

Mililani Golf Club (95-176 Kuahelani Avenue, Mililani; 623-2222) offers 18 holes at moderate rates. Its driving range is open until 10 P.M., and it has a pro shop and restaurant. Par 72; 6,360 yards.

Pearl Country Club (98-535 Kaonohi Street, 'Aiea; 487-3802) is a hard, hilly course overlooking Pearl Harbor with moderate fees. Par 72; 6,230 yards.

Royal Kunia Country Club (Waipahu; 671-7885 or 676-1116) is an 18-hole championship course. This Robin Nelson–designed gem is closed as of this writing, but it is likely to open soon. Its designer considers it the best course in Hawai'i. Par 72; 7,060 yards.

Ted Makalena Golf Course (93-059 Waipi'o Point Access Road, Waipahu; 296-2000), located in the Pearl City area, is an inexpensive municipal course. Par 71; 5,946 yards.

Waikele Golf Club (94-200 Paioa Place, Waipahu; 676-9000), with views of Diamond Head and Pearl Harbor, is a Ted Robinson–designed championship course noted for its water features and sweeping views. A reasonably priced course, it has 18 holes, a pro shop, driving range, and restaurant. A shuttle picks up golfers in Waikīkī. Par 72; 5,983 yards.

Tennis

Tennis has long been a staple sport in Honolulu. Convenient public courts can be found at **Ala Moana Park** (10, lighted), **Diamond Head Tennis Center** (9), including one paddle tennis court, **Kapiʻolani Park** (4, lighted), and, a little farther away, **Koko Head** (6). Reservations are not available at these courts, which operate on a first-come, first-served basis.

Hotels in Waikīkī that have courts and allow nonguests to play for a modest fee include the **Renaissance ʻIlikai** (5) (949-3811) and the **Pacific Beach Hotel** (2) (922-1233). On the north shore, the **Turtle Bay Resort** (10) (293-8811) allows nonguests to use its courts for a fee.

Tennis lessons are available from **Alan's Tennis Etc.** (395-4341) and the **Hawaiʻi Tennis Academy** (373-1282).

Sightseeing Tours

There are so many tours and tour operators on Oʻahu that it would be impossible to list them all or to keep up with their continually changing schedules and fees. If you want your trip precisely planned, a travel agent can book tours for you through the larger companies. However, many of the best tours are offered by small operators not linked to mainland or foreign travel agencies. Do not be concerned about not being able to get onto a particular tour, since so many are available.

Most tour operators offer reduced fares for children. Advance reservations should be made for all tours; most hotels have courtesy desks in their lobbies where these can be arranged quickly and easily. Hawaiʻi's tour bus drivers and guides are usually well versed in knowledge of Hawaiiana and are eager to share their knowledge of the islands. Visitors should feel free to ask questions.

Tours of Oʻahu follow two basic routes: circle island (around the eastern tip of the island, all the way up the windward coast, around the north shore, across the Leilehua Plateau, and back to Waikīkī via the freeway), and little circle island (around the eastern tip, up the windward coast to Kailua, and through the Pali Highway tunnel back to town, stopping off at the Nuʻuanu Pali lookout).

Considering how few roads there are on the island, the variety of tours is amazing. This is because there are so many good places to stop along the way that no single tour stops at all of them; to do so would take a week rather than the customary day for the full circle.

The short circle eliminates most of the drive through rural countryside but still includes so many points of interest that it could take all day, though it is usually done as a half-day tour. Visits to the Polynesian Cultural Center or Waimea Falls Park can easily occupy half a day. Shorter tours take in selected spots such as Chinatown, ʻIolani Palace, Punchbowl, Hanauma Bay, Sea Life Park, or Pearl Harbor and the Arizona Memorial.

The best tours are those using the smaller conveyances, though this extra quality and service also costs more. **E Noa Tours** (591-2561) offers many different routes to most popular destinations such as Bishop Museum, Waimea Valley, Pearl Harbor, Polynesian Cultural Center, Mount Tantalus, and Chinatown. Hotel pickup is included in the reasonable rates. **Discovering Hidden Hawaiʻi Tours** (734-4447) also uses smaller vans. Their list of destinations includes all the top spots and also includes the flea market at Aloha Stadium.

Roberts Hawaiʻi (539-9400) can accommodate those seeking general sightseeing routes aboard big buses. One of the state's leaders in tours and transportation, the family-owned company has been in business for over sixty years and offers a variety of tour packages.

In the Air

Mo'o Kapu o Hāloa Ridge
from the air, looking
toward Mokoli'i Island
(Chinaman's Hat).

Gliding

To fly like a bird, glider plane rides are available at Dillingham Airfield in Mokulēʻia on the north shore through **Original Glider Rides** (677-3404), which operates a regular flight schedule from 10:30 A.M. to 5 P.M. daily, including holidays. Original Glider Rides has been in business for more than 30 years, offering views 2,000 feet above the north shore in a motorless airplane. The 20-minute flights usually run $100 for one passenger or $60 each for two passengers. However, in the present stagnant economy, rides are offered at $35 a person. An aerobatics flight is $85. Reservations are helpful but not required; flights take off every 20 minutes, but they are dependent on weather. If you call, you'll always get a person, usually "Mr. Bill" himself, the man in charge.

Another glider outfit is **Skysurfing Glider Rides** (256-0438), also at Dillingham Airfield.

Air Tours

A great introduction to the island is a circle tour by air, allowing you to get the lay of the land so that you'll better know where you are. Scenic flights, providing a totally new perspective of the island, are not inexpensive, but they offer good value for the price. The best air tours are in helicopters, which can slide deep into narrow valleys, allowing sightseeing in remote areas that are difficult or impossible to enter by land. On Oʻahu the leading company for such tours is **Rainbow Pacific Helicopters** (834-111), departing from Honolulu airport (with free pickup from Waikīkī hotels). A trip on a Rainbow Pacific flight is fun, exciting, and safe. Every passenger has a window seat. The pilot points out attractions, with the emphasis on the major tourist sites as well as places where movies and TV shows have been filmed (there's not much in the way of cultural history). Tours are given in English, Japanese, and German.

Also providing helicopter tours are **Makani Kai Helicopters** (834-5813), which offers day and night tours of Oʻahu, with multilingual inflight narration. Tours depart from Honolulu airport and range from a 10-minute Waikīkī or Pearl Harbor flight to a comprehensive 60-minute tour of the entire island. **Cherry Helicopters** (293-2570) departs from the north shore's Turtle Bay, offering a surfing tour of the north shore and a Sacred Falls tour along the Koʻolau Mountains, Kahana Valley, and Chinaman's Hat.

Propeller-powered seaplanes provide a fun and romantic way to view Oʻahu's sights. Tours offered by **Island Seaplane Service** (836-6273) take off and land in the protected waters of Keʻehi Lagoon, next to the Honolulu airport. Half-hour and hour flights are available, with complimentary van service from hotels.

Neighbor Island Tours

To see six islands in 3 hours, take a Volcano flight from **Eco Air** (839-1499). Flying in a twin-engine turbocharged Piper Chieftain with large, unobstructed windows, you'll see spectacular views of Oʻahu, Molokaʻi, Maui, Kahoʻolawe, Lānaʻi, and Hawaiʻi with its active volcano. Flights leave from the Honolulu airport, and hotel pickup is part of the deal.

Premier one-day tours of Hawaiʻi, Maui, Kauaʻi, and Molokaʻi are offered by **Aloha Vacations** (735-9009) via Hawaiian Airlines jet service to the specific island. Once there, visitors are taken on a narrated tour of the island aboard a minicoach. Tours are either all-inclusive circle trips or in-depth visits to specific places, such as Kīlauea Volcano on Hawaiʻi or lovely Hāna on Maui. The Molokaʻi tour includes a mule ride to Kalaupapa Peninsula.

Shopping

Rare is the visitor who doesn't go shopping for something during a Hawaiian holiday. Waikīkī has the greatest concentration of shops and the widest variety of goods for sale, but there are shopping centers and boutiques elsewhere that are worthy of note. Except for smaller neighborhood shops, most stores are open until 9 P.M., and in Waikīkī many of them stay open until 11 P.M., including the Waikīkī branch of Macy's (formerly Liberty House).

Shopping Centers

The shopping center Waikīkī visitors are most likely to encounter is the **Royal Hawaiian Shopping Center** (2201 Kalākaua Avenue) with three interconnected four-story buildings occupying a three-block area. There are 150 shops and restaurants in the center, including upscale shops like Chanel, Celine, and Hermès, and many Japanese and Korean restaurants. Daily events include ukulele lessons, lei making, and coconut frond weaving. The Visitor Information Center on the first floor is staffed with friendly personnel who will answer your questions. The center is open daily from 10 A.M. to 11 P.M. (some shops close earlier). A parking garage is entered via Royal Hawaiian Avenue.

Our favorite shop in this center is the **Little Hawaiian Craft Shop** (926-2662), one of the few places in Waikīkī where you can get authentic made-in-Hawai'i crafts, including wood carvings, Ni'ihau shell lei, Hawaiian quilts, clay windchimes, Christmas tree ornaments, and much more. The shop also carries a good selection of tapa and other handcrafts from the South Pacific. Another interesting shop is the **Ukulele House** (923-8587), which has a large selection of locally made ukuleles for sale; vintage ukuleles are on display, reminders of the instruments played by Hawaiian *paniolo,* whose first ukuleles were brought here in 1879 by Portuguese immigrants.

Opposite the Royal Hawaiian Shopping Center is **DFS Galleria Waikīkī** (330 Royal Hawaiian Avenue), which opened recently to much fanfare. A hodgepodge of ersatz architecture and faux nostalgia, this center is notable as a tax-free shopping zone and has a duty-free shopping section for international travelers. There's a much-touted two-story walk-through aquarium; the few fish (they seem to all be yellow tang) tend to stay on the first-floor level where merchandise displays block the view of the aquarium. Nightly half-hour shows at 7 P.M. continue the phony "Old Hawai'i"

An assortment of flower lei.

theme. Several excellent local chains are located in the center—among them Tori Richard, Cinnamon Girl, Crazy Shirts, and Island Soap & Candle Works—and are its saving grace. Parking at the Waikīkī Trade Center is validated with purchase.

Opposite the Royal Hawaiian center is the **Waikiki Shopping Plaza** (2270 Kalākaua Avenue), a multilevel conglomeration of small shops carrying a variety of merchandise (including Waikīkī's only bookstore), centered around a towering plastic water "sculpture," enhanced with colored lights, which is most striking when viewed from the escalators. A large *koi* pond is at the lower level of the escalator courtyard.

The center for souvenir shopping is the **International Market Place** (2330 Kalākaua Avenue), with scores of little kiosks in the

International Market Place, Waikiki.

open space under a huge banyan tree between Kalākaua and Kūhiō Avenues. You can buy a freshly strung flower lei here for $5, except for which one would be hard pressed to find something authentically from Hawai'i amid the tacky souvenirs. A minor repetition of the same theme is the narrow pedestrian walkway nearby called **Duke's Lane**, also between the two main thoroughfares. Opposite this is another arcade called **Waikīkī Town Center** (2301 Kūhiō Avenue) with the usual assortment of aloha wear, beachwear, and souvenir shops. The **Waikīkī Trade Center** (2255 Kūhiō Avenue) provides a modern setting for the shops on its ground level.

A little of the flavor of Disneyland can be found at **King's Village** (Ka'iulani Avenue between Kalākaua and Kūhiō). Built on the same three-quarter scale as that famous theme park, the "village" shops sell souvenirs, jewelry, and clothing as well as fast foods.

The Hilton Hawaiian Village's **Rainbow Bazaar** houses a range of shops and also creates a little world of its own. Nearby **Eaton Square** (400 Hobron Lane) is a small, European-flavored shopping area with several art, antique, and clothing shops as well a fine French restaurant, Chez Michel.

Ala Moana Center, the world's largest open-air shopping center.

Located at the edge of Waikīkī, **Ala Moana Center**, the world's largest open-air shopping center, offers an enormous variety of fashion, food, and fun shopping. At last count there were more than 200 businesses offering everything from diamonds to dictionaries to dining. The center is home to five large department stores: Macy's (formerly Liberty House), Neiman Marcus, J. C. Penney, Sears, and Shirokiya. All the top designer and chain stores are here as well as numerous local establishments. Free entertainment is provided regularly at the stage at the center of the complex. Regular hours are Monday through Saturday, 9:30 A.M. to 9 P.M.; Sunday, 10 A.M. to 7 P.M.

The **Ala Moana Shuttle** (955-9517) runs a bus between the center and six stops in Waikīkī for $1 per ride.

A little farther down Ala Moana, **Ward Centre** (1200 Ala Moana Boulevard) offers quality shopping for clothing, art, and unusual gift items. Paul Brown Salon & Day Spa is a fashionable women's and men's hair salon, and the Gallery at Ward Centre shows some of the island's finest artists. Honolulu Chocolate Company has excellent candies. There are a number of popular family-type restaurants in the center as well as Keo's Thai Cuisine and Mocha Java Café. Borders Books and Music anchors one end of the center.

Across the street from Ward Centre, a small strip mall called **Ward Village** houses several nice shops, including a Crazy Shirts store where discontinued styles and irregular tee shirts are sold at a considerable discount.

Almost next door, **Ward Warehouse** (1050 Ala Moana Boulevard) occupies former warehouse buildings opposite the docks at Kewalo Basin. Its casual atmosphere provides relaxed shopping for clothing, art, pastries, epicurean cookware, and much more, as well as a variety of eating establishments. Not to be missed here is Native Books & Beautiful Things, a coopera-tive, run by local artists, selling only made-in-Hawai'i clothing, crafts, and books, most of them made by native Hawaiians (see also page 226). Blue Ginger sells clothing for women, men, and children made from well-designed cotton batik fabrics, as does Noa Noa, which also has a selection of Oceanic artifacts. Cinnamon Girl has elegant casual clothing for women and children. Nohea Gallery has one of the largest selections around of fine art by local artists, including beautifully crafted wood items.

From Ward Warehouse, mov-ing toward downtown on Ala Moana, you'll find **Restaurant Row** (500 Ala Moana Boulevard), with its boutiques, restaurants, and nine movie theaters. Restau-rants include Ruth's Chris Steak House, Sansei Seafood Restau-rant and Sushi Bar, and Sunset Grill. The salon Chop is where Honolulu's hip young crowd goes to get their hair coifed.

Aloha Tower Marketplace, which opened in 1994, is the newest of Honolulu's shopping centers, a beautiful Mediter-ranean-style complex situated right on the waterfront at Hon-olulu Harbor. It has a number of restaurants, galleries, and retail stores, as well as sidewalk kiosks, many of which sell Hawai'i-made products. Notable restau-rants here include Big Island Steak House, Chai's Island Bistro, Don Ho's Island Grill, Kapono's, and Gordon Biersch Brewery. There is a clean and comfortable food court as well, offering a range of inexpensive fast foods. Live entertainment is presented regularly in the center court.

On the eastern side of Diamond Head, the very pleasant **Kāhala Mall** (4211 Wai'alae Avenue; exit 26B from H1 going east) has the

Aloha Tower Marketplace, with a bronze sculpture by Pegge Hopper and Leo Rijn.

likes of Banana Republic, the Gap, and Barnes & Noble. Eateries include California Pizza Kitchen. For an excellent selection of stylish objects for the home, garden, and bath, a shop called Following Sea is one of our favorites. There's a branch of Macy's department store here, and there is a large Longs Drugs. A nine-screen movie complex rounds out the offerings.

The **Waikele Center**, beyond Pearl City and situated off the H 1 freeway (exit 7), is a bargain-hunter's dream. This huge complex of discount warehouse stores includes factory outlets for Saks Fifth Avenue, Anne Klein, Banana Republic, Levi's, Carter's for Kids, and Donna Karan, among others. Borders, Comp USA, and K-Mart are also here.

Department Stores

Hawai'i's only remaining home-grown department store is **McInerny's**, whose largest store is now at the Royal Hawaiian Shopping Center. **Liberty House**, which was founded in Honolulu in 1849, was bought out by **Macy's** in 2001. Macy's is promising to keep the island flavor for which Liberty House

Mu'umu'u in a variety of tropical patterns.

was so loved. If so, it will remain a great source for made-in-Hawai'i fashions and gifts. **Shirokiya**, at Ala Moana Center, is a Tokyo-based department store and a favorite among Honolulu's Japanese community.

Neiman Marcus, also at Ala Moana Center, is the latest department store to have arrived in Hawai'i, opening in 1998. It's a beautiful place to shop or browse, with incredibly elegant clothing and jewelry. There are three superb restaurants in the store, including the casual Espresso Bar on the first level, perfect for coffee and a snack or light lunch. The busy, friendly Mermaid Bar on the next level has an appealing selection of salads and sandwiches. Mariposa, on the top floor with a spectacular ocean view, is noted for its fine cuisine. Best of all, Neiman Marcus has one of the finest collections of works by Hawai'i artists in the state. Throughout the store are paintings, sculptures, and works on paper by all the best artists active today, including Satoru Abe, Brendt Berger, Ken Bushnell, Yvonne Cheng, Helen Gilbert, Hans Ladislaus, Hanae Uechi Mills, Mary Mitsuda, Hiroki Morinoue, Timothy Ojile, and Tadashi Sato, among others.

Sears and **J. C. Penney** differ little from their mainland branches

except that they carry aloha wear and Hawaiian souvenirs.

Aloha Wear

Mu'umu'u (long, loose dresses) and shirts in bright, flowery prints put visitors in the light-hearted aloha spirit quicker than a mai tai can. People in Hawai'i really do wear these casual, comfortable clothes, although couples with matching outfits are found only at masquerade parties, on stage, or in Waikīkī.

A fine selection of reasonably priced aloha wear for men, women, and children is available at **Hilo Hattie** (700 North Nimitz Highway), which runs a free shuttle every 20 minutes (8:20 A.M.–3:30 P.M.) from Waikīkī hotels and the Duke Kahanamoku statue to its store, open daily. (If you want to get off at Aloha Tower or Ala Moana Center on the way back, you may.) Hilo Hattie also has a smaller store in Ala Moana Center.

Macy's also has a good selection of aloha wear for women and men, with some quite sophisticated styles. Teens find the latest in youthful aloha wear at **Local Motion**, with stores in Waikīkī and elsewhere. Vintage and used aloha wear can be found at **Bailey's Antiques** (517 Kapahulu Avenue). **Reyn's**, with locations at Ala Moana and the Kāhala Mall, is noted for its inside-out aloha shirts.

For a dress to wear to an island-style wedding or *lū'au*, the place to go is **Design by Michele Henry** in Chinatown (1026 Nu'uanu Avenue; 521-9596). Michele creates *mu'umu'u* in authentic '50s styles, using her mother's old dress patterns and vintage-patterned cotton fabrics. If there's nothing on the rack just right for you, Michele will make something to your specifications. (If you're there during lunch or tea time, go to her adjoining café for a delicious homemade treat.)

Tee Shirts

There is no shortage of those ubiquitous souvenirs, tee shirts proclaiming that one has visited the Aloha State. Some of the best designed tees are made by **Crazy Shirts**, all 100 percent cotton. Crazy Shirts has a dozen outlets on O'ahu, so you're sure to stumble across one. But if you really like their shirts (and who doesn't?), it's worth the trip to go to one of their three outlet stores: at Ward Village (116 Auahi Street, across from Ward Centre), at Waikele Center (94-798 Lumiaina Street), and at Costco Commercial Center near Aloha Stadium (call 422-4552 for directions).

Fabric

There are good selections of printed fabrics and Hawaiian prints at **Iida** (Ala Moana Center),

The loose-fitting, gaily patterned aloha shirt, short-sleeved, with a collar and buttoned down the front, has been a staple of Hawai'i's men's wear since the 1930s. Aloha shirts have been virtually unchanged since designs of the '30s and '40s captured the hearts of those who were drawn to the romantic aura of things Hawaiian. Today they look much like the shirts described in the *Honolulu Advertiser* in 1939 as "exotic prints, over which tumble in delightful confusion tropical fish and palm trees, Diamond Head and the Aloha Tower, surfboards and leis, ukuleles and Waikiki beach scenes."

A perennial question among the men is if aloha shirts should be worn with the shirttails hanging out or tucked in and with a belt. The answer seems to be that they can be worn however one wants, though for a formal occasion, such as a wedding, or for a fancy restaurant, the shirt probably should be tucked in.

Invitations to the premiere of the film *Pearl Harbor* indicated that the preferred attire was "aloha crisp," which caused much merriment in the local press as well as puzzlement as to what on earth Hollywood meant by the phrase. Most people attending the function decided to iron their shirts, at least.

Kuni Island Fabrics (2563 South King Street), **Fabric Mart** (1631 Kalākaua Avenue, near the Convention Center), and **Kaimukī Dry Goods** (1144 10th Avenue). For unique fabrics from Indonesia, there's **Toko Kain** (Kilohana Square, near the Convention Center), which translates as "fabric shop." This small shop also has home furnishings from Indonesia, the likes of which you won't find back home.

Art *and* Artists

Artists of every ilk flourish in the tranquil, tropical environment of Hawai'i. Many internationally known artists have come to Hawai'i and have recorded their visits by means of their art. Among these are **John La Farge** (1835–1910), who made watercolor views of Kīlauea Crater in 1890, and **Georgia O'Keeffe** (1887–1986), who came to Hawai'i in 1939 to paint plant-life for advertisements for the Hawaiian Pineapple Company, later known as Dole Pineapple.

Among the artists who came to Hawai'i and never left are printmaker **Charles W. Bartlett** (1816–1940), who arrived in 1917, and the Frenchman **Jean Charlot** (see page 109), who came in 1949 and was to exert major influence on the art and artists of his adopted home.

Many renowned artists were born here, studied in New York or Europe, and returned to make their mark in Hawai'i, including Hilo-born **D. Howard Hitchcock** (1861–1943), Honolulu-born **Juliette May Fraser** (1887–1983), and **Isami Doi** (1903–1965), who was born in 'Ewa on O'ahu.

Madge Tennent (1889–1972) came to Hawai'i in 1923, stopping en route on her return home to England after a stay in Samoa. She and her husband were taken with the charm of the people and environment and decided to stay. Tennent's bold oil paintings of monumental Hawaiian women are in the collection of the National Gallery of Art as well as in numerous other museums and private collections. Her paintings are now available only through private sale and fetch six-figure prices. A collection of her paintings and drawings can be viewed at the Tennent Gallery in Honolulu (see page 151), which was once her home.

Another internationally known Hawai'i artist is **Louis Pohl** (1915–1999), whose contributions to Hawai'i's contemporary art earned him official recognition as a "Living Treasure" by the Hawaii State Legislature. His works include powerful volcanic landscapes as well as serene seascapes. **Masami Teraoka** (b. 1936), who paints darkly satirical canvases inspired by his Asian roots, American culture, and European artistic traditions, is another Hawai'i artist with an international reputation.

You may find works by many of these artists at some of the galleries listed below. Louis Pohl's works are shown at the **Louis Pohl Gallery** (1056 Fort Street Mall; 566-6644; open Monday–Saturday, 10 A.M.–4 P.M.).

Art Galleries

Honolulu's fine art museums are described on pages 143–51. Here we describe galleries where works by contemporary artists living and working in Hawai'i are displayed and may be purchased. There are a great many galleries that sell "tourist art"—saccharine, factory-produced sea- and landscapes or overpriced giclée prints on canvas. Those galleries are not included in our survey of art emporiums in Honolulu.

Our favorite gallery is **Bibelot** in Kaimukī (1130 Koko Head Avenue, above the Post Office; 738-0368), run by Tom Tierney, Paul Sakai, and Paul's mother, Beverly. The work of local artists is shown with a schedule of monthly changing exhibitions. Many emerging artists are selected for Bibelot shows, and prices are far below what they would be elsewhere. In addition, the gallery has a choice selection of gift-type items, all original and many one-of-a-kind. Especially strong are the ceramics, though there are superb paintings and other artworks.

In the tradition of capturing the beauty of Hawaiian women, the large canvases of **Pegge Hopper** depict native women in all their strength and grace. Although Hopper's prints and posters are available in many places, the largest selection of paintings can be seen in her Chinatown gallery (1164 Nuʻuanu Avenue; 524-1160). **Ramsay Galleries** (1128 Smith Street; 537-2787), also in Chinatown, exhibits pen-and-ink architectural drawings by Ramsay that capture many of Chinatown's historically significant structures. Ramsay Galleries also exhibits the work of other artists from time to time.

New to the Chinatown scene is the **Arts at Marks Garage** (1159 Nuʻuanu Avenue; 521-2903), an avant-garde space for both visual and performing artists. All sorts of events are held in the space, as well as exhibitions of contemporary crafts and cutting-edge art.

Cedar Street Galleries (817 Cedar Street; 589-1580) represents nearly every living artist of note in Hawaiʻi—over one hundred of them. Owner Mike Schnack is extremely knowledgeable about local artists and will help you locate just what is to your liking and fits your pocketbook. Also with many years experience working in the local arts community, Greg Northrop of **Fine Art Associates** (591-2489) knows everyone and can help set up commissions for specific artworks.

The **Gallery at Ward Centre** (1200 Ala Moana Boulevard; 597-8034) is a cooperative venture with a fine group of artists and craftspeople. **Nohea Gallery** (596-0074), with the main store in Ward Warehouse and small shops in several hotels, has a good selection of Hawaiiana paintings as well as *koa* wood objects and unique jewelry.

In addition, art is exhibited at a variety of venues around the island. For a complete listing of current exhibitions, see the Island Life section of the Sunday *Honolulu Advertiser*.

Antiques

For a huge selection of vintage aloha shirts and aloha wear for the ladies, there is no better place than **Bailey's Antiques and Aloha Shirts** (517 Kapahulu Avenue; 734-7628). They also have vintage Levi's and fabrics as well as collectibles with a Hawaiiana flavor.

Robyn Buntin (848 South Beretania Street; 523-5913), just half a block from the Honolulu Academy of Arts, offers a good selection of antiques and artifacts from the Far East. **Antique House** (923-5101), at the Royal Hawaiian Hotel, specializes in Oriental arts and antiques and features Chinese jade carvings, snuff boxes, and ceramics. One of the largest Japanese antique stores in the U.S., **Garakuta-Do** (1833 Kalākaua Avenue; 955-2099) offers *tansu, imari,* baskets, *netsuke,* kimono, obi, bronze, hibachi, scrolls, and modern Japanese woodblock prints. **Mellow's Antiques** (841 Bishop Street; 533-6313), downtown in Davies Pacific Center, carries 18th- and 19th-century antique jewelry, furniture, paintings, and porcelain. **Anchor House Antiques** (471 Kapahulu Avenue; 732-3884) specializes in European and Oriental antiques, silver, jewelry, *koā* furniture, and Hawaiian paintings and artifacts. In Kilohana Square on Kapahulu Avenue, **Miko Oriental Art Gallery** (1022 Kapahulu Avenue; 735-4503) specializes in old ceramics, Buddhas, Asian furniture, and cabinet pieces.

On the windward side, in Kailua, **Windward Antiques** (760 Kailua Road; 262-5526) carries an excellent selection of European, Asian, and American antiques, primitive Hawaiiana, weapons and silver, as well as a large inventory of estate jewelry.

Handcrafts

Leaves of *hala,* called *lauhala,* were traditionally woven and plaited by Hawaiians into all manner of useful items, including floor mats and baskets. Today the range has been expanded to include handbags, lampshades, place mats, and much more. Similar items are made of tapa (*kapa* in the Hawaiian language). Though the tapa you buy here is not from Hawai'i, it is authentic, having been produced by hand using the ancient methods in Samoa, Tonga, and Fiji.

Allan Camara's Hawaiian-style quilt booth at an island craft fair.

Another traditional craft still very much alive is the making of permanent lei. These were and are made from feathers, seeds, or shells. Ni'ihau shell lei, made from tiny, varicolored shells found only on the island of Ni'ihau, are collected by museums and command high prices (see page 19). Feather lei are expensive too, and they require much time and care in the making. Feather neck and head lei were traditionally worn by the *ali'i,* as were *lei palaoa,* hook-shaped pendants that originally were made of whale ivory.

Indigenous woods such as *koa, milo,* and monkeypod are carved into decorative bowls and other utensils, as well as mundane figures such as fish and pineapples. The traditional *akua ki'i* wooden images representing gods, are today carved in modern renditions.

Perhaps the best selection of authentic crafts is at **Native Books & Beautiful Things** (1050 Ala Moana Boulevard; 596-8885) in Ward Warehouse. This huge store carries a full range of gifts and clothing made in Hawai'i. There are authentic gourd *ipu,* or drums, and bamboo nose flutes. Tee shirts and aloha wear are made from fabrics printed in Hawai'i with motifs related to native plants and authentic tattoo designs. Moderately priced children's clothing and toys are available here, as well as jewelry, art, items for the home, and gourmet foods.

Another great source for carefully selected, high-quality crafts is the Ku'u Home ("my home") department at **Macy's** in Ala Moana, where local buyers select fine items for the home, both useful and decorative, made only by Hawai'i artisans.

Many crafts can be found at the **International Market Place** in Waikīkī (but, if you want something *made in* Hawai'i, check the label to make sure you're not buying something from China or the Philippines). The **Little Hawaiian Craft Shop** (2233 Kalākaua Avenue; 926-2662) in the Royal Hawaiian Shopping Center has a broad selection of unusual objects and can be relied on for authenticity. In Ala Moana Center, **Irene's Hawaiian Gifts** (946-6818) has a good selection of fine Hawaiian woodcarving. **Blair** (860 Halekauwila; 593-9207), in Kaka'ako off Ward Avenue, carries a wide selection of quality carved wooden articles from Hawai'i and the Philippines. **Lanakila Crafts** (1809 Bachelot; 531-0555), part of a rehabilitation center in Nu'uanu, has pieces crafted by workers with disabilities.

Fine furniture of local woods is crafted by local artisans in the workshops of **Martin & MacArthur**, with locations in Kapālama near Sand Island (1815 Kahai Street; 845-0160), where office furniture and picture-framing supplies are available, and in the more accessible Aloha Tower Marketplace (524-6066) and Ala Moana Center (941-0074).

For a wide variety of handcrafts,

visit a **Pacific Handcrafters Guild** fair (see Calendar of Events) or some other local crafts fair. If you happen to be here in the fall, check for the **Hawai'i Craftsmen**'s annual exhibition at the Honolulu Academy of Arts.

Markets

O'ahu has an abundance of open-air markets, selling everything from locally grown fruits and vegetables (at much lower prices than in the supermarkets) to crafts of every sort. Just watch for them as you explore the island, and stop when you can. The **Aloha Flea Market**, held at Aloha Stadium parking lot in 'Aiea from 6 A.M. to 3 P.M. on Wednesdays, Saturdays, and Sundays, is a great place to shop for souvenirs at bargain prices.

Fruits, Flowers, *and* Foliage

Many people wish to ship fresh fruits to friends, or to themselves, or to take back with them flower lei or cuttings and seeds of colorful tropical plants. This is easy to arrange; many vendors will ship purchases for you, including **Royal Hawaiian Leis** (441-5347) and **Lins Lei Shop** (537-4112).

Some fruits and flowers are subject to quarantine regulations imposed by the U.S. Department of Agriculture and are prohibited from entry to mainland states. Guavas, mangoes, and passionfruit *(liliko'i)* are not allowed. Be cautious when buying lei to take home. Certain flowers, such as roses, *maunaloa,* and jade; berries, such as mock orange and *mokihana;* and leaves, such as *hala,* are prohibited, and lei containing them will be confiscated. You may take coconuts with you, as well as pineapples and papaya that have been inspected.

Sterile cuttings and seeds of many tropical and semitropical plants are sold in sealed packages that have been passed and certified by the Department

Orchids are plentiful at O'ahu flower markets.

of Agriculture, and these will pass inspection without difficulty. They are sold in many souvenir-type shops and in plant and garden shops. An ideal shop for such purchases is the **Foster Botanical Gardens Gift Shop** (180 North Vineyard Boulevard; 522-7065).

Coconuts are a fine and fun souvenir to take home. You can pick them up off the ground if you find yourself in an area where they don't trim the trees. (But beware of falling coconuts; they can kill.) Don't bother wrapping them; just keep the outer husk, an excellent natural packing that has served to float coconuts for thousands of miles across open oceans to be dashed by waves, unharmed, upon foreign shores. Not only that, they survive the rough handling of the U.S. Postal Service. Just write the address with a felt-tip pen on the coconut itself—unwrapped—and paste on the necessary postage stamps. The post office actually accepts these unorthodox parcels.

Music *and* Books

The big chain stores—such as **Borders Books and Music** (Ward Centre and Waikele), **Barnes & Noble** (Kāhala Mall), and **Tower Records** (Kāhala Mall and next to Ala Moana Center)—carry large selections of Hawaiiana in their Oʻahu stores. **Rainbow Books and Records** (1010 University Avenue at King Street; 955-7994) specializes in Hawaiian records, both new and used, as well as used textbooks.

The best place in town for art books is the **Academy Shop** at the Honolulu Academy of Arts (900 South Beretania Street; 532-8700). The Bishop Museum's **Shop Pacifica** (1525 Bernice Street; 848-4158) carries a large selection of works on Hawaiian and other Polynesian cultures and natural history. But the best selection of Hawaiiana books is at **Native Books** (1244 North School Street; 845-8949).

Young shopper with ukulele at the International Market Place.

This is the warehouse and office for the Ward Warehouse store Native Books & Beautiful Things as well as the main bookstore for the company. If you have a deep interest in things Hawaiian, it's a wonderful place to browse. Artwork by native Hawaiians is usually displayed in the bookstore.

Good shops within their limited range of historical works are the **Mission Houses Museum Shop** (553 South King Street; 531-0481) and the **ʻIolani Palace Shop** (King and Richards Streets; 532-1050). Both also carry excellent selections of gift items. Nearby is the **Book Cellar** (222 Merchant Street; 523-3772), a gem of a little shop that has an outstanding and reasonably priced selection of Hawaiiana and used and rare books. In the same building is a small branch of **Native Books & Beautiful Things** (599-5511).

If you enjoy New Age, metaphysical, and self-improvement books, **Sirius Books & Crafts** (2320 Young Street; 947-4910) carries a good selection, along with music and videos.

For books related to hiking and camping and for helpful information about the great outdoors in Hawaiʻi, the **Hawaiʻi Geographic Society** (49 South Hotel Street; 538-3952) is the place to go.

If you want to buy a book in Waikīkī, good luck. There is, however, a branch of **Waldenbooks** tucked away on the second floor of Waikīkī Shopping Plaza (2270 Kalākaua Avenue; 922-4154), open 365 days of the year from 9:30 A.M. to 9:30 P.M.

Over on the windward side, there's an excellent independent bookstore, **Bookends** (600 Kailua Road; 261-1996), in the Times Shopping Center in Kailua.

Discount Warehouses

Honolulu has in recent years sprouted two warehouse-sized wholesale "members only" stores, where food and a multitude of other discounted consumer goods are sold, many packaged in large volume or multiple containers. These stores are **Costco**, located in Hawaiʻi Kai (333 Keāhole Street; 394-3312), Honolulu (opening soon at Dole Cannery in Iwilei, off Nimitz Highway), and Waipiʻo (94-1331 Ka Uka Boulevard; 678-6100), and **Sam's Club** (10000 Kamehameha Avenue, Pearl City; 456-7788). Members of their mainland counterparts may shop at the Hawaiʻi branches. These mega-stores offer good prices on such items as local specialty foods, surf wear, and Hawaiiana books and CDs.

Specialty Food Stores

Local supermarket chains, such as **Star Market** and **Times Super Market**, devote many aisles to locally produced foods and produce that reflect the ethnic diversity of the islands. For fresh local fish and an array of Polynesian staples not found in most stores (such as apple bananas, Okinawan sweet potatoes, and, in season, breadfruit), **Tamashiro Market** (802 North King Street; 841-8047), in Pālama, can't be beat. A good fish market is **Slow Poke** (45-1048 Kamehameha Highway, Kāne‘ohe; 235-0048); *poke* means "to slice" in Hawaiian and refers to the raw-fish dish called *poke* (see Glossary). Prepared concoctions of sliced octopus (*tako poke*) and other fish, as well as flavorful and generous plate lunches, are the drawing card for **Fort Ruger Market** (3585 Alohea Avenue; 737-4531); people come for miles for popular local delicacies prepared at this grocery store on the slopes of Diamond Head. Even mainland chains, such as **Safeway**, offer exotic local produce and fish in their Hawai‘i

stores. The Japanese department store **Shirokiya**, next to Macy's in Ala Moana Center, has a huge grocery (973-9235) with foods from Japan as well as freshly prepared Japanese specialty items.

For the gourmet food lover, **Strawberry Connection** (Dole Cannery, 650 Iwilei Road; 521-9777), off Nimitz Highway, has an excellent selection of top-of-the-line fresh produce, French patés, gourmet cheeses, fine chocolates, pasta products of every shape and color, and European jams. The store started as a wholesale supplier for local restaurants and has expanded to accept retail business. A deli features gourmet salads and sandwiches. For the epicure of European taste, another shop worth mention is **R. Field Wine Company** (1460 South Beretania Street; 596-9463), located within a Foodland supermarket, offering hard-to-find deli items and rare cheeses, gourmet canned and bottled goods, and fresh produce from local farms, along with a divine selection of the vintner's art. Chocolate lovers will be in heaven at **Honolulu Chocolate Company** (1200 Ala Moana Boulevard; 591-2997), in Ward Centre, which offers an excellent selection of premium chocolate candies. Also catering to the chocoholic is **Ghirardelli** in

Waikīkī (2131 Kalākaua Avenue; 922-3766), where there is an old-fashioned soda fountain (with very modern prices).

Health Food Stores

The title to Honolulu's best health food store goes to **Down to Earth** (2525 South King Street; 947-7678), in Mō‘ili‘ili. The nearby **Kokua Market Natural Foods Co-op** (2643 South King Street; 941-1922) and **Huckleberry Farms** (1613 Nu‘uanu Avenue; 524-7960), in lower Nu‘uanu, are also excellent. Down to Earth is the largest of the markets, with a food bar and a few eat-in tables; a separate shop sells home products and clothing made only from natural fibers.

Drugstores

The local "drugstore" here is **Longs**, with twenty-two locations on O‘ahu. They sell hardware, housewares, souvenirs, greeting cards, office supplies, electrical and automotive supplies, cameras and film; cosmetics, slippers ("sleepahs," in other words, rubber thongs or flipflops), aloha shirts, food, appliances, and much more—not to mention drugs and other pharmacy items. Longs is hands down the hometown favorite drugstore.

Fun for Children *(of all ages)*

MOST ACTIVITIES IN HAWAI'I are fun for children as well as adults. Those listed here are perhaps more geared to children, but they are fun for adults as well, and you don't have to be a kid to have a great time at them.

The **Honolulu Zoo** (151 Kapahulu Avenue; 971-7195), at the edge of Kapi'olani Park, has, in addition to its regular exhibits of fascinating creatures, a mini-zoo of farm-type livestock especially for children where they can handle and interact with the animals. Moonlight tours of the zoo are offered several nights a month, suitable for *keiki* over 5 years of age. There are a great many other family programs at the zoo; call for current information.

Nearby, the **Waikīkī Aquarium** (2777 Kalākaua Avenue; 923-9741) provides a close look at the marine world. Many of its activities, such as guided walks along reef and shore and after-dark tours of the aquarium, are ideal for curious youngsters. Call for a current schedule.

Sea Life Park (41-202 Kalaniana'ole Highway, Makapu'u; 259-7933), an outstanding example of this genre, offers spectacular viewing of undersea creatures and the environments in which they live. Here one can witness the high intelligence of marine mammals such as dolphins and sea lions. For an extra fee you can get right in the water with tropical fish, stingrays, and dolphins. Roundtrip trolley service from Waikīkī is available for a reasonable fee.

Another memorable visit for the children is to the **Kāhala Mandarin Oriental** (see page 272) to watch the daily dolphin feedings and educational programs conducted by a trainer from Dolphin Quest. Three Atlantic bottlenose dolphins, as well as sea turtles and an array of tropical fish, are permanently kept in the hotel's large lagoon. The daily programs are open to the public and are free of charge

Opposite: Activities for children at the Waikīkī Aquarium.

Right: Hawaiian reef fish at Sea Life Park.

Dolphin in the lagoon at the Kāhala Mandarin Oriental.

Below: The Children's Discovery Center, in Kaka'ako, not far from Ala Moana.

(hotel guests may get in the water with the dolphins). Parking in the hotel's garage ($2) will be validated if you make a purchase at the hotel; otherwise, it's $3 per half hour.

The **Polynesian Cultural Center** (page 128) and **Waimea Falls Park** (pages 130–32) are excellent places for families to spend a full afternoon, and their rural locations provide the opportunity of swimming and picnicking en route. There are also a number of easy hiking trails that are suitable for families with children, including **Maunawili** (pages 200–1), **Mānoa Falls** (pages 197–98), and **Diamond Head** (pages 64–65).

The **Bishop Museum Planetarium** (page 144) is a terrific

educational attraction for children and adults alike. The new **Bishop Museum at Kālia**, at Hilton Hawaiian Village (949-4321), focuses on interactive exhibits that young people will enjoy and is open daily from

9 A.M. to 9 P.M. In the Activities Area, cultural interpreters share stories and legends and teach Hawaiian crafts like the making of *kapa*. The **Children's Discovery Center** (111 'Ohe Street; 522-8910), off Ala Moana Boulevard in Kaka'ako, is a *keiki* wonderland, loaded with hands-on interactive displays ranging from virtual volleyball to do-it-yourself television news.

Attracting children of all ages is **Hawaiian Waters Adventure Park** (400 Farrington Highway, Kapolei; 674-9283), a state-of-the-art waterpark featuring a wave pool and a variety of slides, including a six-story-high waterslide called the Cliffhanger. There's an adults-only area with a bar and a whirlpool spa. The price of admission allows a full day of fun with use of all water attractions. Food concessions sell pizza, hot dogs, and

local-style fare, and there are changing rooms with showers and lockers. Roundtrip bus packages from Waikīkī are available; TheBus also makes a stop here.

The *Magic of Polynesia* show nightly at the Waikīkī Beachcomber Hotel (971-4321), featuring magician John Hirokawa, is entertaining for older children. Kids and adults might be amused by a cool spin on the ice at the **Ice Palace** (4510 Salt Lake Boulevard, 'Aiea; 487-9921), near Aloha Stadium. This popular rink is open daily; the admission fee includes rental of skates.

Hawaiian Waters Adventure Park in Kapolei is a family favorite.

For restaurants that cater to families with children, see page 301.

Activity Programs

The **Hawai'i Nature Center** (2131 Makiki Heights Drive; 955-0100) runs an environmental education program aimed primarily at schools, but it occasionally has fascinating weekend programs and workshops on Hawaiiana—such as making ancient Hawaiian toys like *kukui* nut tops and jacks and carving nose flutes out of bamboo—and it offers an extensive nature-oriented summer program for children and families. The center

guides hikes along the nature trails in the Ko'olaus near Honolulu twice a month. They also provide maps to the extensive hiking trails at their backdoor on Mount Tantalus, easily walked by even young children and rewarding for the splendid views.

Fairs

Annual favorites that are fun for the entire family are the **Punahou Carnival** in February and the **50th State Fair** weekends in May and June (see Calendar of Events). Both have midway rides with kiddy sections for younger children—and thrillers for those so inclined.

Entertainment

ENTERTAINMENT AND NIGHTLIFE are, for an overwhelming majority of visitors, as much a part of a holiday on O'ahu as are the ocean and beaches. A Polynesian show or a *lū'au* is on almost every first-time visitor's agenda, and most seek out Hawaiian music, knowing they're not likely to find it anywhere else. But there's also plenty of international fare, sometimes with a local flair.

The biggest stars in the entertainment business like to come here, too, often appending their Hawaiian holidays to concert engagements. Local entertainers are adept at the wide variety of musical styles popular in the world today, and there are plenty of venues affording them opportunities to display their talents. Music, dance, and comedy abound.

The classics are not forgotten here in Hawai'i: theater, opera, ballet, symphony, and chamber music are offered in regular seasons by local repertory companies, and visiting classical artists come to Honolulu on tour. There are also frequent performances of a variety of ethnic music and dance from the traditions of Hawai'i's many immigrant groups.

Depending on your taste, there are sedate restaurants with entertainment, elegant lounges,

A dancer performs hula *'auana*, modern-style hula.

rowdy crowds, club dancing, or just plain partying. O'ahu has it all, and Waikīkī is the entertainment center of the island.

Details of what is going on while you are here are available from free tourist publications (many listing only advertisers) and from local newspapers. Reliable sources include the calendars of events in the entertainment sections of the daily *Honolulu Advertiser* and *Honolulu Star-Bulletin.* Also, *Honolulu Weekly,* an excellent free newspaper, has listings of events. We suggest you always call ahead, especially if you are relying on a listing in a weekly or monthly publication.

Polynesian Shows

On nearly every island in the Pacific, Polynesian or not, the "Polynesian Show" has become virtually de rigueur for tourist entertainment. These shows stage performances based on the traditional music, dance, and costumes of Hawai'i, Tahiti, Samoa, New Zealand, and, occasionally, Tonga and the Cook Islands; sometimes Melanesian Fiji is included.

Available on O'ahu at all *lū'au* and dinner shows, these spectacles are glitzy, show-biz interpretations.

The Tahitian *tamure* almost invariably highlights the evening with its fast-paced hip-swiveling, its grass skirts, tall headdresses, and wildly beating drums. Another showstopper is the Samoan fire dance or its close kin, the knife dance (often combined as the fire-knife dance). Hawaiian hula is usually the *'auana,* or modern variety, though some shows include a traditional *'ōlapa* or *kahiko* hula as well. The Maori (New Zealand) contributions are always a *poi* dance (*poi* in Maori are the white balls on string that the women manipulate so expertly in their dances) and the fierce *haka,* in which men challenge each other (and their audience) with spears and protruding tongues.

The biggest and best known of these shows is the dazzling extravaganza at the Polynesian Cultural Center in Lā'ie (see page 128).

Lū'au

Undoubtedly, the *lū'au* is the most famous feast on visitors' entertainment menus. This highly civilized Polynesian custom resembles the American Thanksgiving feast, except that the *lū'au* can be given at any time, for any reason. One good traditional reason for a *lū'au* is to honor and entertain visitors, so your attendance at one is entirely appropriate. The feast is named after the *kalo* tops (*lū'au*) that are always served. Cooked with coconut cream, they are delicious.

Other traditional fare on such occasions includes a whole pig (or even chicken or fish), which is baked (*kālua*) in a pit in the ground (*imu*), and such dishes as *laulau,* small packages of fish, pork, chicken, or beef, with *kalo* tops, wrapped in *ti* or banana leaves and baked; *poi,* a thick, purplish gray paste made from the cooked and pounded base of the *kalo* plant (the nutritious staple food of the Hawaiians); sweet potatoes; *lomilomi* (smashed) salmon with chopped tomatoes and onions; and *haupia,* a thick, creamy coconut pudding. The introduction of European and Asian foods to Hawai'i has added great variety to the culinary concoctions that are now traditional at a *lū'au.* There is usually so much to choose from that the *lū'au* can please the palate of almost anyone.

Though the focus of the feast is food, a *lū'au* includes a host of entertainment. Music, dance, and usually a bit of comedy enhance the festive atmosphere and add to the fun. Prices at the different venues range from about $50 to $85 per person; there is usually an open bar, or tickets are given for two or three drinks; prices for children are reduced, and under five is usually free.

The only *lū'au* in Waikīkī is the **Royal Lū'au** (931-7194) at the Royal Hawaiian, and it's only on Mondays. Slightly more expensive than most, it enjoys the romance of Waikīkī sunsets with Diamond Head as a backdrop—and you don't have to travel to get there.

Germaine's Lū'au (941-3338 or 949-6625) is held every night on a sandy beach near Barbers Point, about 40 minutes from Waikīkī. The fun begins on the buses (included in the price) that transport visitors to the *lū'au* site, where the pig is roasting in the *imu.* As the sun sets, you watch the pig being removed for serving; then there's an all-you-can-eat buffet. There's lots of audience participation as part of the entertainment, which includes traditional dances from Hawai'i, Tahiti, New Zealand, Fiji, and Samoa. The whole event is low-key and slightly hokey, but also a barrel of fun for those so inclined.

Paradise Cove Lū'au (842-5911) is in the same general area on the leeward coast as Germaine's, and it too provides free transportation from Waikīkī. On arrival, guests are treated to demonstrations of ancient Hawaiian games and crafts.

Guests may watch or join a traditional *hukilau* (seine net fishing party), which is followed by the feast and a Polynesian show. A variety of dinner packages are available, including the most expensive, steak and lobster.

Polynesian Cultural Center (293-3333), on Oʻahu's north shore, offers several packages in which a *lūʻau* can be combined with a tour of seven authentically recreated Polynesian villages (see page 128). Transportation from Waikīkī is an extra fee.

Hula

If a *lūʻau* epitomizes the culinary traditions of our island culture, hula captures its heartbeat. Dance was an integral part of the ritual life of the ancients, and the old hula has never died. New dances derived from it became popular entertainment for visiting sailors in the 19th century, who paid well to witness these altered performances, but Hawaiians didn't fundamentally connect this new and lucrative enterprise with

their sacred dance. Reviled by missionaries as obscene, the old dance was taken underground and taught in secret, while the new dance thrived in places where religious reformers held no sway. Thus there developed two distinct classes of hula, the ancient and the modern.

Hula *ʻōlapa,* more recently known as hula *kahiko,* the old style, is performed to the accompaniment of chanting and percussion only. Traditionally, the dance was done to accompany

Traditional *lūʻau* fare, clockwise from top left: *hālua* pork, *poi, lomilomi* salmon, and *haupia.*

"Poi looks like common flour paste, and is kept in large bowls formed of a species of gourd, and capable of holding from one to three or four gallons. Poi is the chief article of food among the natives, and is prepared from the taro plant. The taro root looks like a thick, or, if you please, a corpulent sweet potato, in shape, but is of a light purple color when boiled. When boiled it answers as a passable substitute for bread. The buck Kanakas [native men] bake it under ground, then mash it up well with a heavy lava pestle, mix water with it until it becomes a paste, set it aside and let it ferment, and then it is poi—and an unseductive mixture it is, almost tasteless before it ferments and too sour for a luxury afterward. But nothing is more nutritious. . . . I think there must be as much of a knack in handling poi as there is in eating with chopsticks. The forefinger is thrust into the mess and stirred quickly round several times and drawn as quickly out, thickly coated, just as if it were poulticed; the head is thrown back, the finger inserted in the mouth and the delicacy stripped off and swallowed—the eye closing gently, meanwhile, in a languid sort of ecstasy. Many a different finger goes into the same bowl and many a different kind of dirt and shade and quality of flavor is added to the virtues of its contents." —Mark Twain, 1866

the chant, which was of primary importance, and it was performed on most occasions by men. Though many hula groups today have a preponderance of women, the men's hula is every bit as beautiful and is energetic with a virile grace that seems absent from the aggressive men's dances of other Polynesian cultures. Chanting, too, is an art that has experienced a revival,

Keiki **hula dancers from Hālau Hula o Hōkūlani at a Lei Day celebration.**

along with an upsurge of interest in the Hawaiian language, which is always used in the chants.

The women's hula, though often softer than the men's, still has strength and precision. Precision is a vital element of this hula style, and while there is ample scope for the enactment of modern tales in the ancient mode, the rules of the dance are strict and are strictly followed.

It is interesting to note that the most famous symbol of the

hula, indeed, of Hawai'i—the grass skirt—is not Hawaiian at all. The grass skirt was introduced from Micronesia by laborers from the Gilbert Islands in the early 19th century. Hawaiians subsequently used native materials, such as *ti* leaves, in a similar fashion, but they were always fresh and green, out of respect for the gods, a strictly Hawaiian innovation.

Prior to European visitations, the garments worn by Hawaiians were made of barkcloth *(kapa)*. During the reign of King Kalākaua, when by royal decree the hula was again performed in public (helping to earn him the nickname "the Merrie Monarch"), European clothing of the time was worn in the dance, and hula dating from that era are still performed in costumes of the period.

Hula *ku'i*, a transitional form that combines traditional hula movements with those of 19th-century European ballroom dance, arose at this time. Prior to this innovation, men and women seldom danced together; in most ancient hula performed today, they still do not.

Hula *'auana,* the modern style, is much more flexible than its ancient forebear, just as modern ballet more freely extends the forms of classical ballet. Its costuming is keyed to the story

being told and is limited only by the imagination. Modern hula is usually accompanied by both melody and lyrics as well as ukuleles, guitars, and other instruments, and the songs may be in any language, though English and Hawaiian are most common.

There are several *hālau* on O'ahu that perform both modern and traditional hula, but performances are not regularly scheduled. Among the most appealing sights you'll see, if you're fortunate, is a well-trained hula troupe of *keiki*.

The most famous hula show is the **Pleasant Hawaiian Hula Show**, formerly known as the **Kodak Hula Show** (see page 62). This Waikīkī institution (free) should not be missed. Another free show takes place at **Kūhiō Beach**, near the Duke Kahanamoku statue, nightly from 6:30 to 7:30 P.M., featuring a torchlighting ceremony and hula. There are often hula performances on the center stage at Ala Moana Center and on weekends at the Aloha Tower Marketplace.

Check tourist publications and the Friday *TGIF* section of the *Honolulu Advertiser* for listings of when and where *ho'olaule'a* or other community events are scheduled that feature hula, because what you see can be significantly different from what you may see in a Polynesian revue, especially if you catch a good *kahiko*.

Ka Pā Hula Hawai'i is a superb group, dancing primarily to chants from the Kalākaua period, in both *'olapa* and *ku'i* styles. **Hālau Hula o Kukunao-kala** dances more than one style of *kahiko* and specializes in chants from the island of Moloka'i. **Nā Pualei o Likolehua** and **Pua Ali'i 'Ilima** dance a variety of *kahiko* and *'auana*. **Hālau Hula o Maīki** dances mostly *'auana,* as does **Nā Kamalei**; the subjects of their hulas vary widely. Notable *keiki* groups on O'ahu are **Hālau Hula Olana Ai** and **Hula Hui o Kapunahala**.

Hawaiian Music

There is no sound more clearly associated with the tropical beauty of these islands than the lovely Hawaiian melody accompanied by the ukulele. Though neither melody nor harmony had existed in Polynesian tradition prior to European contact, the people of the islands demonstrated remarkable natural affinity and talent for both. They also enthusiastically adopted the stringed instruments the visitors introduced, and each Polynesian group has developed a distinctive musical style during the past century or two.

Island musicians with their instruments.

The guitar is probably the instrument most commonly used by contemporary Hawaiian musicians, but its baby brother, the ukulele, is most strongly identified with Hawai'i. *'Ukulele* is, in fact, a Hawaiian word. It means "leaping flea" and was first applied as a nickname to Edward Purvis, a popular 19th-century player of the instrument who jumped around while he strummed. Brought to Hawai'i by Portuguese laborers in 1879, the diminutive instrument was known to them as *braquinho*.

The other stringed instrument immutably linked with Hawai'i is the steel guitar, played horizontally with a metal slide. The distinctively Hawaiian slack-key guitar derives from a tuning effect achieved by loosening the strings of a guitar.

Today's island music has continued to evolve and is now less stereotypical—more grounded in true expression of the feelings of island life—than the so called *hapa-haole* music written in the '30s and '40s, much of it by composers who had never even set foot in the islands.

Most of the large resort hotels have live Hawaiian music in their cocktail lounges and often in restaurants during dinner hours. Hawai'i's equivalent of the Grammies, the Hōkū Hanohano awards, called the Hōkūs, are presented annually to the hottest local stars. If you notice that a Hōkū-winning performer or group is playing somewhere, by all means make an effort to take in the show. Among favorite performers and groups are Daniel Ho, Keali'i Reichel, Henry Kapono, Moe Keale, Willy K, Power of 4, Manu Mele, Kalapana, Kapena, Ho'okena, and Olomana.

The **Honolulu Zoo** hosts weekly Wednesday evening concerts during the summer, sponsored by AT&T Hawai'i, for which there is a charge of $1 per person to benefit the zoo. Top island performers are featured. For information, call AT&T at 531-0101. The **Waikīkī Aquarium** also hosts a summer concert series, with such Hawai'i favorites as the Brothers Cazimero and Keola Beamer. Call 923-9741 for a current schedule.

Hawaiian music can be heard on radio station **KCCN** (AM 1420 and FM 100.3), on **KDNN** (FM 98.5), and on **KINE** (FM 105.1).

Dinner Shows

Not all dinner shows are "Polynesian" shows, though all have some Polynesian content and a distinctive island touch. All have a late, after-dinner seating, which is significantly less expensive, and a few have a second show.

A number of Hawaiian "stars" headline their own shows and have been longtime fare on the visitor nightlife calendar. They include the inveterate "Tiny Bubbles" singer **Don Ho**, appearing Sundays through Thursdays at the Waikīkī Beachcomber Hotel (923-3981). Ho, the Dean Martin of Waikīkī, communes with his audience, singing the "Hawaiian Wedding Song" for honeymooners and urging everyone to "suck 'em up."

The **Society of Seven** at the Outrigger Waikīkī (922-6408), Tuesdays through Saturdays, has, like the Don Ho Show, been a Waikīkī regular for over 40 years, so they're obviously doing something right. The Waikīkī Beachcomber features illusionist John Hirokawa in his *Magic*

of Polynesia show (971-4321), a family favorite.

The premier dinner show is *Creation: A Polynesian Journey* (931-4660), a spectacular revue that tells the ancient legends of the islands through song and dance. At the 'Āinahau Showroom of the Sheraton Princess Ka'iulani, this show has been a Waikīkī staple for three decades. The Sheraton Moana Surfrider presents its popular **Nā Kūpuna Night** dinner show (922-3111). Hawaiian entertainers perform "old Hawai'i" tunes and ancient styles of hula. The setting, on the Banyan Veranda, could scarcely be more pleasant.

Dinner Cruises

A number of operators offer dinner offshore, complete with live entertainment; all offer prices that are comparable, and all the cruises last about 2 hours. Transportation from Waikīkī is provided, sometimes for an extra fee.

The outfit with the best reputation for quality food, entertainment, and comfort is the *Navatek I* (848-6360), which offers a nightly sunset buffet cruise and a moonlight dinner or cocktail cruise. The unique construction of the vessel's hull prevents seasickness, making the ride as comfortable as you can get on the water.

The huge *Star of Honolulu* (983-7827), cruising Honolulu

waters since 1992, holds 1,600 passengers and offers a full range of dinner cruises. The *Ali'i Kai* (539-9495), Hawai'i's largest catamaran, offers sunset dinner cruises that include a Polynesian show. A dinner cruise and Polynesian revue can be combined with a Waikīkī show in a money-saving package offered by the *Starlet* (983-7827). **Dream Cruises** (592-5200) offers a more intimate experience aboard the *American Dream,* a 100-foot yacht that cruises the waters off Waikīkī. Friday nights they take in the fireworks off Duke Kahanamoku Beach.

Cocktails

Our favorite romantic spots for cocktails enhanced by traditional Hawaiian music and hula are **House without a Key** at the

Sonny Kamahele of the Islanders at the House without a Key, Halekūlani Hotel.

Halekūlani Hotel (2199 Kālia Road; 923-2311) and the **Banyan Courtyard** at the Sheraton Moana Surfrider (2365 Kalākaua Avenue; 922-3111). Both are perfect for watching the setting sun. The **Ocean Terrace Bar** at the Waikīkī Beach Marriott Resort (2552 Kalākaua Avenue; 922-6611) also books top local entertainers, including Ledward Ka'apana and Auntie Genoa Keawe. The **Mai Tai Bar** at the Royal Hawaiian (2259 Kalākaua Avenue; 923-7311) is also very popular. They have a nice sunset view and are well known for their mai tais as well as a recent innovation, pink beer. In the downtown area, **Palomino Restaurant Rotisseria Bar** (66 Queen Street; 528-2400), in the mezzanine of Harbor Court, draws a large after-work crowd.

Nightclubs

Just as soon as a club is anointed as the in spot, it's out, so the club scene is difficult to keep up with. We include here (mostly) those that have been around for some time. Most clubs levy a small cover charge. All stay open until between 2 and 4 A.M. on weekends, most closing earlier during the week. Check the listings in the local newspapers, especially the Friday editions, for current club events. *Honolulu Weekly,* a free tabloid, has espe-

Genoa Keawe (b[...] been captivatin[g audi]ences for over [...] an unrivaled falsetto tech[...]nique, facile yodeling skill, and her ability to hold a high note for over two minutes. Born in the Kaka'ako section of Honolulu, she began singing at age ten in a Mormon Church choir. Marrying at age sixteen, she had twelve children. She began to appear on the stage and to be heard on radio in the 1940s. Many of her songs, recorded from the late '40s to the early '60s, have become mainstays of the Hawaiian music repertoire. Over the years she has received many Hōkū awards, the Hawai'i equivalent of the Grammy, and she was recently awarded a National Heritage Fellowship from the National Endowment for the Arts. Now in her eighties, Auntie Genoa continues to perform regularly in Waikīkī hotels.

cially complete listings of musical events broken up into categories like alternative, blues, contemporary, Hawaiian—you get the picture. However, mistakes have been known to appear, so it would be good to call ahead. More accurate are the listings in the *TGIF* section of the *Honolulu Advertiser.*

The younger crowd and often a celebrity or two can be found Friday nights after 9 P.M. at W Honolulu's **Wonder Lounge** (2885 Kalākaua Avenue; 922-3734), which provides a sophisticated, upscale club scene. Currently hot

too is the **Green Room** at Indigo in Chinatown (1121 Nu'uanu Avenue; 521-2900), with both DJs and live entertainment, depending on the night of the week. The Green Room is known also for its various kinds of martinis.

The most popular bar in Waikīkī is **Duke's Canoe Club** (2335 Kalākaua Avenue; 922-2268), at the Outrigger Waikīkī Hotel. All sorts of beach events are held here, and it's crowded day and night. *Pūpū* and standard mainland bar food are served. Duke's attracts a young crowd

Duke's Canoe Club is right on Waikiki Beach.

who don't want to pay the high cost of hotel food and who enjoy the great local entertainers—the likes of Kapena, Henry Kapono, Jonah Cummings, Haumea Warrington, and Makana.

New on the scene and drawing big crowds is the **Spy Bar** at John Dominis Restaurant (43 ʻAhui Street; 523-0955), open only on Friday nights after 10:30 P.M. Another popular nightspot is **Anna Bannana's** (2440 South Beretania Street; 946-5190), near the University of Hawaiʻi, which has live music and is frequented by a young crowd. The funky decor is reminiscent of an American roadhouse. Also popular are **Auntie Pasto's Kapahulu** (559 Kapahulu Avenue; 739-2426),

where on Friday and Saturday nights young people line up on the sidewalk waiting to get in; and **Wave Waikiki** (1877 Kalākaua Avenue; 941-0424), which features many mainland bands.

For local color, there's **Hank's Café** in Chinatown (1038 Nuʻuanu; 526-1410).

For the older set, there are a number of nightlife options, most of them restaurants with entertainment, usually featuring local musicians of the first order. Recommended are **Chai's Island Bistro** (Aloha Tower Marketplace; 585-0011); **Don Ho's Island Grill** (Aloha Tower Marketplace; 528-0807); and **Kapono's** (Aloha Tower Marketplace; 536-2161).

Scruples Beach Club (2310 Kūhiō Avenue; 923-9530) and **Rumours** at the Ala Moana Hotel (410 Atkinson Drive; 955-4811) are popular among fans of music of the '60s and '70s. **Esprit** at the Sheraton Waikīkī (2255 Kalākaua Avenue; 922-4422) has been a popular gathering spot for years.

For jazz, there's **Duc's Bistro** in Chinatown (1188 Maunakea Street; 531-6325) and the **Veranda** at the Kāhala Mandarin Oriental (5000 Kāhala Avenue; 739-8888), where the Betty Loo Taylor Trio plays Tuesdays through Saturdays accompanied by vocalist Loretta Ables. This is a wonderful place to while away an evening, with *pūpū* from Hōkū's next door and a glass of great wine.

David Swanson tickles the keys at W's **Diamond Head Grill** (2885 Kalākaua Avenue; 922-1700). Devoted jazz buffs might want to try **Studio 6** (949 Kapiʻolani Boulevard; 596-2123), where members of the local musician's union often get together weekday nights to jam. Also watch for performances by Jimmy Borges, Azure McCall, and Gabe Baltazar, three noted Honolulu jazz musicians who play at various locations throughout the city.

The classiest *karaoke* bar can be found at **Sansei Seafood**

Restaurant and Sushi Bar
in Restaurant Row (500 Ala
Moana Boulevard; 536-6286).

Hula's Bar and Lei Stand
in the Waikīkī Grand Hotel (134
Kapahulu Avenue; 923-0669)
is a popular gay bar and dance
club at the edge of Waikīkī.

Theater

The historic **Hawai'i Theatre**
(1130 Bethel Street; 528-0506),
built in 1922 in downtown
Honolulu's Chinatown district,
has recently undergone a $22-
million facelift. Nicknamed the
Carnegie Hall of the Pacific, this
lovely old theater has a richly
appointed and elegant interior,
in the tradition of a grand
Broadway theater. Reopened
in the spring of 1996, the theater
has a seating capacity of 1,400.
The extensive restoration has
upgraded the facility to a state-
of-the-art center that hosts a
variety of productions throughout the year.

The history-rich and distin-
guished **Diamond Head Theatre**
(520 Makapu'u Avenue; 734-
0274) runs its season from
October through August and
includes large-scale musicals as
well as dramatic productions,
often with cast members who
have played on Broadway. The
smaller **Mānoa Valley Theatre**
(2833 East Mānoa Road; 988-

6131) presents well-known plays
as well as locally written productions. Internationally known for
outstanding Asian productions,
the East-West Center's **Kennedy
Theatre,** on the University of
Hawai'i campus (1770 East-West
Road; 956-7655), presents shows
from September through May.

Many traveling Broadway
shows come to Honolulu's
Blaisdell Center. These have
included such popular productions as *Cats, Miss Saigon,
Chicago,* and *Rent.*

Classical Music

Honolulu's thriving music scene
encompasses a variety of classical
presentations in the finest European tradition. Some of these
are offered in regular seasons,
while others are staged at irregular intervals throughout the
year. Announcements of visiting
classicists will be found in the
local press as well as on Hawai'i
Public Radio (FM 88.1 and 89.3).

The **Honolulu Symphony
Orchestra** (524-0815), conducted
by Samuel Wong, is one of
the oldest symphonies in
the country and the oldest
west of the Rockies. Based
at the Blaisdell Concert
Hall, the orchestra presents
regular seasons of classics as well
as a pop series, from September
through May. Guest artists have

included Yoyo Ma, Marilyn
Horne, Pinchas Zukerman, and
Vladimir Feltsman. Some of the
orchestra's most popular concerts
are "pops under the stars" evenings
presented at the Waikīkī Shell
in Kapi'olani Park.

The **Hawai'i Chamber
Orchestra Society** (734-0397)
gives concerts in a season
running from October through
May. High-quality chamber
music also is presented by
groups comprised of Honolulu
Symphony Orchestra members,
including the **Galliard String
Quartet** and **Honolulu Brass**.

The **Hawai'i Opera Theatre**
(596-7372; box office 596-7858)
stages three full-length operas
in midwinter (January–April)
at Blaisdell Concert Hall. Past
performances have included
Bizet's *Carmen,* Verdi's *Il
Trovatore,* and Donizetti's
Daughter of the Regiment.

A sunset cruise.

Calendar
of Events

THE EVENTS LISTED HERE occur annually, sometimes varying from one month to another. Current information may be obtained from the Oʻahu Visitors Bureau (733 Bishop Street, Suite 1872, Honolulu, HI 96813; 877-525-OAHU, 808-524-0722; www.visit-oahu.com).

January

Ala Wai Canoe Challenge, Ala Wai Canal (outrigger canoe competition)

International Body-Boarding Championships, Banzai Pipeline, North Shore (the world's top body boarders take on giant waves)

Narcissus Festival, Chinese Cultural Plaza, Honolulu, beginning with the second full moon after winter solstice, sometime between mid-January and mid-February (the Chinese New Year is celebrated with a queen pageant, coronation ball, Chinese cooking, lion dances, firecrackers, food booths, and arts and crafts)

Sony Open PGA Golf Tournament, Waiʻalae Country Club ($525,000 tournament featuring top professionals)

February

Cherry Blossom Festival, February and March (various Japanese cultural events throughout Oʻahu)

Great Aloha Run/Walk, Aloha Tower to Aloha Stadium, Presidents' Day, the third Monday in February (8.2-mile fun run)

NFL Pro Bowl, Aloha Stadium (annual all-star football game involving the National and American conferences of the NFL)

Punahou Carnival, Punahou School, Mānoa (rides and ethnic foods; art, plant, book, and white elephant sales)

March

Kamehameha Schools Song Contest, Blaisdell Center (competition among students of Hawaiian ancestry)

Kite Festival, Kapiʻolani Park (competition and festival with many unusual and gigantic kites flown by pros)

Prince Kūhiō Day, March 26 (state holiday honoring Hawaiʻi's Prince Kūhiō)

Saint Patrick's Day Parade, Fort DeRussy to Kapiʻolani Park, March 17

April

Aloha Basketball Classic, Neal Blaisdell Arena (collegiate tournament)

Buddha Day Celebration, the Sunday closest to April 8 (flower festival pageant at island temples to celebrate the birth of Buddha; sponsored by the Hawaiian Buddhist Council)

Easter Sunrise Service, National Memorial Cemetery of the Pacific, Punchbowl (sponsored by Hawaiʻi Council of Churches)

Metric Century Ride, Haleʻiwa (100-km bicycle ride along the north shore)

Pacific Handcrafters Spring Fair, Thomas Square Park, late April or early May

May

50th State Fair, Aloha Stadium, weekends through June (commercial exhibits, produce, food booths, entertainment)

Lei Day, May 1 (lei competitions, celebrations, and exhibits)

Memorial Day Services, National Memorial Cemetery of the Pacific, Punchbowl, last Monday in May

Visitor Industry Charity Walk, Ala Moana Beach Park (a popular fundraiser sponsored by businesses in the visitor industry)

World Fire Knife Dance Competition, Polynesian Cultural Center, Lāʻie

World Ocean Games, Waikīkī (international teams compete in such events as outrigger canoeing, paddleboarding, kayaking, and surf lifesaving in this 10-day event)

June

Betsuin Bon Dance, Honpa Hongwanji Temple (a celebration with dance and food at this Shin Buddhist temple)

Festival of Hawaiian Quilts, Mission Houses Museum (quilt exhibit, living history program, craft demonstrations, entertainment, and food)

Kamehameha Day, June 11 (state holiday honoring King Kamehameha the Great, Hawai'i's first monarch; lei-draping ceremony at Kamehameha statue, opposite 'Iolani Palace; parade with floral floats)

King Kamehameha Hula and Chant Competition, Neal Blaisdell Center, mid-June (*hula kahiko* on Friday night; *hula 'auana* Saturday night)

Pan-Pacific Festival–Matsuri in Hawai'i, Waikīkī (street party and parade celebrating Japanese culture)

Taste of Honolulu, downtown (charity fundraiser sponsored by the Easter Seal Society of Hawai'i, with entertainment and food booths from top local restaurants)

July

Artists of Hawai'i, Honolulu Academy of Arts, through August (juried exhibition of works by Hawai'i artists)

Collectors Show, Blaisdell Exhibition Hall (collectibles and antiques from Hawai'i, mainland, and international vendors)

Dragon Boat Race, Ala Moana Beach Park (16-paddler teams propel colorful Taiwan-built wooden boats; entertainment and food and craft vendors participate in the 2-day event; sponsored by AT&T)

Fourth of July (fireworks at Ala Moana Beach Park and Kailua Beach)

Friends of the Library Book Sale, McKinley High School (a 4-day event with thousands of books, sheet music, records, and more, most priced between $1 and $2)

Hale'iwa Arts Festival, Hale'iwa (over 60 visual artists display and sell their works, from oils and watercolors to ceramics and jewelry)

Hawai'i International Jazz Festival, various locations (for four days all over town, top musicians participate in concerts, clinics, and jam sessions)

Hawai'i State Farm Fair, Aloha Stadium, end of July or early August (carnival, produce and livestock, and entertainment)

Pacific Handcrafters Summer Craft Fair, Thomas Square Park (arts and crafts, ethnic foods, and entertainment)

Prince Lot Hula Festival, Moanalua Gardens, third Saturday of July (*hula hālau* perform; concessions and tee shirts)

Queen Lili'uokalani Keiki Hula Competition, Blaisdell Arena (dancers six to twelve years old participate in this competition, which has taken place for over twenty-five years; sponsored by the Kalihi-Palama Culture and Arts Society)

Quicksilver Paddleboard Race, Kaluako'i Resort on Moloka'i to Maunalua Bay, O'ahu (32 miles on a paddleboard across the Kaiwi Channel, perhaps the world's most challenging water event)

Ukulele Festival, Kapi'olani Park (Hawai'i's top entertainers and a ukulele orchestra of 300 children)

August

Admission Day, third Friday in August (state holiday recognizing Hawai'i's statehood, August 21, 1959)

Floating Lantern Ceremony (Toro Nagashi), Ala Wai Canal, August 15 (final event of the Japanese O-Bon festival)

Greek Festival, McCoy Pavilion, Ala Moana Beach Park (Mediterranean cuisine, entertainment, jewelry, and clothing)

Pacific Island Taro Festival, Windward Community College, Kāne'ohe, July or August (storytelling, music, dance, arts and crafts, and a farmers' market)

Slack Key Guitar Festival, Ala Moana Park (features Hawai'i's top performers)

September

A Day at Queen Emma Summer Palace (Hawaiian arts and crafts, food, and entertainment)

Aloha Festival (native Hawaiian events, including pageantry, royal ball, canoe races, ho'olaule'a in Waikīkī and downtown, parades with floral floats and pā'ū riders, and entertainment)

Bankoh Nā Wāhine o Ke Kai, Hale o Lono Harbor on Moloka'i to O'ahu (women's 40.8-mile six-person outrigger canoe race)

International Bed Race and Parade, Kalākaua Avenue and Kapi'olani Park (charity fundraiser featuring a zany race with beds preceded by a parade through Waikīkī)

O'ahu Century Ride, Kapi'olani Park (100-mile bicycle race up the windward coast and back)

Okinawan Festival, Kapi'olani Park

Pacific Handcrafters Fall Fair, Thomas Square Park (arts and crafts, ethnic foods, and entertainment)

Waikīkī Rough Water Swim, Sans Souci Beach to Duke Kahanamoku Beach at Hilton Hawaiian Village (2-mile swim for all ages and categories, sponsored by the American Lung Association)

October

Bankoh Moloka'i Hoe, Moloka'i to O'ahu (40.8-mile six-person championship outrigger canoe race)

Discoverers' Day, the second Monday in October (Hawaiian equivalent of Columbus Day)

French Festival, Waikīkī and Honolulu, end of October or early November (culinary workshops, cultural events, and entertainment)

Makahiki Festival, Waimea Falls Park (the historic harvest time is celebrated with Hawaiian games, crafts, music, and foods)

November

Christmas Craft Fair, Mission Houses Museum (open-air bazaar with Hawai'i's top crafters)

Hawai'i International Film Festival, Hawai'i Theatre and other theaters throughout Honolulu (crosscultural films by award-winning filmmakers from Asia, the Pacific, and the U.S.)

Triple Crown of Surfing, through December (Hawaiian Pro at Hale'iwa; World Cup of Surfing at Sunset Beach; Pipeline Masters at Banzai Pipeline)

Veterans Day Parade, Fort DeRussy to Kapi'olani Park, November 11 (sponsored by the American Legion)

December

Honolulu City Lights and Festival of Trees, downtown (Christmas celebration)

Honolulu Marathon (one of the largest marathons in the world, with over 30,000 runners)

Jingle Bell Run, Honolulu Hale to Aloha Tower (2-mile fun run/walk featuring costumed teams)

New Year's Eve, December 31 (firecrackers are set off everywhere; First Night, downtown, celebrates New Year's with an alcohol-free street party)

Pacific Handcrafters Christmas Fair, Thomas Square Park (arts and crafts, ethnic foods, and entertainment)

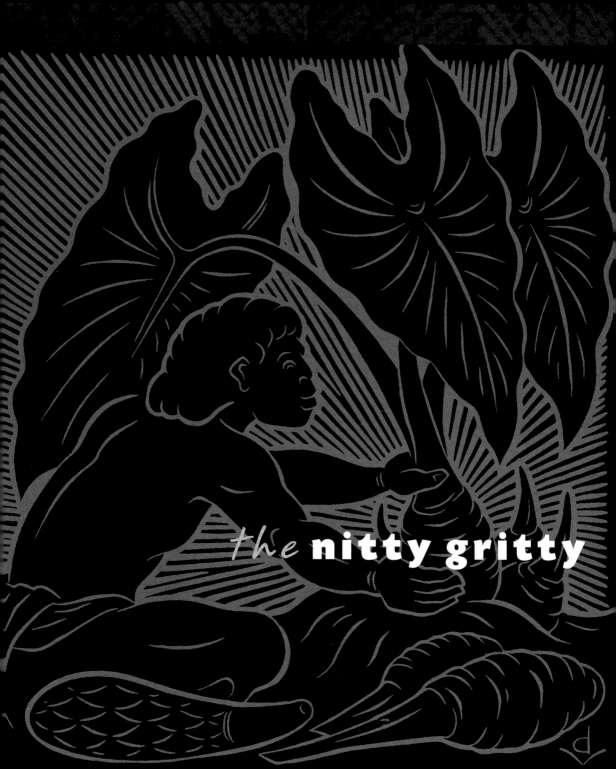

the **nitty gritty**

Telephone

THE AREA CODE for all of the Hawaiian islands is 808, and that must be dialed if you are calling to or from a neighbor island. Toll-free numbers have the area code 800, 887, or 888. For emergency calls, dial 911. Public coin telephones require 50¢ for local calls (except for emergency calls to 911).

Getting *to* O'ahu

Airlines

Hawai'i is such a popular destination that airfares are kept relatively low through volume and competition. There are many airlines serving the islands, most arriving at Honolulu International Airport on O'ahu. Here passengers heading for a neighbor island may switch to interisland aircraft to continue their journey.

Flight times are roughly 5 hours from California, 9 hours from Chicago, 11 hours from New York, 8 hours from Tokyo, and 9.5 hours from Sydney. Return flights to the U.S. mainland, taking advantage of the jet stream, are often somewhat

Page 255: Dietrich Varez, *Taro*, linocut.

shorter. Domestic carriers providing service to and from the U.S. mainland are Aloha, America West, American, Continental, Delta, Hawaiian, Northwest, and United. Foreign carriers currently serving Honolulu are Air Canada, Air New Zealand, All Nippon Airways, Canadian Airlines, China Airlines, Japan Airlines, Korean Air, Philippine Airlines, and Qantas, among others.

Carriers providing service between the Hawaiian islands are **Aloha Airlines** (800-367-5250; www.alohaairlines.com); **Hawaiian Airlines** (800-367-5320; www.hawaiianair.com); **Island Air** (800-323-3345); and **Pacific Wings** (888-575-4546; www.pacificwings.com).

Airport

Honolulu International Airport, serving as a gateway between East and West, is one of the busiest airports in the world. Passengers arriving from the U.S. mainland or from other countries emerge from this vast complex on the ground level of the main terminal building. Monitors with arrival information are located throughout the area. The airport's second level services mainland and overseas departures and

includes ticket counters for reservations and check-in, monitors with departure information, agricultural inspection stations for departing passengers, and all departure gates.

If you arrive on Hawaiian or Aloha, you will pick up your baggage at the **Interisland Terminal**, located at the 'ewa end of the main terminal, where these airlines are based. You can walk or take the free Wiki Wiki (Hawaiian for "quick") buses. Just past the interisland terminal is what is called the **Commuter Terminal** (it's the old interisland terminal). This is where Island Air and Pacific Wings are based.

Adjacent to the main terminal is a large parking structure with easy access to and from both ground and upper levels. Car rental agencies are located on the ground level; their rental return areas are in the same vicinity as the lei stands. Both the lei stands and car rental return areas are clearly marked by signs on the roads that circle through the airport. The Interisland Terminal has its own parking structure adjacent to the building, and there is ample outdoor parking next to the Commuter Terminal.

For additional airport visitor information, call 836-6413.

Airport Amenities

O'ahu's airport has all the standard conveniences of large airports everywhere: restaurants, coffee shops, cocktail lounges, fast food counters, duty free shops, currency exchange, barbershop, business services, and newsstands. It is worth noting that many items are more expensive at the airport than they may be elsewhere.

A unique feature of Honolulu airport is the area in the center of the complex containing lei stands, offering a variety of fresh flower lei for sale at reasonable prices. There is also a beautiful, tranquil garden where those with long airport waits can relax.

Within the airport, the free Wiki Wiki buses transport people from faraway gates to the escalators leading to the baggage claim areas on the lower level. Buses also transport people between the main terminal and the Interisland Terminal, normally operating between 7 A.M. and 10 P.M., depending on the interisland flight schedules.

For those who wish to get some rest before or after a flight or simply to freshen up, the **Shower Tree**, 3085 North Nimitz Highway (833-1411), offers showers and/or private, Pullman-like sleeping cubicles (single or double occupancy) for a modest fee. Day rates are under $40 for two; less for single occupancy. Weekly rates are offered as well, for the thrifty visitor who doesn't mind the less convenient, no-frills digs in return for travel dollars saved. There are only 32 cubicles available, so reservations are suggested.

Customs and Immigration

All passengers arriving from other countries must pass through Customs and Immigration, located in the International Arrivals Center at the 'ewa end of the main terminal building. Passports are required for citizens of foreign countries except Canadians, who must provide proof of residence. Many foreign nationals no longer need visas for entry into the United States, providing their stay is less than 90 days. Check with the U.S. embassy or consulate for information. After clearance by customs and quarantine inspectors, passengers exit the airport on the ground level, as do U.S. mainland arrivals.

Quarantine

Do not plan to bring your pet with you for a Hawaiian holiday. Quarantine regulations in Hawai'i are among the strictest in the world, and all arriving passengers must declare any animals or plants they are bringing to the islands. Failure to do so is punishable by law, and the penalties are severe.

The Hawaiian islands are free of many plant and animal diseases that cause problems in other parts of the world, and the quarantine laws are designed to prevent the introduction of those problems here. The importation of live animals is strictly prohibited except by permission; this includes all household pets, which must be boarded for a period of 120 days at the state quarantine station on O'ahu, located in Hālawa Valley, a 15-minute drive from the Honolulu airport. Dogs and cats meeting certain pre-arrival requirements may have the quarantine period reduced to 30 days. For information about importing domestic animals, contact the Animal Quarantine division at 99-951 Hālawa Valley Road, 'Aiea, HI 96701 (483-7171).

If you wish to import live plants to Hawai'i, contact the Hawai'i Department of Agriculture, Plant Quarantine Inspection, at 701 Ilalo Street, Honolulu, HI 96813 (586-0844 or 837-8413) for details and permits.

Cruise Ships

Arriving in Hawai'i by cruise ship is far more complicated now than it was decades ago when most visitors sailed into island ports. Today, the cruise lines that make stops at Hawai'i ports are of foreign registry and are forbidden by U.S. law to transport American citizens from one U.S. port to another. However, it is possible to travel on a majestic cruise ship between the islands (see page 195).

What *to* Bring

Visitors should pack warm-weather clothing to wear in Hawai'i's perpetual spring and summer climate. The usual attire on O'ahu is casual, and apparel known elsewhere as summer clothing is worn year round. Shorts are acceptable almost anywhere; most businesses require customers to wear shoes (though rubber thongs will usually suffice). Comfortable walking shoes are a must. Sleeveless or short-sleeved shirts are usually best for day wear, but long sleeves, or even a jacket or sweater, may be needed for cool winter evenings and for air-conditioned buildings. Deluxe restaurants occasionally have a dress code requiring men to wear jackets but usually not ties. Until the last decade, men wore jackets and ties to work in offices, but today an aloha shirt suffices.

Once here, there's no shortage of places to buy sunscreen, bathing suits, sandals, and the like. Prices do tend to be slightly higher than on the mainland.

Leaving Hawai'i

Though the Hawai'i Visitors Bureau and the state certainly hope you will purchase souvenirs while you're here, there's no point in trying to take home many agricultural products, as they won't pass agricultural inspection, designed to prevent certain insects from traveling to the mainland. Coffee, jams, and salsas will pass. But don't try to slip through the inspection line with fresh limes, avocados, bananas, or the like. You will definitely be stopped (we know from experience).

If you're leaving the United States, you may take whatever you like, but there's no guarantee of its passing quarantine inspection in your country of arrival.

For specific inquiries and further details, you may telephone the O'ahu office of the State of Hawai'i Department of Agriculture (948-0145 or 836-3827) and ask for mainland export information.

Getting Around

HONOLULU INTERNATIONAL Airport is 4 miles from downtown and 8 miles from Waikīkī. Public and private buses, taxis, and limousines provide airport service, and several car rental agencies have offices at or near the airport. Limited helicopter transfer service is also available.

There are myriad options for getting around on land. Buses come in several varieties, and numerous types of private vehicles can be rented.

Taxis *and* Shuttles

Taxicabs at the airport are situated just outside of the baggage claim area. They are regulated by the City and County of Honolulu. The cost of a metered trip to Waikīkī averages between $20 and $25, depending on which end of Waikīkī your hotel is situated. Incidentally, taxi drivers are directed to offer passengers a receipt, but if you are not presented a receipt when you reach your destination, ask for one.

Charley's Taxi (531-2333 or 531-1333) will arrange a lei greeting for you if you call them in advance. **Super Shuttle** (841-2928) provides airport transportation for $6 each way.

Limousines

Private limousine or car service is provided by some of the luxury hotels for arriving guests, or visitors can arrange to be met at the Honolulu airport. Limousine services offer private sightseeing excursions as well, driving you anywhere on the island at any time for as long as you like. The leaders on O'ahu are **Americabs** (591-8830), **Cloud Nine Limousine** (524-7999), and **Elite Limousine Service** (735-2431).

TheBus

The public bus on O'ahu, called **TheBus**, has been nationally recognized as one of the top bus systems in the U.S. These yellow and white leviathans carry passengers all over the island for $1.50. A bus pass for four consecutive days, which allows a person unlimited rides, is $15, available at ABC stores. A pass for a month is $27, available at many supermarkets and convenience stores and at any Satellite City Hall.

The #19 and #20 buses, labeled "Waikīkī Beach and Hotels" when inbound and "Airport" when outbound, stop at the second level of the main terminal at regular intervals throughout the day. Between Ala Moana Center and Waikīkī, take the #8, #19, or #20 bus. For current schedules and route information, call 848-5555 between 5:30 A.M. and 10 P.M. To inquire about bus passes or bus service for physically challenged persons, call 523-4083. Also, bus timetables for the entire island are available at the Ala Moana Satellite City Hall,

which is open daily.

It should be noted that passengers on city buses are not supposed to carry on anything that will not fit onto their laps. This rule is not strictly enforced, but if you are carrying luggage, it would be wise to avoid buses during rush hour.

Taking TheBus to get around the island can be time consuming, but the price is right. Valid transfers are accepted when a passenger is changing from one route to another and traveling in one general direction via the most direct route. Bus operators are generally helpful in telling visitors which buses to catch to reach their destinations. Buses are equipped to transport bicycles. Passengers cannot wear wet bathing suits.

Trolleys

The **Waikiki Trolley** (593-2822), an open-air conveyance, is supposed to be reminiscent of the old Waikīkī trolley that once linked downtown Honolulu with rural Waikīkī, just 4 miles away. The original trolley was mule drawn. This self-propelled replica operates from 8 A.M. to 10 P.M. There are a number of routes for shopping, dining, and sightseeing. You can get on and off as many times as you like. Ticket and route information is

available at the following stops: Royal Hawaiian Shopping Center, DFS Galleria, Hilton Hawaiian Village, Ala Moana Center (*mauka* side), Ward Warehouse, and Aloha Tower Marketplace. An all-day pass is $18 for adults and $8 for children ages 12 and under; four-day passes are avail-

able for $40; children $10.

The **Rainbow Trolley** (539-9495), operated by the tour company Roberts Hawai'i, runs every 20 minutes with over 25 stops at hotels, shopping centers, and sightseeing attractions. Tickets are available from trolley operators. A one-day pass is $10 for adults and $5 for children under 12; four-day passes are $30; children $10.

Driving

Any visitor who drives in Hawai'i must have a valid driver's license from another state or a Canadian province or a current international driver's license issued in another country. Wear your seatbelt. Hawai'i police are known to issue tickets to beltless drivers and riders. Posted speed limits should be followed.

O'ahu has more cars per capita than anywhere else in the nation. Between 6:30 and 8:30 A.M. and 3:30 and 5:30 P.M., it appears that all of them are trying to drive into or out of Honolulu. Visitors are well advised to avoid driving in urban areas during those hours if possible. Friday and Saturday nights in Waikīkī are also packed with traffic.

Parking is severely limited in Waikīkī and downtown. Unless you plan to do a lot of exploring, it would probably be easiest to use public transportation on O'ahu, possibly renting a car for a day or so of touring around the island.

Many street parking spaces are in areas that become tow-away zones during rush hour, usually between 6:30 and 8:30 A.M. and 3:30 and 5:30 P.M. Read parking signs carefully, and be sure to heed the restrictions. Tow trucks are at the ready to haul away illegally parked cars within 5 minutes of the start of rush hour.

Driving Times

Sample distances in both miles and driving time from Waikīkī are:

Honolulu International Airport
 8 miles, 30 minutes
Arizona Memorial
 11 miles, 30 minutes
downtown Honolulu
 4 miles, 15 minutes
Hanauma Bay
 11 miles, 30 minutes
Sea Life Park
 15 miles, 35 minutes
Kualoa Ranch
 30 miles, 60 minutes
Polynesian Cultural Center
 35 miles, 75 minutes
Waimea Falls Park
 36 miles, 75 minutes
Hale'iwa
 32 miles, 60 minutes
University of Hawai'i
 3 miles, 10 minutes
Pali Lookout
 11 miles, 30 minutes

Car Rentals

A number of car rental agencies have service desks fronting the baggage claim areas on the ground level of the main terminal of the Honolulu airport. Many others have offices near the airport and courtesy phones in the baggage claim area. Those not on the premises will pick up customers at the terminal. If you wish to rent a car in Waikīkī, you can be picked up at your hotel, though most agencies are within walking distance, as Waikīkī is not that big. Hotel concierges can be of assistance if you need a single-day rental.

Most of the agencies provide current standard American and Japanese models. Many visitors elect to rent a convertible during their Hawai'i stay. If your fancy runs to Jeeps or other sporty four-wheel-drive vehicles or to fancy sports cars, your wish will be granted—for a price.

In addition to the license requirements, renters usually must be at least 21 years of age; those under 25 must also hold a major credit card.

Nationally known rental agencies at or near the Honolulu airport include: **Alamo** (800-327-9633; 833-4585); **Avis** (800-321-3712; 834-5536); **Budget** (800-527-7000); **Dollar** (800-800-40000; 944-1544); **Enterprise** (800-736-8222; 836-7722); **Hertz** (800-654-3011; 831-3500); **National** (800-227-7368; 831-300), and **Thrifty** (800-367-2277; 831-2277). We like Budget and Avis, but all of the companies are good.

Among local companies, **Paradise Rent-a-Car** (926-7777 or 946-7777) offers Jeeps, VW Bugs, and exotic cars like BMWs and Corvettes. **JN Car & Truck Rentals** (831-2724) features economy and luxury cars, convertibles, and vans and trucks.

Mopeds *and* Motorcycles

Renters of mopeds or motorcycles must possess a valid driver's license and be over the age of 18. Those not holding major credit cards must leave a cash deposit. Mopeds are illegal on the freeways (H1, H2, and H3).

Island Moped Rentals (924-3422) has three Waikīkī locations. Other moped rental agencies, all in or near Waikīkī, are **Blue Sky Rentals** (947-0101), **Moped Zone** (732-3366), **Paradise Isle Rentals** (946-7777), **Surf & Turf Rentals** (923-5544), and **Wiki Wiki Wheels** (951-5787).

Thrifty Car Rental (971-2660) also rents motorcycles, as does **Paradise Rent-a-Car** (946-7777). Other agencies are **Adventure on 2 Wheels** (944-3131), **Cruzin Hawai'i Motorcycles** (945-9595), and **Wiki Wiki Wheels** (951-5787). In the heart of Waikīkī, **Coconut Cruisers** (924-1644) rents mopeds and motorcycles.

Bicycles

Touring bicycles can be rented from **Blue Sky Rentals** (947-0101), **Paradise Isle Rentals** (946-7777), **Wiki Wiki Wheels** (951-5787), and **Coconut Cruisers** (924-1644). On the north shore, bicycles can be rented in Hale'iwa from **Raging Isle** in the North Shore Marketplace (66-250 Kamehameha Highway; 637-7707). It is also cheap and easy to bring your own as excess baggage; most airlines provide cartons, and some require that handlebars be rotated and pedals removed for transport.

If you need emergency repairs, the following shops offer service in a half-day to a day, depending on the problem and how busy they are: **McCully Bicycle** (955-6329), at 2124 South King Street; **Eki Cyclery** (847-2005), at 1603 Dillingham Boulevard; the **Steady Wrench** (949-1711), at 1407 Kalākaua Avenue; and **Kailua Bike Shop** (266-6730) on the windward side at 354 Hahani. The **Bike Shop**, a well-respected outlet, makes rentals and repairs from its shops in Honolulu (596-0588), 'Aiea (487-3615), and Kailua (261-1553).

Tips are an essential element of income for many who serve Hawai'i's visitors.

Tipping

MANY PEOPLE who work in the tourist industry in Hawai'i hold down more than one job and count tips as essential to their income. At restaurants, bars, and nightclubs, tip 15 percent of the bill before tax; up to 20 percent for exceptional service and in fine-dining establishments. The same tip applies to taxi drivers, hairdressers and beauticians, and massage therapists.

Give tour guides a 10 or 15 percent tip. Give airport and hotel porters $1 or $2 per bag (at least $5), and leave $1 or $2 per day in the room for housekeeping services. The attendant who valet parks your car should be given $2 each time you take the car out. If the hotel concierge is helpful during your stay, leave a $5 or $10 tip.

Traveling *with* Children

HAWAI'I IS an ideal destination for family vacations. The near-perfect climate allows for plenty of time outdoors at the beach or in a park. And there are plenty of things to do on O'ahu that are educational as well as enormously entertaining.

It should be noted, however, that while many neighbor island hotels offer special all-day programs for children, that is not so common on O'ahu. O'ahu hotels with programs for *keiki,* either year round or during vacation periods, include Hilton Hawaiian Village Beach Resort and Spa, Hyatt Regency Waikīkī, Kāhala Mandarin Oriental, Outrigger Reef, Sheraton hotels (including the Royal Hawaiian), J. W. Marriott Ihilani Resort and Spa, and Waikīkī Beach Marriott Resort.

Most hotels offer babysitting services through the concierge. If you want a night out without the children and your hotel doesn't have an in-house babysitter, call **Aloha Babysitting Service** (732-2029). This reliable operation has been providing visitors in the Waikīkī area with fully licensed and bonded sitters for more than twenty-five years. Sitters travel to the hotels with books and toys in tow. The service has a 4-hour minimum and charges for transportation to the hotel.

For a listing of family-friendly restaurants, see page 301.

Keiki **checking out the flamingos at the Honolulu Zoo.**

Gay *and* Lesbian Travelers

FOR GAY AND LESBIAN travelers, **Gay Hawaiian Excursions** (800-311-4460; www.gayexcursions.com) will set up a wide variety of tours and activities, including whale watching, horseback riding, kayaking, windsurfing, snorkeling, scuba diving, surfing, dinner cruises, and much more.

Physically Challenged Travelers

CITY BUSES are fitted to handle passengers in wheelchairs. The City and County of Honolulu provides curb-to-curb service through **Handi-Van**. To obtain a free pass, call the eligibility office at 523-4083 or pick up an application at any Satellite City Hall. The vans run from 5 A.M. to 11 P.M., and fares are $2 each way for all distances. Visitors who have obtained a pass during their stay may use this service to return to the airport.

Aloha State Cab (847-3566) has accessible vehicles. Accessible vans are available for rental from **Accessible Vans of Hawai'i** (800-303-3750; www.accessiblevans.com), which will meet you at the airport.

Two Honolulu travel agencies specialize in providing travel arrangements for visitors with physical or mental disabilities, including booking reservations for cruises and sightseeing tours: **Access Aloha Travel** (545-1143) and **Accessible Adventures of Hawai'i** (951-4948).

Services

Website *and* Newspapers

An award-winning Website for ecotourism and general information about Hawai'i is: www.alternative-hawaii.com

At the moment Honolulu has two daily newspapers: the *Honolulu Advertiser* and the *Honolulu Star-Bulletin*. Both provide national and world news as well as schedules of current events that are of interest to visitors as well as locals. In addition, the less mainstream *Honolulu Weekly*, available free in newspaper boxes all over the city, provides a hip take on local affairs. It too has listings of events, especially those related to the arts and musical scene in Honolulu.

Shoe Repair, Dry Cleaning, *etc.*

Being a cosmopolitan center, Honolulu is replete with businesses that provide all sorts of necessary services. For one-stop services, there's nothing better than **Sear's** in Ala Moana Center, which offers reliable shoe repair (947-0235), dry cleaning (947-0384), alterations (947-0528), and watch repair (947-0343). **Waikīkī Laundromats** (923-2057) has self-service facilities at eight locations in Waikīkī. The **Waikīkī Ena Road Laundry** (478 Ena Road; 942-3451), one block from the Hilton Hawaiian Village, has self-service machines as well as same-day drop-off service.

Business Services

There are three branches of **Kinko's** in Honolulu: 1500 Kapi'olani Boulevard (944-8500), across from Ala Moana Center; 590 Queen Street (528-7171), close to the downtown business district; and 2575 South King Street (943-0005), in the university area. You can get photocopies; ship via FedEx; have business cards and brochures printed; use PCs and Macs; and access the Internet. All locations are open 24 hours.

Civic Clubs

A lot of visitors who belong to civic clubs back home inquire with tourist service desks about local chapters. Most frequently sought are **Lions Club International** (524-7025) and **Rotary Club of Honolulu** (922-5526). Visiting members from other districts are welcome to call for information about local meetings and activities.

Libraries

O'ahu's public libraries offer lending rights to visitors who obtain a local library card during their stay. The **Waikīkī-Kapahulu Public Library** (400 Kapahulu Avenue; 733-8488) is conveniently located at the Diamond Head end of the Ala Wai Canal. The **Hawai'i State Library** (586-3500), worth visiting for the building alone, is located on the edge of the downtown capitol district, at the corner of King and Punchbowl Streets, adjacent to 'Iolani Palace. There is a section devoted to historical books about Hawai'i, and the librarians are very helpful in locating material.

Post Offices

Most branches of the **U.S. Postal Service** are open Monday through Friday, 8 A.M. to 4:30 P.M., and Saturday, 9 A.M. to noon. The telephone number for all is 800-275-8777. The Waikīkī branch (300 Saratoga Road) is located next to Fort DeRussy, in the same block. Another convenient branch is at Ala Moana Center, on the *mauka* side just *'ewa* of the central mall. The Downtown Station is at the corner of Merchant and Richards Streets, opposite 'Iolani Palace, in the beautiful Old Federal Building. Honolulu's main post office is at the airport (3600 Aolele Street), where there is window service Monday through Friday, 7:30 A.M. to 8:30 P.M.

Medical Services

Honolulu has a number of excellent hospitals. **Queen's Medical Center** (1301 Punchbowl Street; 538-9011) has state-of-the-art facilities, including a top-rated emergency room. Queens will provide physician referrals; call 537-7117. **Kapi'olani Medical Center for Women and Children** (1319 Punahou Street; 983-6000) is a well-regarded facility not far from Waikīkī; for physician referral, call 535-7000. **Kaiser Permanente** (432-0000) has a number of clinics on O'ahu and a large medical center—open only to Kaiser members. On the windward side, **Castle Medical Center** (263-5500) has 24-hour emergency care and provides physician referrals (263-5400). There are walk-in physician services in Waikīkī, to which your hotel's concierge can refer you, but they tend to be pricey.

Two of them are **Urgent Care Clinic** (2155 Kalākaua Avenue; 597-2860), in the building near Beach Walk, and **Hawai'i Medical Ueno Clinic** (1777 Ala Moana Boulevard; 926-9911), in the Renaissance 'Ilikai hotel. The latter is open 24 hours.

The best thing medically you can do for yourself while you're in Hawai'i is check into **Holistica Hawai'i Health Center** (951-6546) at the Hilton Hawaiian Village. The center embraces all aspects of wellness—mind, body, and spirit. Holistica uses cutting-edge medical technology, such as the electron beam tomography (EBT) scanner and high-resolution 3-D ultrasound, to assess your body's condition. Board-certified physicians and medical specialists conduct a thorough assessment of each client's health, focusing on such areas as cardiology, endocrinology, and metabolism, as well as concerns specific to men and women. Residential programs are available, ranging from half a day to a week. Accommodations are in the world-class Kālia Tower of Hilton Hawaiian Village, and the spa services of Mandara Spa, in the Kālia Tower, complement the health center's program. Programs can be individualized for executives and their families, athletes, and multigenerational families.

Island Weddings

AN ACTIVITY popular among visitors to Hawai'i is either getting married or renewal of vows. Numerous enterprises are engaged in the business of making people's romantic dreams of ceremonies in tropical settings come true. There are so many spots that are splendidly suited to the purpose that the difficulty is in the choosing. Some of the most favored locations are Waikīkī Beach, Ha'ikū Gardens, Moanalua Gardens, and Foster Botanical Gardens. There are also, of course, many lovely indoor settings.

Waimea Falls Park (638-8511) will arrange weddings on the grounds of this tropical north shore paradise, and **Kualoa Ranch** (237-7321), on the windward side, offers personalized weddings either oceanfront or in a tropical garden. Both of these places will arrange for receptions as well. The **Dillingham Estate** in Mokulē'ia (on the north shore near Hale'iwa) is a beautiful site for a wedding; however, you will have to make your own arrangements for the ceremony and reception. For information, call the Mokulē'ia Land Company (637-8088).

In town, one of the nicest settings for a wedding is the grounds of the **Mission Houses Museum** (see pages 83–84), perfectly restored to their 19th-century ambiance. Call 531-0481 for information. The **Honolulu Academy of Arts** (pages 144–49) has several open courtyards that offer perfect wedding sites, from the intimate Asian courtyard with its serene lily pond to the large courtyard at the Luce pavilion, where the Pavilion Café can cater your reception.

All the large hotels provide wedding services, arranging for everything from the minister to the champagne. They provide beautiful settings for weddings, including intimate gazebos and beachside pavilions. Just ask about wedding services. You may get more information by calling the local (808) telephone number rather than the toll-free number.

Our favorite hotel wedding site is the exquisite garden at the **Halekūlani Hotel** (pages 262–63), where the hotel will erect a flower-bedecked canopy for your ceremony. A particularly lovely place for a reception is the upper floor of the hotel's House without a Key. The **Kāhala Mandarin Oriental** (page 272) also is a beautiful site for a wedding. Their director of weddings can be reached at 739-8715.

Numerous local companies specialize in wedding arrangements, among them **Affordable Weddings of Hawai'i** (923-4876 or 800-942-4554), **Aloha Wedding Planners** (943-2711), and the **Wedding Connection** (923-9734 or 800-388-6933). An option that's a little different is a wedding

at sea, offered by **Royal Hawaiian Cruises** (848-6360) aboard the *Navatek I* and by **Dream Cruises** (592-5200), **Hawai'i Sailing Adventures** (596-9696), and **Honolulu Sailing Co.** (239-3900).

Marriage licenses are available from the State of Hawai'i Department of Health (1250 Punchbowl Street, Honolulu, HI 96813; telephone 586-4545). Licenses are issued immediately after application and expire after 30 days. They are valid only in Hawai'i, and the fee ($50) is payable at the time of filing. Both parties must be 18 years old and of the opposite sex (the Hawai'i legislature and the voters have refused to sanction same-sex marriages).

A wedding party at Makapu'u Point on the windward coast is led by a Hawaiian *kahuna*, or priest.

accommodations

THERE IS NO SHORTAGE of hotels, condominiums, or private vacation homes on Oʻahu. Guestrooms and cottages are available throughout the island, mostly in areas that are not populated with a lot of tourists. For nature lovers and the budget minded, rustic cabins and tent camping are available but should be reserved well in advance as they are limited in supply. Camping permits are required for public parks that allow camping.

If you wish to stay in a bed-and-breakfast accommodation or a private vacation home, there are several local reservation services and real estate agents available to assist you (see page 275). Many of these services charge a nominal booking fee, which can turn out to be a savings in the long run. Many B&Bs and vacation rentals require a minimum stay and offer reduced rates for longer periods.

Accommodations are listed alphabetically in the following four categories:

- Hotels and condominiums
- Bed-and-breakfasts and inns
- Studios, cottages, and house rentals
- Campsites

Pages 258-59: Dietrich Varez, The Moana Hotel (ca. 1930), linocut

Hotels *and* Condominiums

BOTH TOLL-FREE AND LOCAL telephone numbers are provided. Very often the toll-free number (area code 800, 887, or 888) is for a nationwide reservation system. Sometimes if you call the local number you may get better rates. Or a travel agent may be able to book a hotel at rates below what is quoted by the hotel to you.

Don't forget to check out hotels' websites, where special rates are often posted. For instance, one Waikīkī budget hotel cites a rack rate of $136, a discounted rate of $93 (AAA, seniors, military, *kamaʻāina*), and an Internet rate of $79 for a premium-category room. The average room rate on Oʻahu in 2001 was $128.

Rates given here are for one night and are usually for two people. There is usually a fee for an additional person, though many hotels allow children under a certain age to stay free in the room with their parents. We've listed the lowest and the highest rates provided to us. Don't be frightened by the highest rates; they're often for what is called the Presidential Suite or some such. A standard room is fine for most of us mortals. Also, be sure to ask about packages or special rates. Except in high season, nearly every hotel has special rates for the asking. If you'll be on your honeymoon or will be celebrating an anniversary, be sure to tell the hotel.

Rates do not include Hawaiʻi taxes of 11.25% (7.25% room tax and 4% excise tax).

Waikīkī Hotels *and* Condominiums

Ala Moana

410 Atkinson Drive, Honolulu, HI 96814-4722.
800-367-6025; 808-955-4811; fax 808-944-2974 (www.ala moanahotel.com). $125–$2,300

Ideally situated on the edge of Waikīkī and steps away from Hawaiʻi's new convention center, the Ala Moana Hotel offers guests the fun and romance of Waikīkī without the hustle and bustle. The hotel has been a preferred choice for visitors and *kamaʻāina* since it opened in 1970. Overlooking Ala Moana Beach Park, this 1,152-room hotel is conveniently connected to the world-famous Ala Moana Center and is the closest major hotel to downtown Honolulu. Most guestrooms open onto a private lanai overlooking the Pacific Ocean, the Koʻolau Mountains, or the parks and beaches of paradise. The hotel offers seven concierge floors featuring rooms with upgraded amenities. Guests of these rooms are indulged with a Thermasol spa (sauna and whirlpool in one), complimentary continental breakfast, and nightly turndown service. Dining and entertainment facilities in the Ala Moana Hotel satisfy a variety of tastes, from romantic dinners at the sky-high penthouse restaurant Aaron's, to discotheque action at Rumours nightclub or piano music in the hotel's lobby at the Mahina Lounge, a favorite *pau hana* (after work) gathering place.

Ambassador Hotel of Waikīkī

2040 Kūhiō Avenue, Honolulu, HI 96815. 800-923-2620; 808-941-7777; fax 808-951-3939 (www.ambassadorwaikiki.com). $105–$625

This comfortable high-rise at the intersection of Kūhiō and Kalākaua Avenues (the so-called gateway to Waikīkī) is two blocks from beautiful Fort DeRussy Beach. Rooms range from studios to three-bedroom suites, with kitchenettes in all but the smallest studios. There is a swimming pool, and ADA-equipped rooms are available.

Aston Aloha Surf

444 Kānekapōlei Street, Honolulu, HI 96815. 800-922-7866;

808-923-0222; fax 808-922-8785 (www.aston-hotels.com). $95–$180

Aston is a local Hawaiian chain that offers excellent values. Newly renovated, the Aloha Surf is located on a quiet side street near the Ala Wai Canal in Waikīkī, three blocks to the beach. Amenities include complimentary continental breakfast, a swimming pool, and laundry facilities. Children stay free.

Aston at the Waikīkī Banyan

201 'Ohua Avenue, Honolulu, HI 96815. 800-922-7866; 808-922-0555; fax 808-922-8785 (www.aston-hotels.com). $165–$240

Located on the Diamond Head side of Waikīkī, one block from the beach, this condominium hotel has 330 one-bedroom apartments, each with a fully equipped kitchen. There are a pool, sauna, tennis court, playground, laundry facilities, and outdoor barbecues. Children stay free.

Aston Waikiki Beach Tower

2470 Kalākaua Avenue, Honolulu, HI 96815. 800-922-7866; 808-926-6400; fax 808-922-8785 (www.aston-hotels.com). $455–$1,100

This luxurious, newly renovated AAA Three-Diamond condominium resort has studio, one-, and two-bedroom apartments overlooking Kūhiō Beach. Large living rooms, state-of-the-art kitchens, in-room washer/drier, twice daily maid service, spa, sauna, pool, and valet parking are just some of the amenities. Children stay free.

Aston Waikiki Grand

134 Kapahulu Avenue, Honolulu, HI 96815. 800-922-7866; 808-923-1511; fax 808-922-8785 (www.aston-hotels.com). $85–$125

Across from Kapi'olani Park, this budget property has 175 studio units, each with refrigerator or kitchenette, one-half block to Waikīkī Beach. Children stay free.

Aston Waikiki Sunset

229 Paokalani Avenue, Honolulu, HI 96815. 800-922-7866; 808-922-0511; fax 808-922-8785 (www.aston-hotels.com). $180–$615

One- and two-bedroom condominium apartments have been newly renovated and are an excellent choice for families. The location is at the Diamond Head side of Waikīkī, one block to the beach and near the zoo, aquarium, and Kapi'olani Park. There are a heated pool, sauna, tennis, and outdoor barbecues. Children stay free.

The Big Surf

1690 Ala Moana Boulevard, Honolulu, HI 96815. 808-946-6525; fax 808-949-1142. $33–$75

This is true budget territory, with one- and two-bedroom units having full kitchens and studio rooms having refrigerators. Rooms have individual a.c. units and ceiling fans. There is daily maid service (with weekly linen change). The hotel is a short walk from Ala Moana Center and beaches.

The Breakers

250 Beach Walk, Honolulu, HI 96815. 800-426-0494; 808-923-3181; fax 808-923-7174; breakers@aloha.net (www.breakers-hawaii.com). $91–$135

This older, 2-story hotel is a bit of old Waikīkī tucked away inside walls and tropical gardens. One- and two-bedroom units all have compact kitchenettes. Situated just half a block from the beach, the hotel has a nice pool and an outdoor snack bar and lounge.

Diamond Head Beach Hotel

2947 Kalākaua Avenue, Honolulu, HI 96815-4697. 800-535-0085; 808-922-1928; fax 808-924-1982; marc@aloha.net (www.marcresorts.com). $168–$560

On a quiet beach at the foot of Diamond Head, at the less bustling end of Waikīkī, this small, 56-room gem is a moderately priced European-style hotel. Complimentary continental breakfast is included, and there is a nice sunning and swimming beach. Kapiʻolani Park is nearby, with tennis courts, picnic areas, and the zoo.

Doubletree Alana Waikīkī

1956 Ala Moana Boulevard, Honolulu, HI 96815. 800-222-TREE; 808-941-7275; fax 808-949-0996 (www.alana-doubletree.com). $195–$2,000

This elegant boutique hotel has 268 rooms and 45 suites. Amenities include a 24-hour fitness center with Universal equipment and sauna, heated outdoor swimming pool, a reading room with national and international magazines and newspapers, a business center and support services, and a contemporary art gallery on the mezzanine level. Padovani's Bistro and Wine Bar, celebrated for its fine dining, is located in the hotel and also serves excellent breakfasts and lunches. The hotel is within easy walking distance of Waikīkī beaches.

Hale Koa

2055 Kālia Road, Honolulu, HI 96815. 800-367-6027; 808-955-0555; fax 800-HALEFAX; information@halekoa.com (www.halekoa.com). $66–$169

Here is hands down the best deal in town, but there's a catch: you have to be active or retired military or employed by the Department of Defense. On 72 acres of lush, beautifully landscaped grounds (one of the largest open spaces left in Waikīkī), the 817-room hotel is on lovely Fort DeRussy Beach and minutes from shopping and nightlife. The hotel boasts a large health club, sauna, three swimming pools, post exchange, and a military discount travel office.

Halekūlani

2199 Kālia Road, Honolulu, HI 96815. 800-367-2343; 808-923-2311; fax 808-926-8004 (www.halekulani.com). $325–$1,725

Halekūlani means "house befitting heaven," and that this hotel surely is. If we had to pick one hotel as our favorite in Waikīkī, it would be the Halekūlani. Not overly large, with serene courtyard gardens, a gorgeous swimming pool, outstanding architecture, rooms furnished with impeccable taste, superb food at all of its restaurants (La Mer, Orchids, and House without a Key), and friendly, attentive service, the

Halekūlani is an oasis of tranquility in busy Waikīkī, even with its prime beachfront location. Guestrooms are housed in tiered towers, the highest 17 stories, while the open-air reception area and the restaurant buildings are no more than 2 stories, replicating the original main building of 1932 (the hotel actually opened in 1917 with a beach house and five cottages). Evenings the refrains of Hawaiian music by the islands' top entertainers waft through the air, and graceful hula is performed beneath a towering *kiawe* tree. There is no more romantic spot to relax and watch the setting sun while day turns to night. Personal touches and attention to the smallest detail make every guest feel like an honored member of the Halekūlani family. Original artworks, including large-scale sculptures, by Hawai'i's finest artists grace the public areas. Committed to supporting the arts in Honolulu, the hotel offers complimentary admission to Honolulu's top museums and tickets for performances of the Honolulu Symphony during its season. The hotel continues to earn the AAA Five-Diamond award year after year, and it earns a place on nearly every list of the world's top hotels.

More than one million glass tiles in various shades of blue, white, and green—crafted by an Italian mosaic artist following the graphic design of Ryo Urano—form the spectacular cattleya orchid mosaic in the Halekūlani's pool. Completed in 1981, the pool was over a year in the making.

Hawaiiana

260 Beach Walk, Honolulu, HI 96815. 800-367-5122; 808-923-3811; fax 808-926-5728 (www.hawaiiana hotelatwaikiki.com). $85–$190

You'll find lots of aloha here, from the daily complimentary coffee and juice served poolside to the Sunday evening hula show and the friendly and accommodating staff. Every room has a kitchenette and lanai, and there are outdoor barbecues. Posh it isn't, but with a location half a block from the beach, this garden oasis among high-rises is an excellent economical choice.

Hawaiian Monarch

444 Niu Street, Honolulu, HI 96815-2351. 800-535-0085; 808-949-3911; fax 800-535-0085; marc@aloha.net (www.marc resorts.com). $87–$119

At the gateway to Waikīkī, this value-priced hotel offers rooms and studio suites with complete kitchens or kitchenettes. It's a short walk to Ala Moana Center, the Hawai'i Convention Center, and beaches.

Hawai'i Prince Hotel Waikiki

100 Holomoana Street, Honolulu, HI 96815. 800-321-6248; 808-956-1111; fax 808-944-4491; reservationsHPHW@Hiprince.com (www.princeresortshawaii.com). $300–$950

Awarded Four Diamonds by AAA, this is one of Waikīkī's newer luxury hotels. Situated overlooking the Ala Wai Yacht Harbor, between Ala Moana Center and Waikīkī Beach, it has 521 oceanfront guestrooms and suites, each with floor-to-ceiling windows and attractively decorated. The Prince Court is a favorite dining spot for visitors and locals alike. The hotel has its own golf course and provides complimentary transportation to there as well as to beaches and central areas of Waikīkī.

Hilton Hawaiian Village Beach Resort and Spa

2005 Kālia Road, Honolulu, HI 96815. 800-221-2424; 808-949-4321; fax 808-947-7898 (www.hiltonhawaii.com). $179–$4,130

With some 3,000 rooms in six towers encompassing 22 acres, the Hawaiian Village is Hawai'i's largest hotel. This self-contained mega-oasis is a family-oriented resort offering guests an endless list of amenities. There are over 90 designer and specialty shops; four swimming pools, including a 10,000-square-foot superpool; fine dining with 18 restaurants, including Bali by the Sea and the Golden Dragon; a fitness center and exercise classes; a fully equipped, 24-hour business center; Polynesian shows and lounge performances; and a grand stretch of beach. Penguins, swans, and other exotic wildlife frequent the lush gardens and meandering streams. Rooms are generously sized, and many offer sweeping views from Diamond Head to the airport. Both the

Aliʻi and Kālia Towers have their own private pools and offer personalized luxury services. The $95-million Kālia Tower, newly opened in 2001, also includes the Mandara Spa (page 210), Holistica Hawaiʻi (page 256), and a branch of the Bishop Museum (page 144). The Niumalu Café and Bar in the Kālia Tower, open from breakfast on, features island cuisine, distinctive coffees, and favorite cocktails in a pleasant indoor-outdoor setting, amid spectacular murals by Yvonne Cheng and Roy Tabora. The Lagoon Tower offers condominium-style units, each with a full kitchen and up to three bedrooms. The family plan allows children to stay with parents or grandparents at no extra charge, and there is a well-managed *keiki* club, providing exciting daylong activities for children.

Holiday Inn Waikiki

1830 Ala Moana Boulevard, Honolulu, HI 96815. 800-HOLIDAY; 808-955-1111; fax 808-947-1799 (www.holiday-inn.com). $120–$310

Situated two blocks from the Ala Moana Beach Park, this Holiday Inn has 200 relatively spacious rooms, a swimming pool, fitness center, and laundry facilities. Children 19 years and under stay free with parents.

Hyatt Regency Waikiki

2424 Kalākaua Avenue, Honolulu, HI 96815. 800-233-1234; 808-923-1234; fax 808-923-7839 (www.hyattwaikiki.com). $265–$4,000

Twin 40-story towers, connected by an open-air great hall, house 1,230 spacious rooms and 18 suites in this AAA Four-Diamond resort. The Regency Club offers special services, including complimentary breakfast and cocktails in a 39th-floor lounge. There are five restaurants, a variety of cocktail lounges, business services, an elegant spa (see page 210), and a Camp Hyatt evening program for children.

ʻIlima

445 Nohonani Avenue, Honolulu, HI 96815. 808-923-1877; fax 808-924-2617; mail@ilima.com (www.ilima.com). $99–$330

This small condominium hotel with 17 floors has studios, one- and two-bedroom suites, and a three-bedroom penthouse. It is located near the Ala Wai Canal, two blocks from Waikīkī Beach. Each room has its own kitchen and private lanai. Heated swimming pool, sunning decks, sauna, and exercise room are available, and economical features include free local telephone calls and parking. Special programs at this friendly hotel include the sixth night free and low rates for "mature" visitors.

Imperial of Waikiki

205 Lewers Street, Honolulu, HI 96815. 800-347-2582; 808-923-1827; fax 808-923-7848 (www.imperialofwaikiki.com). $109–$209

Across from the Halekūlani and just 100 yards from the beach, this budget-priced timeshare condominium complex offers 270 units: studios and one and two bedrooms, all with mini or full kitchen facilities and all hotel services. A pool and spa are located on the rooftop sundeck.

Island Colony

445 Seaside Avenue, Honolulu, HI 96815. 800-535-0085; 808-923-2345; fax 800-535-0085; marc@aloha.net (www.marc resorts.com). $119–$175

Spacious units include hotel rooms with refrigerators and coffeemakers, studios with kitchenettes, and one-bedroom suites with complete kitchens. Located on the Ala Wai Canal, the Island Colony is known for its breathtaking views of Waikīkī from upper floors. It has a pool, jet spa, sauna, and restaurant.

A group of bronze hula dancers by sculptor Kim Duffett, at the Hilton's entrance, welcomes visitors to Waikiki.

Miramar at Waikīkī

2345 Kūhiō Avenue, Honolulu, HI 96815. 800-367-2303; 808-922-2077; fax 808-926-3217 (www.miramarwaikiki.com). $115–$375

In the heart of Waikīkī, with 357 guestrooms and suites, the Miramar offers great value. Onsite restaurants and lounges as well as a sparkling pool provide a place to unwind after a day of shopping or exploring. There is no charge for children sharing the same room with an adult. Waikīkī Beach is a block away.

New Otani Kaimana Beach Hotel

2863 Kalākaua Avenue, Honolulu, HI 96815. 800-356-8264; 808-923-1555; fax 808-922-9404; rooms@kaimana.com (www.kaimana.com). $138–$1,017

On one of Oʻahu's nicest beaches at the quiet end of Waikīkī, far from the crowds in central Waikīkī, this 124-room boutique hotel is one of our favorites. In the 19th century this was the site of the Sans Souci Hotel, where Robert Louis Stevenson lolled beneath the *hau* tree that shades the hotel's beachside café today. *Kamaʻāina* dine at the hotel's Japanese restaurant, Miyako, and enjoy get-togethers with friends and family at the Hau Tree Lanai on the beach—

surely one of Waikīkī's most romantic spots for outdoor dining. Rooms have refrigerators, and many have microwaves.

Ocean Resort Hotel Waikīkī

175 Paoakalani Avenue, Honolulu, HI 96815. 800-367-2317; 808-922-4671; fax 808-924-1982; res@oceanresort.com (www.oceanresort.com). $98–$300

Just one block from Waikīkī Beach, this budget property has single rooms (some with kitchenettes), studios, and one-bedroom suites with private lanais. It is near Kapiʻolani Park, the zoo, and the aquarium.

Ohana Maile Sky Court

2058 Kūhiō Avenue, Honolulu, HI 96815. 800-462-6262; 808-947-2828; fax 808-943-0504 (www.ohanahotels.com). $109–$209

With 43 floors and 596 guestrooms and suites with kitchenettes and full hotel service, this hotel offers a pool, spa, shuffleboard, and spectacular views from high floors. Ask about special rates.

Ohana Waikīkī Malia

2211 Kūhiō Avenue, Honolulu, HI 96815. 800-462-6262; 808-923-7621; fax 808-921-4804 (www.ohanahotels.com). $129–$189

This busy, friendly hotel, with 327 rooms and suites, is centrally located and just two blocks from the beach. There are a rooftop tennis court, 24-hour coffee shop, lounges, and shops. Ask about special rates.

Outrigger East

150 Kaʻiulani Avenue, Honolulu, HI 96815. 800-688-7444; 808-922-5353; fax 808-926-4334 (www.outrigger.com). $175–$375

This action-oriented hotel, situated two blocks from the beach, has 445 rooms and an escalator entrance. Some rooms have kitchenettes. Keoni's restaurant, serving American and Thai cuisine, is located in the hotel, and there is an espresso bar in the lobby. Outrigger's family of hotels also includes Ohana Hotels of Hawaiʻi, offering affordably priced guestrooms in convenient Waikīkī locations, starting at just $99.

Outrigger Islander Waikīkī

270 Lewers Street, Honolulu, HI 96815. 800-688-7444; 808-923-7711; fax 808-924-5755 (www.outrigger.com). $175–$205

This 287-room high-rise is smack in the center of Waikīkī, one block from the beach. It has a swimming pool, shops, and a cocktail lounge. All-connecting rooms are great for families.

Outrigger Reef

2169 Kālia Road, Honolulu, HI 96815. 800-688-7444; 808-923-3111; fax 808-924-4957 (www.outrigger.com). $220–$750

One of only seven hotels right on Waikīkī Beach, with 883 guestrooms and the exclusive Voyagers Club, this hotel offers island hospitality in an informal atmosphere. A large freshwater pool forms a wall of Harry's Underwater Bar, one of five bars and lounges. There are two restaurants, including the popular Shorebird Beach Broiler, live entertainment, a state-of-the-art business center, and shops galore. The Cowabunga kids club offers supervised activities for children ages 5–13.

Outrigger Waikīkī

2335 Kalākaua Avenue, Honolulu, HI 96815. 800-688-7444; 808-923-0711; fax 808-921-9749 (www.outrigger.com). $230–$645

Among the features of this hotel are a Waikīkī beachfront location, 530 rooms and suites, multiple dining and entertainment choices, a swimming pool, and all beach activities. The main showroom headlines the Society of Seven, one of Waikīkī's most popular acts. And lively Duke's Canoe Club is a favorite watering hole for Waikīkī beachgoers.

The top three floors are the Voyagers Club, with keyed elevator access, concierge services, and a weight room.

Pacific Beach Hotel

2490 Kalākaua Avenue, Honolulu, HI 96815. 800-367-6060; 808-923-4511; fax 808-922-8061; reservation@hthcorp.com (www.pacificbeachhotel.com). $185–$310

This busy, friendly 830-room hotel is across from Kūhiō Beach. It has an amazing 280,000-gallon, 3-story indoor "oceanarium" that is the focal point of three levels of dining. Amenities include private lanais, a pool and whirlpool spa, tennis courts, onsite 24-hour fitness facility, and shops.

Park Shore

2586 Kalākaua Avenue, Honolulu, HI 96815. 800-426-0670; 808-923-0411; fax 808-923-0311; sales@theparkshore.com (www.westcoasthotels.com/park shore/). $165–$250

On the corner between Kūhiō Beach and Kapi'olani Park, this friendly, 227-room hotel offers good views, two restaurants, a swimming pool, and shops in one of Waikīkī's premier locations. The zoo and aquarium are within easy walking distance.

Queen Kapi'olani

150 Kapahulu Avenue, Honolulu, HI 96815. 800-367-2317; 808-922-1941; fax 808-922-2694; res@queenkapiolani.com (www.queenkapiolani.com). $120–$405

Situated at the less-congested Diamond Head end of Waikīkī, one block from the beach, this small hotel has 308 rooms and 11 one-bedroom suites. Most rooms have lanais; some have kitchenettes. Complimentary *pūpū* are served nightly in the Queen's Lounge. Decor is reminiscent of the traditions of old Hawai'i.

Radisson Waikīkī Prince Kūhiō

2500 Kūhiō Avenue, Honolulu, HI 96815-3696. 800-333-3333; 808-922-0811; fax 888-656-4422 (www.radisson.com). $185–$790

Modern elegance distinguishes this 620-room deluxe hotel situated one block from Kūhiō Beach. The Kūhiō Club, with keyed elevator access, occupies the top four floors. There are a tenth-floor recreation deck, pool, Jacuzzi, modern fitness center, 24-hour business center, two specialty restaurants, lobby bar, and nightly entertainment. Guestrooms are newly renovated and have Wayport Internet access.

Renaissance 'Ilikai Waikīkī

1777 Ala Moana Boulevard, Honolulu, HI 96815. 800-245-4524; 808-949-3811; fax 808-947-0892; sales@ilikaihotel.com (www.ilikaihotel.com).
$210–$1,200

Situated next to the Ala Wai Yacht Harbor, this popular hotel has 783 spacious guestrooms, 52 suites, and 25,000 square feet of meeting rooms. Eighty percent of the rooms offer ocean views. Most rooms have full kitchens for extended stays and families. There are two pools, lighted tennis courts, a night-club, a poolside lounge, a fitness center, and a golf practice range. Three superb restaurants—Canoes, Sarento's, and Tanaka of Tokyo—offer first-class dining. It is a short walk to Ala Moana Center, the Convention Center, and beaches.

Royal Hawaiian

2259 Kalākaua Avenue, Honolulu, HI 96815. 800-782-9488; 808-923-7311; fax 808-924-7098 (www.luxurycollectionhawaii.com).
$310–$800

A member of the Starwood Luxury Collection, the elegant Royal Hawaiian has been a widely recognized landmark since its opening in 1927. It has 526 large, old-fashioned rooms and suites situated in the original 6-story structure or in the newer 17-story tower. The Royal is steeped in romantic history. Hilo Hattie got her start here in the 1930s as a member of the Royal Hawaiian Girls' Glee Club, and by the 1940s the hotel was the playing ground of the likes of Mary Pickford and Douglas Fairbanks, the Rockefellers, Fords, and DuPonts. Although Waikīkī high-rises today loom nearby, the hotel manages to keep an intimate, old-world ambience, with beautifully landscaped grounds and a lovely (though crowded) beach. The Monday evening Royal Lū'au, complete with orchid lei, mai tais, and a Polynesian show, is the only *lū'au* on Waikīkī Beach—a reminder of earlier days. A business center opened in 2000, and in 2001 the Abhasa Resort Spa (page 211) opened in space previously used for a salon, bringing the hotel's facilities into the 21st century.

Sheraton Moana Surfrider

2365 Kalākaua Avenue, Honolulu, HI 96815. 800-782-9488; 808-922-3111; fax 808-923-0308 (www.sheraton-hawaii.com).
$195–$950

Step back into Hawai'i of a century ago at this glorious update to Waikīkī's very first stylish, courtly hotel, the Moana, which opened in 1901. Recent renovation has restored the hotel to its turn-of-the-century charm. The veranda lounge and dining room represent everything loved by those who flocked to the hotel in its heyday. Tea, cocktails, and Sunday brunches on the veranda are favorites of *kama'āina*. Today there are 793 rooms and suites, including a 428-room modern tower. Highlights of the hotel include a magnificent lobby, luxury boutiques, a pretty pool, four restaurants, and the popular Beach Bar under the historic banyan tree, where there is nightly Hawaiian entertainment on the veranda.

Sheraton Princess Ka'iulani

120 Ka'iulani Avenue, Honolulu, HI 96815. 800-782-9488; 808-922-5811; fax 808-931-4577 (www.sheraton-hawaii.com). $150–$550

Across the street from Waikīkī Beach, this hotel has 1,150 rooms, three international restaurants and lounges, a showroom staging *Creation: A Polynesian Journey,* a large pool and restaurant in a tranquil garden, spacious lobbies, and a variety of shops. The Sheraton's Keiki Aloha program provides day and evening entertainment for children staying at any of the Sheraton properties, including the Royal Hawaiian.

Sheraton Waikiki

2255 Kalākaua Avenue, Honolulu, HI 96815. 800-782-9488; 808-922-4422; fax 808-923-8785 (www.sheraton hawaii.com). $225–$705

Front and center on the beach with 1,852 rooms and 130 luxury suites, the Sheraton Waikīkī is known for oceanfront views from 80 percent of its rooms. The hotel offers four specialty restaurants, two coffee shops, the popular Esprit nightclub, lounges, and nightly entertainment. For fine dining, there are spectacular views from the rooftop Hanohano Room. There are a large beachfront pool, an array of shops, and large convention facilities. A five-year, $20-million renovation project was completed in 2000.

Waikiki Beachcomber

2300 Kalākaua Avenue, Honolulu, HI 96815. 800-622-4646; 808-922-4646; fax 808-923-4889; beach@dps.net (www.waikiki beachcomber.com). $200–$850

Across Kalākaua Avenue from the Royal Hawaiian, this hotel has 500 rooms and suites, a swimming pool, shops, restaurants, live entertainment nightly, and lounges. Shopping abounds, with Macy's (formerly Liberty House) on property, the Royal Hawaiian Shopping Center across the street, and numerous upscale boutiques lining Kalākaua Avenue. Noted particularly for its friendly staff, the Waikīkī Beachcomber is the perfect place to find island aloha. It hosts the Don Ho show, a Hawai'i tradition for over forty years, as well as *Magic of Polynesia,* starring illusionist John Hirokawa in a spectacular stage show.

Waikiki Beach Marriott Resort

2552 Kalākaua Avenue, Honolulu, HI 96815. 800-367-5370; 808-922-6611; fax 808-921-5255 (www.marriott.com). $209–$2,100

This 1,304-room hotel is the Marriott's flagship resort in Hawai'i, directly across from famed Kūhiō Beach and convenient to Waikīkī nightlife as well as the zoo and aquarium in Kapi'olani Park. With two towers rising above arcade shops and lush courtyards, the hotel occupies five acres of prime Waikīkī property—once the summer home of Queen Lili'uokalani. There are eight restaurants and lounges, two pools, a championship tennis court, a fitness center, and a business center with PC workstations. Children stay free, and cribs or cots are provided without a charge. A childcare center is available.

Waikiki Gateway

2070 Kalākaua Avenue, Honolulu, HI 96815. 800-247-1903; 808-955-3741; fax 808-923-2541; reserve@waikiki-hotel.com (www.waikiki-hotel.com). $93–$136

This 186-room budget hotel, shaped like a Mayan pyramid, is located in the new Kalākaua District at the gateway to Waikīkī. It is home to the award-winning Nick's Fishmarket Restaurant, across the street from the Kalākaua Shopping Plaza, two blocks from the beach and the new Convention

Center. Daily complimentary continental breakfast is served on the 16th floor with a spectacular view. Look for Internet specials.

Waikīkī Marc

2425 Kūhiō Avenue, Honolulu, HI 96815-2351. 800-535-0085; 808-922-7777; fax 800-535-0085; marc@aloha.net (www.marcresorts.com). $111–$208

This intimate boutique hotel with studios and one-bedroom units is one block from the beach. Some rooms have kitchenettes or full kitchens. Adjoining the swimming pool are a jet spa and sauna.

Waikīkī Parc

2233 Helumoa Road, Honolulu, HI 96815. 800-422-0450; 808-921-7272; fax 808-923-1336 (www.waikikiparc.com). $190–$270

One of Waikīkī's newer hotels, the affordable, luxury Waikīkī Parc is located 100 yards from the beach, adjacent to its sister hotel, the Halekūlani. A boutique hotel with 298 rooms, it features sophisticated accoutrements, two fine restaurants, lounges, a recreation area and swimming pool, and extremely fresh and tasteful rooms, many with ocean views. There is a self-service laundromat, and each of the guestrooms

has a compact refrigerator. Rates include full American breakfast at Parc Café or Japanese breakfast at Kacho. Meals at the Halekūlani may be charged to your Waikīkī Parc account. We recommend this hotel as a quiet and safe alternative to larger Waikīkī properties.

Waikīkī Parkside

1850 Ala Moana Boulevard, Honolulu, HI 96815. 800-237-9666; 808-955-1567; fax 808-955-6010; aloha@waikikiparkside.com (www.waikikiparkside.com). $125–$275

Across from the Hilton Hawaiian Village, this 255-room, moderately priced hotel is close to beaches, shopping, and the Convention Center. Nearby are Starbucks, Hard Rock Café, Sizzler's, Outback Restaurant, and McDonalds. The hotel features a fitness room, pool with sundeck, and laundry facilities.

Waikīkī Sand Villa

2375 Ala Wai Boulevard, Honolulu, HI 96815-3448. 800-247-1903; 808-922-4744; fax 808-923-2541; reserve@waikiki-hotel.com (www.waikikisandvillahotel.com). $93–$166

Fronting the Ala Wai Canal, this hotel offers complimentary

continental breakfast served poolside and views of rainbow-clad mountains. The onsite Green Dolphin Dive Shop provides scuba lessons in the safety of the hotel's pool, then arranges for an exciting ocean dive.

Waikīkī Shore

2161 Kālia Road, Honolulu, HI 96815. 800-688-7444; 808-971-4500; fax 808-971-4580 (www.outrigger.com). $205–$315

The only condominium property on Waikīkī Beach, this 83-unit hotel offers one- and two-bedroom units with kitchenettes or full kitchens and washer/dryer. It is managed by the Outrigger chain, and guests may use the new Serenity Spa at the Outrigger Reef.

W Honolulu

2885 Kalākaua Avenue, Honolulu, HI 96815. 800-877-WHOTELS; 808-922-1700; fax 808-923-2249 (www.whotels.com). $350–$3,000

The famed W chain of hotels offers modern, sophisticated accommodations in major cities for discriminating travelers. At the quiet end of Waikīkī, nestled at the foot of Diamond Head, W Honolulu is a 48-room hotel with all the amenities for which the W brand is famous: in-room data ports, Web TV, high-speed Internet access, CD players, and the luxurious W signature bed with 250-thread count sheets and goose down pillows. The spacious, two-bedroom penthouse, with a large lanai facing Diamond Head and the Ko'olau Mountains, is the ultimate in tasteful accommodations. The hotel is partnered with the Ko'olau Golf Club, one of O'ahu's finest courses.

Hotels *and* Condominiums *outside* Waikīkī

Estates at Turtle Bay

P.O. Box 366, Kahuku, HI 96731. 808-293-0600 (www.turtlebay-rentals.com). $85–$180

Nestled on the grounds of the Turtle Bay Resort, this condominium complex has five swimming pools and four regulation tennis courts. The championship Palmer and Fazio golf courses surround the property. Unit sizes range from studios to three bedrooms. Each has a full kitchen and washer/dryer. Two-night minimum stay; longer during holiday periods. Surfing, swimming, and snorkeling beaches are nearby.

J. W. Marriott Ihilani Resort and Spa

92-1001 Olani Street, Kapolei, HI 96707. 800-626-4446; 808-679-0079; fax 808-679-0080; reservations@ihilani.com (www.ihilani.com). $289–$4,500

This extraordinary, world-class resort opened in December 1993. Part of the 640-acre Kō 'Olina Resort along O'ahu's western *('ewa)* shore, the hotel was designed as the ultimate luxury vacation and business retreat. The focal point of this 387-room hotel is a 15-story glass-domed atrium.

Amenities include large (680 square feet) guestrooms with private lanais, two swimming pools, pristine beaches, four restaurants, a cocktail lounge, upscale boutiques, a full-service health spa (see pages 210–11), fitness programs, an 18-hole championship golf course at Kō 'Olina Golf Club, a tennis club, beauty salon, and children's program. The golf course is consistently rated among the top resort courses in the country. Kō 'Olina Marina is the base for sport fishing and other ocean activities.

The J. W. Marriott Ihilani Resort and Spa.

Kāhala Mandarin Oriental

5000 Kāhala Avenue, Honolulu, HI 96816-5498. 800-526-6566; 808-739-8888; fax 808-739-8800; reserve-mohnl@mohg.com (www.mandarin-oriental.com/kahala). $310–$4,070

Formerly known as the Kāhala Hilton, this AAA Five-Diamond beachfront hotel and celebrity hideaway underwent a yearlong $75-million renovation in the mid-1990s and reopened under new ownership as the Kāhala Mandarin Oriental. Located just 10 minutes from Waikīkī, it is neighbor to the Wai'alae Country Club and the tony residential neighborhood of Kāhala. Its seclusion offers a tranquil respite from the bustle of Waikīkī. With the friendly and accommodating staff, lush gardens, and tropical furnishings, visitors get a glimpse of old Hawai'i, a more genteel ambience before tourism became king. The hotel has 368 rooms with panoramic mountain and ocean views, tastefully decorated

with rich furnishings and Asian accents. A tranquil lagoon provides guests the rare opportunity to observe resident Atlantic bottlenose dolphins, cared for by Dolphin Quest. There are a lovely 800-foot white sand beach, a swimming pool and children's pool, business center, fitness center, and upscale boutiques. (A spa and new fitness center are in the planning.) A *keiki* club provides half- and full-day programs. Three excellent restaurants—Hōkū's, the Plumeria Beach Café, and Tokyo Tokyo—as well as the Veranda, an elegant cocktail lounge where tea is served afternoons and a jazz trio plays most evenings, make this hotel an attractive place to visit for nonguests as well.

Pagoda

1525 Rycroft Street, Honolulu, HI 96814. 800-367-6060; 808-923-4511; fax 808-922-8061; hthcorp@worldnet.att.net (www.pagodahotel.com). $110–$195

A favorite of neighbor island residents who come to O'ahu to shop, this older, truly Hawaiian-style hotel is not for everyone, as it is a fair distance from beaches and tourist activities. The garden-level Pagoda Restaurant, surrounded by *koi* ponds, has been a local favorite for over thirty years.

Turtle Bay Resort

57-091 Kamehameha Highway, Kahuku, HI 96731. 800-203-3650; 808-293-8811; fax 808-293-9147 (www.turtlebayhotel.com). $139–$1,950

Having undergone major renovations to host the 2001 Senior PGA Tour, this hotel, formerly the Turtle Bay Hilton, regains its stature as *the* place to stay on the north shore, especially for golfers who enjoy the tremendous challenges of the Palmer course (formerly the Links at Kuilima) and the Fazio course (formerly the Turtle Bay Golf Course and host for the original Senior Skins game). The hotel sits on a picturesque point on O'ahu's gorgeous and sunny north shore. Five miles of shoreline; 486 ocean-view rooms, suites, and cottages; a fine-dining and a casual restaurant; tennis courts; and riding stables—all far from the glitz of Waikīkī—make for an enjoyable and relaxing vacation. A $35-million upgrade to facilities is still in the works.

The Kāhala Mandarin Oriental.

Bed-and-Breakfasts *and* Inns

THERE ARE JUST A HANDFUL of bed-and-breakfasts on Oʻahu. Travelers who prefer this type of accommodation will find more choices among studios and cottages (pages 274–75).

Travelers should note that some B&Bs provide breakfast every day, some only on the first day, after which you can stock up at a local supermarket. There is usually a minimum stay of two or three nights, and there is sometimes an added cleaning fee.

Remember that Hawaiʻi time is hours behind mainland times (see pages 22–23), so plan your telephone calls accordingly.

Fairway View B&B

515 Paumakua Place, Kailua, HI 96734. 888-263-6439; 808-263-6439; fairway515@aol.com (www.bnb-hawaii.com/kailua). $55

This traditional B&B is located on a quiet, dead-end street with mountain views. Two bedrooms are available, sharing a bathroom. Breakfast is served on the lanai. Walk to Kailua Beach. $45 single.

Hawaiʻi's Hidden Hideaway

1369 Mokulua Drive, Lanikai, HI 96734. 877-443-3299; 808-262-6560; fax 808-262-6561; hhhideaway@yahoo.com (www.ahawaiibnb.com). $85–$175

In exclusive Lanikai, next door to Kailua, this charming B&B has one suite and two studios, all of which can interconnect. Surrounded with beautiful tropical gardens, each unit has a private entrance and parking area. Kitchens have refrigerators, microwaves, and hotplates (no stoves). The romantic suite has a private outdoor Jacuzzi. Innkeeper Janice provides a welcome breakfast of juices, cereals, pastries, yogurt, fruits, and beverages. It is one and a half short blocks to a stunning beach.

Mānoa Valley Inn

2001 Vancouver Drive, Honolulu, HI 96822. 808-947-6019; fax 808-946-6168; manoavalley inn@aloha.net. $99–$190

This romantic inn is a splendid example of excellence on a small scale. The home, near the University of Hawaiʻi's main campus, is listed on the Hawaiʻi and National Registers of Historic Places and has been painstakingly restored to its 1920s splendor. The setting, decor, and service are superb, and the small size of the inn—there are only seven rooms and a cottage—allows personal service and a sense of intimacy and privacy not possible in large hotels. Diamond Head and Waikīkī views from the garden are spectacular. Aside from the university, the neighborhood has little to offer. It is a 10-minute drive to Waikīkī Beach. Rates include continental breakfast, afternoon fruit and cheese, and free local calls. No smoking is permitted.

Sharon's Serenity

127 Kakahiaka Street, Kailua, HI 96734. 800-914-2271; 808-262-5621; sprice@aloha.net (www.bnb-hawaii.com/kailua). $65

One block from Kailua Beach, this spacious home has two nice B&B bedrooms, one with access to a kitchen—continental breakfast is provided for the other. Two dogs and a cat live in the home.

Studios, Cottages, *and* House Rentals

Renting a house or cottage on Kailua Beach or on the north shore is a perfect way to experience O'ahu. Unfortunately, finding the right place can be difficult, and what sounds like an idyllic cottage with waves lapping at your doorstep might turn out to be on a busy highway and awkwardly away from the water. Generally, if the price seems too good to be true, it's probably not a great property.

When telephoning from the mainland, be sure to note the time it is in Hawai'i so that you won't disturb people in the middle of the night.

For a listing of agencies that list rental properties, see page 275.

Hale Awakea

348 Awakea Road, Kailua, HI 96734. 808-261-5503; fax 808-262-9662; awakea@mymailstation.com (www.bnb-hawaii.com/kailua). $75

This nicely furnished one-bedroom unit with living area and bedroom has a full bath and kitchenette. It is a 15-minute walk to the beach.

Hale Kai

572 Kaimalino Street, Kailua, HI 96734. 808-254-1101; fax 808-254-5643; coffeyhi@juno.com (www.bnb-hawaii.com/kailua). $95 (studio); $110 (one bedroom)

Near Kāne'ohe Marine Corps Air Station and located on the ocean, this island home offers dramatic ocean and mountain views. Each unit has a private entrance, bathroom, and kitchenette and accommodates two people. There is a 60-foot lap pool on the beautiful property.

Hale Kimo

Sunset Beach, O'ahu. 808-261-5777; fax 808-261-9222; hkimo@halekimo.com (www.halekimo.com). $350–$1,000

This spacious six-bedroom, four-bathroom home faces Sunset Beach and its fabled surf. It can be divided into two private three-bedroom units, or rented as one for a large group (it sleeps up to 16). During the holiday season a 10-day minimum stay is required.

Hale Mele

571 Kaimalino Street, Kailua, HI 96734. 808-254-5566; medolan@aloha.net (www.bnb-hawaii.com/kailua). $125

Across the street from Hale Kai (above), this two-bedroom unit

with one bathroom sleeps six comfortably. There is a kitchenette with range top, microwave, and toaster oven. Crib and highchair are available.

Hale Pohaku

Waimānalo, O'ahu. 808-261-4422 or 808-261-0448; mike@halepohaku.com (www.halepohaku.com). $300

Set on the white sands of Waimānalo Beach, this lava rock house (Hale Pohaku means "house of stone") was built in the late 1920s as a beach hideaway for a wealthy Honolulu family. With three bedrooms and three bathrooms, the house is perfect for large groups. Glass doors in the master bedroom open to the tree-lined beach. Reduced rates are available for stays longer than three weeks.

Kailuana

P.O. Box 841, Kailua, HI 96734. 800-551-0948; 808-261-8903 (www.kailuana.com). $175 (cottage); $350 (house)

One of the nicest of the Kailua Beach properties, this 1.5-acre estate has a comfortable one-bedroom cottage that sleeps four as well as a spacious three-bedroom main house that sleeps up to eight people. Both have fully equipped kitchens and everything needed for a relaxing, fun-filled vacation in paradise. Grassy lawns reach to the edge of world-famous Kailua Beach.

Lanikai Cottage

1350 Aalapapa Drive, Lanikai, HI 96734. 808-261-8656; fax 808-262-3749; greens@lava.net (www.lanikaicottage.com). $100

This cute one-bedroom cottage, half a block from Lanikai Beach, is suitable for a couple or a family with small children willing to share a futon. The small kitchen has a hot plate, microwave, toaster, coffeemaker, refrigerator, and all necessary utensils. An outdoor barbecue and laundry facilities are also provided. The cottage has air-conditioning, though the cooling breezes of the trade winds are usually sufficient. Monthly rate available.

Treasure Island

Laniākea Beach, Oʻahu. 505-821-6698 (San Diego) or 808-780-2222 (www.DWALL.com). $400

This elegant, tastefully furnished oceanfront home sits on almost an acre of tropically landscaped grounds. There are three bedrooms and three baths. When the surf is up, Laniākea Beach has some of the best waves on the north shore. However, the beach is not great for swimming, even on calm days. Lower weekly and monthly rates are available.

Rental Agents

Cathy George and Associates

850 West Hind Drive, Honolulu, HI 96821. 808-373-9844; cga@aloha.net

This agency has a number of north shore listings.

Hawaiʻi's Best B&Bs

www. bnb-hawaii.com

This website provides a listing of luxury vacation homes in addition to B&Bs. Rates for beachside homes range from $385 to $1,000 per day.

Hawaiʻi's Best Bed & Breakfasts

P.O. Box 563, Kamuela, HI 96743. 800-262-9912; 808-885-4550; fax 808-885-0559; bestbnb @aloha.net; www.bestbnb.com

Check here for listings of B&Bs, inns, and cottages throughout the state. Owner Barbara Campbell has been in the travel industry for many years and has personally inspected each property.

Homes and Villas in Paradise

116 Hekili Street, Kailua, HI 96734. 800-282-2736; 808-262-4663; fax 808-262-4817

This agency specializes in upscale properties. If your dream is for an elegant oceanfront home, these are the people to call.

Island Rentals

1226 Mokulua Drive, Lanikai, HI 96734. 800-773-0260 [code 62]; 808-261-2644; fax 808-262-1705; reserve @islandrentals.net; www.island rentals.net

They feature a number of affordable vacation properties.

Sand Sea, Inc., Vacation Homes

P.O. Box 239, Haleʻiwa, HI 96712. 800-442-6901; 808-637-2568; fax 808-637-2569; hawaii @sandsea.com; www.sandsea. com

They list quality beachfront homes on the north and south shores. Rates range from $175 to $700.

Team Real Estate

66-250 Kamehameha Highway, Haleʻiwa, HI 96712. 800-982-8602; 808-637-3507; fax 808-637-8881; TeamRE@hawaii.rr.com; www.teamrealestate.com

The agency lists a lot of north shore properties with prices ranging from $66 to $535.

The following are additional reservation services:

All Islands B&B
800-542-0344; 808-263-2342
B&B Hawaiʻi
800-733-1632; 808-822-7771
B&B Honolulu
800-288-4666; 808-595-7533
Hawaiian Islands B&B and Vacation Rentals
800-258-7895; 808-261-7895

Campsites

Camping is not advised at city and county beachparks owing to thefts and other unpleasant occurrences at these parks. If you want to push your luck and camp out on the beach, you must get a permit from the Department of Parks and Recreation at Honolulu Hale (650 South King Street, Honolulu, HI 96813; 808-523-4525) or from any Satellite City Hall. You must be 18 years of age or older to obtain a camping permit. All parks have restroom facilities and showers.

Ho'omaluhia Botanical Gardens (45-680 Luluku Road, Kāne'ohe, HI 96744; 808-233-7323), however, has a very safe campground under the auspices of the City and County of Honolulu. Tent camping is available from 9 A.M. Fridays through 4 P.M. Mondays. Permits are required and should be applied for well in advance. There is no fee. This 400-acre tropical paradise is gorgeous but gets a great deal of rain; a waterproof tent is essential.

Mālaekahana State Park (56-335 Kamehameha Highway, Kahuku, HI 96731; 808-293-1736), on the north shore near Lā'ie, is one of the nicest state parks on O'ahu for camping.

There is a fee. The wooded beach park is good for swimming, bodysurfing, and fishing. From here you can wade out a half-mile offshore to Goat Island and really feel like you're away from it all. To protect your feet from the sharp rocks, wear athletic shoes or Japanese tabis, socklike footwear with rubber soles available at many Hawai'i general stores (they're also good for hiking on muddy trails).

Other state parks at which camping is permitted are **Kahana Valley State Park, Keaīwa Heiau State Park**, and **Sand Island State Park**. Information about state-operated campsites on O'ahu is available from the Department of Land and Natural Resources, Division of State Parks, P.O. Box 621, 1151 Punchbowl Street, Honolulu, HI 96809; 808-587-0166 or 808-587-0300. Permits are required for all state campgrounds.

Camp Mokulē'ia (729 Farrington Highway, Waialua, HI 96791; 808-637-6241) is a private camp on a nine-acre beachfront site on the north shore near Hale'iwa. There you'll find tent, cabin, and lodge camping, with cabins large enough to sleep up to eighteen people.

dining

THE FOLLOWING LISTING is not intended to be inclusive. We figure most of you can find hotel and fast food restaurants without our help. Rather, we're telling you about some of our favorite places to eat on Oʻahu, both those frequented mostly by tourists and great places where the locals eat. We've classified restaurants as inexpensive, moderate, and expensive. Bear in mind that when we say "expensive," we usually mean "expensive but worth every penny."

Since hours and days open are subject to change, we suggest that you call ahead even for those places for which no reservations are required. Some of the neighborhood restaurants are strictly BYOB, so it pays to ask in advance whether liquor is served. Many restaurants will validate parking at certain garages; be sure to ask about parking options.

For a listing of restaurants that cater to families with children, see page 301.

For a listing of restaurants that cater to families with children, see page 301.

Page 277: Dietrich Varez, *Kuʻi Poi (Pounding Poi)* (detail), linocut.

Local Favorites

SEVERAL SPECIAL FOODS bear mention. The first is the refreshing treat known as **shave ice**, available from many roadside stands and refreshment vans parked near beaches. Finely shaved ice with flavored syrup poured over it, this cool thirst quencher closely resembles what is generally known on the mainland as snow cones, but it isn't the same. The texture of shave ice is much finer—more like actual snow—and the rainbow version is a delight to behold. On a hot afternoon this treat is ultra-refreshing. Some vendors will add a scoop of ice cream or sweet black beans under the mound of delicate ice shavings for an extra treat. Shave ice stands frequent the north shore, and in town there is the famous **Waiola Shave Ice**, with two locations: 525 Kapahulu Avenue (735-8886) and 2135 Waiola Street (949-2269). The latter is the original, but it's a lot easier to find the Kapahulu location, where there is also a good bakery.

Also delicious, available from roadside vans, are **hot *malasadas***, rich, puffy Portuguese doughnuts dipped in sugar that are best while they're still warm. Many people swear by **Leonard's** at 933 Kapahulu Avenue (737-5591),

but the winner hands down in our opinion is **Champion** at 1926 South Beretania Street (947-8778), where 45¢ brings you the richest, creamiest warm doughnut imaginable—a true taste treat.

Unique to Hawaiʻi is the **plate lunch**, which consists of a meat, fish, or chicken entrée— teriyaki beef or chicken, deep-fried *mahimahi,* for example— plus two scoops of rice ("two scoop rice") and a scoop of macaroni salad. Plate lunch used to be served on a paper plate covered with aluminum foil to go, but these days it most likely comes in a styrofoam box. Even McDonald's serves plate lunch in Hawaiʻi.

Sweet potato/taro chips from the **Hawaiian Chip Company** are particularly *ʻono*. If you don't find them in local outlets, go by their store at 717 North King Street (845-9868).

Another special treat is homemade ice cream from **La Gelateria**, where Maurice Grasso concocts richly flavored Italian frozen desserts that have much less fat than trendy national brands. You'll find La Gelateria's ice creams at Honolulu's upscale restaurants, but you can also go by the factory at 819 Cedar Street (591-1133), where knowledgeable locals buy their ice cream.

Two Hawai'i chain restaurants where you can get authentic plate lunch and local-style grinds are **L&L Drive-Inn**, with fifty-plus outlets, and **Zippy's**, with twenty-one locations on O'ahu. Both cater to eat-in and take-out, and both are great values. **Ba-Le Sandwich Shops**, with twenty locations around O'ahu, offer great French-Vietnamese sandwiches on a baguette and the best tapioca puddings, in several flavors. Their summer rolls make a tasty light lunch.

High Tea

THE IDEA OF VICTORIAN high tea may seem somewhat incongruous in steamy Honolulu, but the custom actually harks back to the days of royalty, when all things reflecting the British Empire were adored by Hawai'i's rulers. There are several places to partake of tea. Generally, the price is about $15 to $20 per person. Keep in mind that you will have enough to eat to make it a meal. Also, if you'd prefer coffee to tea, most of the places will accommodate you.

The best afternoon tea is served daily on the **Halekūlani's Veranda** (2199 Kālia Road; 923-2311), a charming room overlooking a serene courtyard. Service is friendly and attentive, and the food can only be described as scrumptious. You start with exceptional scones served with Devonshire cream and rich, creamy lemon curd, slightly sweet and slightly tart. This is followed by an assortment of tasty finger sandwiches, each a culinary treat, and exquisite little cakes and pastries to top off the repast.

Tea at the venerable **Moana** (2365 Kalākaua Avenue; 922-3111) is also a delight, on the veranda of this 100-year-old gem of Waikīkī, overlooking a giant banyan and the world's most famous beach. Servers wear white gloves to pour your tea and bring you a very proper three-tiered tray. You eat from the top down: scones with Devonshire cream and preserves; tea sandwiches; and dessert, a selection of cakes and mini tarts. Afternoon tea is served daily.

The Veranda at the Kāhala Mandarin Oriental Hotel (5000 Kāhala Avenue; 739-8780) is extremely civilized for afternoon tea, served daily. Prepared by the staff at Hōkū's, tea includes an assortment of special teas, scones, "not-so-traditional" tea sandwiches, and delicate pastries and confectionary items.

In the Chinatown area, **Tea at 1024** (1024 Nu'uanu Avenue; 521-9596) is a pleasant respite from the busy downtown scene.

Generous servings of freshly made sandwiches, including egg salad and curried chicken salad, and buttery scones with cream and jam are followed by rich brownies and lemon bars. At $12.95, this tea is a great bargain. Open Tuesday–Saturday.

Afternoon tea is served daily at Alan Wong's **Pineapple Room** (Macy's, Ala Moana Center; 945-8881), with unique sandwiches of seared 'ahi and kālua pig. The **Mission Houses Museum** (553 South King Street; 531-0481) also has excellent tea service in its parlor, Winterbourne, with scones, tea sandwiches, pastries, and, of course, a pot of tea.

Afternoon tea on the Halekūlani's Veranda is a delight for young and old.

Restaurants *are listed alphabetically. By area they are:*

Waikīkī
(map pages 67–69)

Arancino
Bali by the Sea
The Colony
Diamond Head Grill
Golden Dragon
Hanohano Room
Hau Tree Lanai
House without a Key
Keo's Thai Cuisine
Kyo-ya
La Mer
Matteo's
Michel's
Miyako
Musashi
Neptune's Garden
Nick's Fishmarket
Orchids
Padovani's Bistro and
    Wine Bar
Prince Court
Rainbow Lanai
Round Table Pizza
Sarento's
Shogun
Shorebird Beach
    Broiler
Singha Thai Cuisine
Surf Room

**Ala Moana/
Downtown/Chinatown**
(map pages 70–72)

Aaron's Atop the Ala
    Moana
Angelo Pietro
Assaggio
Auntie Pasto's
Café VIII ½
Café Sistina
California Pizza Kitchen
Chai's Island Bistro
Compadres Bar & Grill
Duc's Bistro
Gordon Biersch Brewery
Indigo
John Dominis
Kaka'ako Kitchen
Keo's Thai Cuisine
Kincaid's Fish, Chop
    and Steak House
Maple Garden
Mariposa
Mermaid Bar
Mocha Java Café
Onjin's Café
Palomino Restaurant
Rotisseria Bar
Panya Café
The Pineapple Room
Ruth's Chris Steak House
Ryan's Grill
Sansei Seafood Restau-
    rant and Sushi Bar
Scoozee's
Sunset Grill
L'Uraku

Nu'uanu
(map page 100)

Liliha Bakery

Makiki/Tantalus
(map page 103)

Contemporary
    Museum Café
Pavilion Café, Honolulu
    Academy of Arts

Mānoa/Mo'ili'ili
(map page 108)

Alan Wong's
Andy's Sandwiches and
    Smoothies
Beau Soleil
Chef Mavro
Chiang Mai
Donato's
Maharani
Mekong II
Montien Thai
Paesano
Wai'oli Tea Room

**Kapahulu/Kaimukī/
Kāhala** *(map page 113)*

Auntie Pasto's
Big City Diner
Café Laufer
Café Miro
Café Monsarrat
California Pizza Kitchen
Champa Thai
Genki Sushi
Hale Vietnam
Hōkū's

Irifune
JJ French Pastry
Kalei-Tei
Ka 'Ikena
Mr. Ojisan
Ninniku-Ya (The
    Garlic Restaurant)
Olive Tree Café
'Ono Hawaiian Foods
Plumeria Beach Café
Sam Choy's Diamond
    Head
3660 on the Rise
Tokkuri-Tei
Tokyo Tokyo
The Veranda

**Outside Honolulu
proper**

Assaggio, Kailua
Buzz's Original Steak
    House, Kailua
Café Hale'iwa, Hale'iwa
Hale'iwa Joe's, Hale'iwa
    and Kāne'ohe
Jameson's by the Sea,
    Hale'iwa
Lucy's Grill 'n Bar,
    Kailua
Rosie's Cantina,
    Hale'iwa
Roy's, Hawai'i Kai

Guide to Fresh Island Fish

When a waitperson in a Hawai'i restaurant rattles off a selection of island fish on the menu, even we get confused. Here is a guide to a few of the most popular varieties.

'ahi yellowfin or bigeye tuna; a firm fish eaten raw, as sashimi, or broiled in thick filets, preferably rare; blackened *'ahi* is a favorite

aku skipjack tuna; firm red flesh

a'u swordfish or marlin, also known as shutome; a white flesh similar to *mahimahi*

hamachi yellowtail; also known as kamanu and rainbow runner; similar to salmon

kūmū goatfish; a light red reef fish; firm white flesh similar to red snapper

mahimahi dolphinfish (not the marine mammal); a firm white flesh with flaky texture and mild taste; probably the most popular on Hawaiian tables

moana goatfish; firm, sweet white flesh; similar to catfish

moi threadfish; a delicately flavored, light-fleshed fish

monchong also known as the bigscale pomfret; similar to halibut

onaga red snapper; firm and tender white flesh; sometimes used for sashimi; a very decorative looking pink fish when whole

ono also called wahoo; moist and flaky white meat that's *'ono* (delicious); similar to mackerel

opah also known as moonfish; firm pink flesh with a rich, mild flavor; similar to turbot or halibut

'ōpakapaka pink snapper; light pink flesh that is firm in texture

ulua a jackfish; white fatty flesh; similar to pompano; a small *ulua* is known as *pāpio*

Aaron's Atop the Ala Moana, 410 Atkinson Drive. 955-4466. Expensive

Situated on the top (36th) floor of the Ala Moana Hotel, this flashy restaurant/bar provides a terrific view of the city. The cuisine is Continental. For many local regulars, this is the hot spot in which to be seen. Late night live music keeps dancers happy until the wee hours. Open daily for dinner.

Alan Wong's, 1857 South King Street. 949-2526. Expensive

Winner of the 1996 James Beard Chef Award for Best Chef in the Pacific Northwest and Hawai'i, Alan Wong opened his restaurant in 1995 (on King Street near McCully). It has fast become one of Honolulu's most popular dining spots. (For this reason, you'll want to make reservations well in advance.) Wong is a major contributor to the local culinary

style known as Hawai'i regional cuisine, which consists of imaginative and artistically prepared dishes using locally grown vegetables, herbs, Hawaiian fish, poultry, and meats. Entreés, priced from $26 to $30, have an Asian flair. Favorite dishes include hoisin BBQ baby back ribs, grilled lamb chops with coconut macadamia nut crust, ginger-crusted *onaga* with miso sesame vinaigrette, and seared peppered yellowfin *'ahi* with crispy Asian slaw. The garlic mashed potatoes are sublime. California wines are featured. Save room for dessert, which will not disappoint. Also excellent is Kona coffee from McClure Farms in Hōnaunau. The entire menu is so tempting you'll probably want to sample a few appetizers and salads along with your entrée. Though this will run up the bill, this exceptional culinary experience is, in our opinion, worth a big splurge. The service here is attentive and friendly, and the waiters are knowledgeable. Open daily for dinner.

Andy's Sandwiches and Smoothies, 2904 East Mānoa Road. 988-6161. Inexpensive

There is no better place in Honolulu for a fresh fruit smoothie. Breakfast fare is delicious and generous, as are lunchtime sandwiches and salads. The emphasis is on fresh and healthy, with no meat dishes served. They bake their own muffins and cookies, including delicious creampuffs from time to time. You order at the counter, waiting in line with the university crowd, then find a spot at tiny, cramped tables. You'll find this local favorite between Starbucks and a video store, across from Mānoa Marketplace. Open Sunday–Friday for breakfast and lunch.

Angelo Pietro, 1585 Kapiolani Boulevard. 941-0555. Inexpensive

Good pizza, pasta, and salad ($7–$13.95) are served at this funky Japanese-Italian restaurant near Ala Moana Center. Raw potato salad, made with shredded potatoes, is a local favorite. Like many restaurants frequented by locals, the clientele is mostly young and Japanese. Service is friendly and efficient. Open daily for lunch and dinner.

Arancino, 255 Beachwalk. 923-5557. Inexpensive

Excellent Italian pasta dishes and pizzas at very reasonable prices make this casual café a winner. Add to that its prime Waikīkī location, easily walked to from any hotel. There is a good selection of Italian and California wines. Entrées: $6.80–$14.50. Open daily for lunch and dinner.

Assaggio, Ala Moana Center and 354 Uluniu Street, Kailua. 942-3446 and 261-2772. Moderate

Exceptional southern Italian food at moderate prices makes this small local chain a favorite among residents. Dishes are prepared with fresh ingredients, and servings are generous. Baked ziti, roasted chicken, linguine, and lasagna are among the entrées.

There are also locations in Hawai'i Kai (396-0756) and Mililani (623-5115). The Ala Moana restaurant is open daily for lunch and dinner. Kailua is open Tuesday–Sunday for dinner; Tuesday–Saturday for lunch.

Auntie Pasto's, 1099 South Beretania Street and 599 Kapahulu Avenue. 523-8855. Inexpensive

On weekend nights be prepared to stand in line and wait for a table at this very popular Italian eatery. You'll find satisfying food here served in generous portions, and at the right price. The menu, posted on a big board on the wall, features a variety of dishes such as pasta with seafood, eggplant parmigiana, pasta carbonara, and veal Marsala (entrées: $7–$16.95). Salad selections are plentiful, and crusty warm bread accompanies the meal. The Kapahulu Avenue location is a new one (in an old building), while the Beretania Street venue has been around for eighteen years. After 10:30 P.M. Friday and Saturday, the Kapahulu restaurant becomes a hot nightclub. Open daily for dinner; Monday–Friday for lunch.

Bali by the Sea, Hilton Hawaiian Village, 2005 Kālia Road. 941-2254. Expensive

This lovely multilevel restaurant overlooks Waikīkī Beach and is beautifully decorated in pastel colors, with exquisite napery and crystal. Its superb wine list includes both European and American labels and has had rave reviews from *Spectator* and other publications. Favorite entrées ($22.50–$34) include filet mignon with black pepper sauce, *opaka-paka* with Kaffir lime sauce, roasted duck with caramelized apples, and rack of lamb. Recommended fitness selections are noted on the menu. For a dramatic dessert, try the chocolate Diamond Head creation, which spews smoke as it is presented. A magical experience is to watch the Hilton's Friday night fireworks display from the restaurant, 7:30 P.M. October through March and 8 P.M. April through September. Open Monday–Saturday for dinner.

Beau Soleil, 2970 East Mānoa Road. 988-0967. Moderate

This Mediterranean-style café is one of our favorite neighborhood eateries, frequented by the university community and nearby residents. The restaurant's owner bakes his own breads, and continental breakfasts during the week feature warm scones and croissants as well as a great cup of coffee. Weekend brunches offer a feast of hearty dishes, including catch-of-the-day hash and chocolate-chunk pancakes. A variety of imaginative sandwiches and salads is served for weekday lunches. Dinner prices can be high (entrées $12–$27), but well worth the price. Such entrées as grilled rack of lamb with lemon rosemary polenta or rib eye steak with homemade French fries and béarnaise sauce are served. Beau Soleil also caters and will pack a picnic lunch for you. Open Tuesday–Sunday for breakfast, lunch, and dinner.

Big City Diner, 3565 Waiʻalae Avenue. 738-8855. Inexpensive

Local-style comfort foods are the order of the day at this big, family-friendly eatery, serving from morning until late night. TVs tuned to sports hang from the ceiling, and red booths add to the diner ambiance. Huge, juicy burgers and *kim chee* fried rice are favorites. There are a few "expensive" entrées like pan-seared fresh salmon ($14.95) and baby back ribs ($19.95 for a large slab), but for the most part everything is under $10. Children are catered to with a special ($3.99) menu and coloring materials. A full range of spirits are available. After 10 P.M.

Tuesday through Saturday a DJ or *karaoke* holds sway, and the place becomes a happening nightclub. Open daily, 7 A.M.–11 P.M., and later most nights for bar service.

Buzz's Original Steak House, 413 Kawailoa Road, Kailua. 261-4661. Moderate

This casual establishment has been a fixture on Oʻahu's windward side, at the entrance to Lanikai, for more than twenty-five years, serving good salads, steak, lobster, and fresh fish. Their salad bar is legendary, with fresh avocado, pineapple, Maui onions, local greens, potato salad, and Buzz's dressings. The casual, beachside ambiance of old Hawaiʻi adds to the charm. Check out Bill Clinton's table. Open daily for lunch and dinner.

Café VIII ½, 1067 Alakea Street. 524-4064. Moderate

Chef owner Robert Warner, originally from San Francisco, opened this casual mom-and-pop café in 1995, offering simple and excellent northern Italian fare. Vegetables and meats are grilled over *kiawe* wood, providing a fragrant, woodsy odor to the place. Only about a dozen tables are situated inside, with limited patio seating streetside. Open Monday–Friday for lunch.

Café Hale'iwa, 66-460 Kamehameha Highway, Hale'iwa. Inexpensive

Cheap and good food for breakfast is scarfed down by surfer dudes before they head out to the big waves. No frills, just darn good eats—omelets, French toast, pancakes, Portuguese sausage, huevos rancheros, and daily specials. They serve lunch too, with an emphasis on Mexican-style entrées and local-style plate lunch, but close promptly at 2 P.M. Open daily for breakfast and lunch.

Café Laufer, 3565 Wai'alae Avenue. 735-7717. Inexpensive

Friday nights find this local bakery crowded with people waiting wine bottle in hand to savor the dinner special, offered nightly, usually in the $13 to $15 price range. Mornings are for waffles, French toast, and eggs, and lunch and dinner include soups, salads, and sandwiches. And of course there are the cakes—over a dozen different choices—for dessert. Favorites include Linzer torte, Black Forest torte, chocolate macadamia nut tart, and bread pudding. Open Wednesday–Monday for breakfast, lunch, and dinner.

Café Miro, 3446 Wai'alae Avenue. 734-2737. Expensive

Chef Shigeru Kobayashi serves up Asian-inspired French food in a funky, bistro-style setting. As at a French café, there is a set menu of three ($28) or five ($38) courses, all creatively combining fresh local ingredients. Strict vegetarians had better go elsewhere, as the set dinner features beef, chicken, lamb, or fish only. A *keiki* menu is $12. Grape lovers will like the selection of French and California wines; beer and sake are also served. Open Tuesday–Sunday for dinner.

Café Monsarrat, 3106 Monsarrat Avenue. 737-6600. Expensive

This chicly casual neighborhood restaurant is in a safe, middle-class neighborhood, not far from the Honolulu Zoo. Put on your nice clothes or wear shorts—it doesn't matter. The staff is friendly, the noise level high but not unpleasant. The menu is New Orleans inspired and features the likes of seafood gumbo, BBQ shrimp, jambalaya, and *kiawe*-grilled steak. Entrées: $19–$26. Bread is homemade and the house salad has a fresh, light flavor. Lunch features hearty sandwiches with Cajun steak fries. Open daily for dinner; Monday–Friday for lunch.

Café Sistina, First Interstate Building, 1314 South King Street. 596-0061. Moderate

A stylish northern Italian restaurant, on King Street between Ke'eaumoku and Pi'ikoi, Café Sistina is dedicated to good food as well as to Michelangelo, with every available wall and ceiling space painted by chef/owner Sergio Mitrotti, who hails from Turin. Sergio's subject is the frescoes of the Sistine Chapel, which he has copied with awesome verisimilitude. Generously sized entrées include traditional Italian favorites as well as interesting creations like gnocchi with gorgonzola and ravioli stuffed with lobster. Entrées: $8.75–$16.50. Fridays and Saturdays after 10:30 P.M. the tables are cleared away and a Latin-style nightclub, Zona Latina, takes over. Open daily for dinner; Monday–Friday for lunch.

California Pizza Kitchen Ala Moana Center and Kāhala Mall. 941-7715 and 737-9446. Inexpensive

This trendy restaurant, part of a California chain, has a large menu of excellent pasta dishes, salads, and pizzas. The pizzas, made fresh and cooked in a wood-fired stove, are sized small enough to make up a meal for one or can be shared by two and topped off with a salad and the complimentary sourdough bread. Pizzas ($7.99–$11.29) come with an assortment of interesting topping combinations—such as portobello mushrooms, tandoori chicken, or goat cheese with roasted peppers— and are considered by many locals as the best in Honolulu. Salads are available in two sizes (the half-portion is ample for one person) and are made with the freshest greens. The pasta dishes, like Thai linguini and pasta paella, are good choices as well. There is a small list of California wines. Service is friendly and attentive. A special *keiki* menu as well as crayons and paper for coloring make this an ideal place to bring young children. Open daily for lunch and dinner.

Chai's Island Bistro

Aloha Tower Marketplace. 585-0011. Expensive

Thai chef Chai Chaowasaree owns this and Singha Thai, two of O'ahu's best dining spots (at this writing, the U.S. Immigration Service is threatening to deport Chai, so both restaurants may change in the future). The menu at the bistro is decidedly Pacific Rim, the decor has a nice tropical flair, and the indoor-outdoor seating right next to where the SS *Independence* and the MS *Patriot* dock provides a delightful

ambiance. Hawai'i's top musicians such as the Brothers Cazimero and Ho'okena perform here regularly. Open daily for dinner; Monday–Friday for lunch.

Champa Thai, 3452 Wai'alae Avenue. 732-0054. Inexpensive

How many favorite Thai restaurants can you have? Here is another one that we like particularly for their use of lots of fresh vegetables where canned or frozen might be used by other establishments. Curry dishes and the garlic tofu are delicious. We also like entrées that make use of fresh pineapple, like pineapple curry and pineapple fried rice. Entrées range in price from $6.25 to $9.45. There's sometimes a short wait for a table on weekend nights, but never longer than five or ten minutes. Open daily for dinner; Monday–Friday for lunch.

Chef Mavro, 1969 South King Street. 944-4714. Expensive

One of Hawai'i's finest chefs, Marseilles-born George Mavrothalassitis opened his own restaurant in December 1998 (at the corner of King and McCully), and the critics have been agog since. *Gourmet, Wine Spectator,* Zagat's, Gayot's, *Time, Esquire,* the *New York Times,* the *Los Angeles Times,* and the *San Francisco Examiner* all have put Chef

Mavro at the top of their lists. The restaurant is noted for its pairings of *prix fixe* menus with wines selected especially for each course. Diners may select a three-, four-, or six-course feast, or order individual dishes from an à la carte menu (entrées $28–$39). If guests have specific food preferences, Mavro is quick to prepare special requests, even vegetarian entrées and even for the *prix fixe* menus, which begin at $49 for a three-course dinner without the wine selections ($67 with wine). Mavro is noted for his seafood preparations, using freshly caught island fish and drawing from his roots in Provence as well as the cuisine of Hawai'i: *onaga* baked in a crust of Hawaiian salt; grilled Kahuku prawns marinated with cumin; brochette of Keahole lobster. Beef, lamb, and island chicken receive star treatment too. Pastry chef Jeff Walters's *liliko'i malasadas* are famous, and justly so. The restaurant is quiet and intimate, painted in warm, pleasing hues. Paintings by local artists Roger Whitlock and Shelly Ferreira adorn the walls, and even the table vases are raku by Dan Tilton. Chef Mavro has been likened to a three-star restaurant in France; it is the kind of place to which food lovers make a pilgrimage. Open Tuesday–Sunday for dinner.

Chiang Mai, 2239 South King Street. 941-1151. Inexpensive

This nicely decorated restaurant has an excellent menu of northern Thai cuisine. Don't be surprised if you have to wait for a table; this is the favorite Thai restaurant of many locals. Popular dishes include tangy shrimp salad, seafood casserole, whole fish with chili, spicy beef or chicken, broccoli noodles, and pineapple fried rice served in a half pineapple shell. Dishes are prepared mild, medium, hot, or Thai hot, depending on your choice. Open daily for dinner; Monday–Friday for lunch.

The Colony, Hyatt Regency Waikīkī, 2424 Kalākaua Avenue. 923-1234. Expensive

Steak and seafood are the order of the day. All steaks are basted with fresh, locally grown herbs while cooking over a *kiawe* wood fire. Three- and four-course meals ($30–$55) are attractive features of the menu. Open daily for dinner.

Compadres Bar & Grill, Ward Centre, 1200 Ala Moana Boulevard. 591-8307. Moderate

This is the place to be for margaritas at sundown—on the outdoor terrace or at the bar. The restaurant is big, open, and sparkling, with a fun, festive atmosphere. Specialties include turkey enchiladas, crabmeat stuffed avocado, fajita salad, garden quesadilla, and baby back ribs. Open daily for lunch and dinner.

Contemporary Museum Café, 2411 Makiki Heights Drive. 523-3362. Moderate

Mostly only *kama'āina* know about this lovely café nestled below the Contemporary Museum, located above the city in Makiki Heights. A peaceful garden setting provides the backdrop for indoor and outdoor seating. Chef Noreen Lam's menu is small and on the light side, featuring such gourmet delights as hummus and pita and grilled chicken and boursin sandwich. Salads are imaginative, and desserts are luscious. Diners may bring their own wine; corkage fee is $5. This popular café is often full, especially on weekends when groups of local people may book several tables, so reservations are advised. Open for lunch Tuesday–Saturday, 11:30 A.M.–2:30 P.M., and Sunday, noon–2:30 P.M.

Diamond Head Grill, W Honolulu, 2885 Kalākaua Avenue. 922-3734. Expensive

Very cosmopolitan, this is the sort of place to have a martini at the bar while you wait for your table. Tastefully whimsical decor adds to the general sense of a buzz in the air. Hip, young arty types come here to see and be seen and to take in the contemporary jazz of pianist David Swanson after 8:30 P.M. The menu, under the direction of executive chef Todd Constantino, is Pacific Rim inspired and includes such items as a delicious lemon ginger crabcake for a starter and seafood specialties prepared with fresh local fish. The signature *'ōpakapaka* with Kahuku corn and basil mashed potatoes is superb. Grilled prime cuts of beef are perfectly prepared. Entrées: $18–$34. The Diamond Head Grill is noted for its fine selection of wines. A moderately priced breakfast ($7–$14) is served daily, primarily for guests of the hotel, but anyone may go. Open daily for breakfast and dinner.

Donato's, Mānoa Marketplace, 2752 Woodlawn Drive. 988-2000. Moderate

Located upstairs at the Mānoa Marketplace (known locally as the Safeway shopping center in Mānoa), this new location for Donato's is airy and spacious. Specialties include *pappardelle con la papera* (pasta with roasted duck and prosciutto in a tomato sauce), *carpaccio malatesta* (thinly sliced beef tenderloin with portobello mushrooms in a lemon–olive oil dressing), and *spaghetti al cartoccio* (spaghetti with seafood cooked in parchment paper), in addition to traditional Italian menu items. Open daily for dinner.

Duc's Bistro, 1188 Maunakea Street. 531–6325. Moderate–Expensive

This intimate, sophisticated Chinatown bistro specializes in French and Continental cuisine with an Asian touch. Soft jazz, usually live, provides a soothing background for enjoying the excellent food. Entrées ($22–$28) include rack of lamb (flown in from Paris), seafood in a puff pastry shell, and breast of duck, prepared to the specifications of Prince Rainier. A tasty meal in a bowl (spicy rice noodles with shrimp, beef, or chicken), priced at about $12, is an economical alternative. The dessert menu is as adventuresome as earlier courses and includes homemade sorbets and ginger cheesecake. Attentive, friendly service and first-class atmosphere make this a favorite downtown choice for *kama'āina*. Open daily for dinner; Monday–Friday for lunch.

Genki Sushi, 900 Kapahulu Avenue. 735-8889. Inexpensive

Quick, affordable, and fresh sushi for eat-in or take-out are the hallmark of this popular place. Service is via a revolving conveyor belt from which you make your choices, with color-coded dishes to indicate price (about $1.50–$4). Open daily for lunch and dinner.

Golden Dragon, Hilton Hawaiian Village, 2005 Kālia Road. 946-5336. Moderate

One of the best places to go for Chinese cuisine in Honolulu, this elegant restaurant is situated next to a lovely lagoon at the Hilton Hawaiian Village, with tables outside and in. Black lacquer chairs, tables dressed with crisp white tablecloths, and Chinese sculptures and vases all contribute to its exotic setting, richly decorated with striking red and black accents. Chef Steven Chiang's dynamic menu boasts an excellent selection of Szechuan, Cantonese, and nouvelle Chinese cuisine ($12.95–$31.95). Exotic dishes include imperial beggar's chicken and imperial Peking duck (order 24 hours in advance) and lobster tail stir fried with curry sauce. Special wines and beers are available. If you're there on Friday night, ask for a lanai seat on the ocean side, where

you'll be as close as is possible to the Hilton's dramatic fireworks display (7:30 P.M. winter and 8 P.M. summer). Open Tuesday–Sunday for dinner.

Gordon Biersch Brewery Aloha Tower Marketplace. 599-4877. Moderate

Situated in a picturesque waterfront setting, this lively microbrewery restaurant/bar is a great place to go for a drink. Beer is the most popular beverage served here, available in three brewed-on-the-spot German-style lagers. There is a full wine menu as well, offering California wines by the glass or bottle. Menu items range from good old American favorites (steak, pizzas, cheeseburgers, and garlic fries) to island-style cuisine (Asian chicken salad, peppered *'ahi,* and "drunken" *poke*). Entrées: $9.95–$20.95. There is a *keiki* menu. Nonsmoking seating is inside; the harbor-side lanai allows smoking. Live music most nights, local Hawaiian to jazz, R&B, and rock. Open daily for lunch and dinner.

Hale'iwa Joe's, 66-011 Kamehameha Highway, Hale'iwa. 637-8005. Moderate

This is the best place to eat on the north shore, with splendid views of Waialua Bay, site of the short-lived TV show *Baywatch*

Hawai'i. For viewing the sunset, try to get a table on the lanai. Hamburgers and sandwiches are available at lunchtime in addition to most of the dinner entrées, which range in price at dinnertime from $11.75 to $24.95 for a full pound of Alaskan king crab legs. The menu includes chicken curry, *lū'au* fish steamed in *ti* leaves, and whole Hawaiian *moi,* a delicacy once reserved only for the tables of royalty. A *keiki* menu allows for less-expensive dining for the children. Open daily for lunch and dinner. Hale'iwa Joe's also has a restaurant in Kāne'ohe, overlooking the lush Ha'ikū Gardens (247-6671; see page 121).

Hale Vietnam, 1140 12th Avenue. 735-7581. Inexpensive

This casual neighborhood restaurant in Kaimukī is always crowded. The house special is seventeen varieties of *phô,* a hearty beef noodle soup made with brisket and flank steak in a savory broth over rice noodles, with fresh bean sprouts, basil, and chili pepper on the side. A large bowl of *phô* makes an excellent meal. Other dishes include summer rolls, green papaya salad, steamed chicken with peanut ginger sauce, and spicy barbecued pork. Plenty of vegetarian selections are available as well. Open daily for lunch and dinner.

Hanohano Room, Sheraton Waikīkī, 2255 Kalākaua Avenue. 922-4422. Expensive

In Hawaiian *hanohano* means "glorious" or "distinctive"; thus is derived the name of this attractive restaurant, which has magnificent views up and down Waikīkī, especially glorious at sunset. This 30th-floor perch at the Sheraton Waikīkī serves a Continental menu with a Hawaiian touch. The wine list features fine European vintages as well as bottles from California. Sunday brunch includes fresh fruits and juices, Continental entrées, and desserts. Open daily for breakfast, afternoon drinks, and dinner.

Hau Tree Lanai, New Otani Kaimana Beach Hotel, 2863 Kalākaua Avenue. 921-7066. Expensive

Situated right on Sans Souci Beach at the Diamond Head end of Waikīkī, this romantic, open-air restaurant shelters diners beneath the branches of a lovely old *hau* tree. This may be the best dining location on the island. The beachfront setting is breathtaking, especially at night when the lanai is lit by candles, torches, and sparkling lights in the *hau* tree. Breakfast

features eggs, omelets, and French toast as well as authentic Japanese fare. Lunch includes sandwiches, salads, and pastas (average price $15), and dinner features fresh fish as well as pasta, beef, and chicken entrées. While the food is not up to the high prices, the surroundings more than make up for it, and we highly recommend this restaurant. Open daily for breakfast, lunch, and dinner.

Hōkū's, Kāhala Mandarin Oriental Hotel, 5000 Kāhala Avenue. 739-8780. Expensive

This stunning multilevel dining room offers ocean views from every table and an open kitchen where exquisite Euro-Asian/Pacific Rim cuisine is prepared. The *kiawe* grill, Indian tandoori oven, and wok are the primary cooking tools. An imaginative *pūpū* menu features *'ahi poke*

The Hau Tree Lanai.

House without a Key.

musubi (nothing like the spam-and-rice *musubi* you can pick up at the supermarket), oxtail soup, and fresh-baked *naan* bread with Hōkū's dips. A "symphony of *'ahi*" from the sushi bar is a work of art. Dinner entrées ($20–$33) might be, for samplers, Indian chicken curry, wok-seared Maine lobster, or herb-crusted *onaga*. Desserts like melting chocolate cake are to die for. Service is incredibly attentive, making diners feel welcome and comfortable. Open daily for dinner; Monday–Friday for lunch; Sunday 10:30 A.M.–2:30 P.M. for brunch.

House without a Key

Halekūlani Hotel, 2199 Kālia Road. 923-2311. Moderate

Casual poolside dining is offered for breakfast, lunch, and light dinner; *pūpū* and sandwiches average $10 to $15. As with all of the dining options at the Halekūlani, the food is superb. There is no better place for an evening drink than this romantic setting, with Hawaiian entertainers performing under a century-old *kiawe* tree nightly from 5 to 8 P.M.—a sunset ritual that has continued since 1917. Today former Miss Hawai'i Kanoe Miller dances graceful hula Mondays through Saturdays, and former Miss Hawai'i Debbie Nakanelua performs hula on Sundays. Open daily for breakfast, lunch, and dinner.

Indigo, 1121 Nuʻuanu Avenue. 521-2900. Moderate–Expensive

This stylish Chinatown restaurant has everything you'd want for a superb dining experience—exotic decor, gourmet Euro-Asian cuisine at reasonable prices, and excellent service. Ask for a table on the patio, where ceiling fans and a lily pond provide a delightful island ambiance. The menu is full of creative dishes from the hand of chef Glenn Chu, including ten varieties of dim sum dumplings and individual-size pizzas, called "pizzettas," all under $10. Goat cheese wontons and *lumpia*-wrapped shrimp are excellent. Dinner entrées ($12.50–$22.50) include wokked vegetables, fish roasted in banana leaf, and grilled chicken with Indigo peanut sauce (their most requested dish). The dessert menu is large and enticing. Especially delicious is the ginger crème brûlée. The bar, open until 2 A.M., is a gathering place for Honolulu's young, hip crowd who come to be seen and to savor the likes of sake martinis. Restaurant open Tuesday–Saturday for dinner; Tuesday–Friday for lunch.

Irifune, 563 Kapahulu Avenue. 737-1141. Moderate

This funky restaurant with the most down-home waiting room we've ever seen is always packed with locals. The food is decent, and the price is right. Entrées ($9–$12), which have a Japanese flavor, include garlic stir fries with tofu, chicken, or seafood; chicken *katsu;* and a variety of tempuras and curries. Open Tuesday–Saturday for lunch and dinner.

Jameson's by the Sea, 62-540 Kamehameha Highway, Haleʻiwa. 637-4336. Expensive

Tourists and locals flock to this north shore restaurant, with dining on an outdoor lanai or in a more formal dining room upstairs with ocean views. This is a great place for a drink at sunset, when the sky displays its brilliant colors out over Waialua Bay, which is directly across the street. Fresh local fish, chowders, stews, scallops, and oysters are the main attractions. An excellent gift shop stocks a good selection of locally made arts and crafts. Open daily for lunch and dinner.

JJ French Pastry, 3447 Waiʻalae Avenue. 739-0993. Inexpensive

Not truly a restaurant, this French bakery in Kaimukī serves tasty and inexpensive salads that can make a meal. The real reason to come here is for the desserts, especially the luscious chocolate-raspberry pyramid (served at many of Honolulu's fine dining establishments at double the price). The proprietor, "JJ," is a native of Laos who trained at Maxim's. There is a large selection of cakes, tarts, and pastries. Open Monday–Saturday, 9 A.M.–8 P.M.

John Dominis, 43 ʻAhui Street. 523-0955. Expensive

The gorgeous view of boats under way, Waikīkī, and Diamond Head—golden at sunset and sparkling by night—makes this a choice spot. Fresh seafood is the main attraction; the restaurant is adjacent to the local fish auction. Live lobsters and crabs navigate a brook around the dining room. There's also a display of *ulua, onaga,* clams, and oysters soon to be eaten at a dear price. Menu items include fish *en papillote,* tiger prawns, and seafood crepes, as well as salads, steak, lamb, and vegetarian offerings. Preparations are simple and servings are large; prices are high, however, for less-than-spectacular food. Orchid-filled lava rock walls and live entertainment Fridays and Saturdays enhance the island ambiance. Sunday brunch is popular. On Fridays after 10:30 P.M. the restaurant becomes the trendy Spy Bar. Open daily for dinner; 9 A.M.–1 P.M. for Sunday brunch.

Ka ʻIkena, Kapiʻolani Community College, 4303 Diamond Head Road. 734-9488. Expensive

Visitors who find their way to this dining room on the slopes of Diamond Head with a magnificent view are in for a treat. The restaurant is run by students in the culinary arts program at Kapiʻolani Community College, who go all-out in their menu preparations. Dinner prices (about $22–$30) include appetizer, soup or salad, choice of entrée, beverage (but BYOB), and dessert. Recent entrées have included Szechuan-style smoked duck, sake-marinated beef tenderloin, Thai curry, Maine lobster, and minted lamb chops. Lunch and dinner are served Tuesdays through Fridays, though the restaurant is closed between semesters. Reservations are a must; ask for directions when you call.

Kakaʻako Kitchen, Ward Centre, 1200 Ala Moana Boulevard. 596-7488. Inexpensive

This local-style eatery is the brainchild of chef Russell Siu (3660 on the Rise). Gourmet plate lunches are the buzzword here. Breakfasts include the loco moco, a hamburger patty on a bed of rice, topped with brown gravy and two eggs, any style.

All breakfasts come with a homemade biscuit and whipped *liliköʻi* butter. Their signature dish and everyone's favorite is island-style chicken linguine. Entrées average $6, with nothing over $10. Save room for Lisa Siu's homestyle desserts, especially her signature bread pudding. Open daily for breakfast, lunch, and dinner.

Kalei-Tei, 808 Kapahulu Avenue. 734-3868. Inexpensive

This stylish Japanese restaurant is among our favorites. The decor is simple and pleasing, and the food is extraordinary. *Kalei* translates as curry, which is served in a variety of imaginative combinations ($6.75–$8.75): chicken, beef, mushroom, seafood, and, for a real taste treat, tropical fruits. The small menu also includes a couple of very good salads; home-style entrées with an Asian twist, like stuffed baked cabbage and stewed hamburger steak; and several exotic desserts. Good recorded jazz pleases the auditory senses. BYOB, but for a refreshing nonalcoholic drink, try the iced honey-ginger tea. Park in any of the first five spaces on the right in the Running Room lot, across the street. Open Tuesday–Sunday for dinner; Tuesday–Friday for lunch.

Keo's Thai Cuisine, 2028 Kuhiō Avenue and Ward Centre, 1200 Ala Moana Boulevard. 951-9355 and 596-0020. Inexpensive

Say "Thai cuisine" in Honolulu and Keo's is the first restaurant that comes to mind, enjoying its premier ranking since 1977. The tropical ambiance of both locations is enhanced by a profusion of orchids and vases of exotic flowers. Favorite dishes, which can be ordered mild, spicy, or hot, include lemongrass soup, eggplant with tofu, crispy noodles, curries, satay beef or chicken with hot peanut sauce, and green papaya salad. A must-try is the Evil Jungle Prince, a creation of Keo himself that combines lemongrass, Thai basil, and chili peppers with chicken. An excellent wine list complements the sassiness of the food. The Waikīkī location on Kuhiō Avenue is a favorite hangout for celebrity visitors to the islands, as evidenced by the walls full of photographs of famous diners ranging from Robert Redford to Elton John. However, we prefer the Ward Centre restaurant, where the walls are covered with exquisite paintings by local artists, loaned by the Gallery at Ward Centre, and the food is, we think, better. Open daily for lunch and dinner.

Kincaid's Fish, Chop and Steak House, Ward Warehouse, 1050 Ala Moana Boulevard. 591-2005. Expensive

Known for its fine seafood, this lovely harborview restaurant is usually packed with local patrons, making reservations advisable. The menu is made up of à la carte soups and salads, steaks and chops, poultry and pasta, and premium fish. Fresh fish selections change daily. For dessert we suggest their signature creation, the original burnt cream (a custard made with heavy cream and eggs), sure to ravage your cholesterol level. A reasonably priced *keiki* menu also is available. Service is excellent. Open daily for lunch and dinner.

Kyo-ya, 2057 Kalākaua Avenue. 947-3911. Expensive

A Waikīkī institution for fifty years, Kyo-ya offers exquisite Japanese cuisine in equally exquisite surroundings, completely renovated in 1991. Downstairs is the Takeniwa dining room, a modern setting with tables and chairs, and upstairs are private *tatami* rooms that seat from four to seventy guests. Food, under the direction of executive chef Shigeaki Inoue, is as authentic as you can get. This is the premier spot for a remarkable Japanese dining experience. Open daily for dinner; Monday–Saturday for lunch.

La Mer, Halekūlani Hotel, 2199 Kālia Road. 923-2311. Expensive

Perfect for romance and fine dining, this elegant oceanside restaurant has windows that open wide to sounds of the surf and sweet Hawaiian music from below. Chef Yves Garnier, winner of the acclaimed Michelin star, makes full use of Hawai'i's fresh ingredients in his creative Mediterranean menu. La Mer is expensive, there's no doubt about that, with entrées ranging from $36 to $46. Highlights include rack of lamb marinated with thyme and garlic cloves, bouillabaisse La Mer style, and sautéed veal in a light tarragon sauce. Island fish like *hamachi, kūmū* and *onaga* are superbly prepared and presented. For dessert, the signature painter's palette of artfully arranged sorbets is a perfect choice. Complete four- and five-course dinners are available and are highly recommended ($85 and $105). Winner of the coveted Five Diamond Award from the American Automobile Association (and the only Five Diamond restaurant on O'ahu), La Mer is among our top choices for a perfect meal in paradise. Gentlemen note: this is the only place in Honolulu where jackets are still required. Open daily for dinner.

Liliha Bakery, 515 North Kuakini Street. 531-1651. Inexpensive

This local favorite is in the Nu'uanu area, *'ewa* and *mauka* of Chinatown, near the intersection of Liliha and Kuakini Streets. People flock here for the delicious creampuffs, the best anywhere. The most popular variety is the cocoa puff, filled with dense, creamy chocolate pudding. Simple, local-style meals (a meat and two scoops rice) are quite good, but it is the bakery items that keep this place crowded day and night. Diner-style seating is limited, and there is often a wait (no reservations; no credit cards). Open 24 hours from Tuesday at 6 A.M. to Sunday at 8 P.M.; closed Monday.

Lucy's Grill 'n Bar, 33 Aulike Street, Kailua. 230-8188. Moderate

There aren't many good places to eat in the Kailua area; this is one of them. Pizza, chicken, lamb, and pork loin are imaginatively prepared. First courses are especially intriguing, and a meal made up of them can be highly satisfying. Open daily for dinner.

Maharani, 2509 South King Street. 951-7447. Inexpensive

The traditional Indian cuisine served here includes *naan* bread and tasty *masalas,* or curries. The yellow chicken curry, available only on weekends, is a special treat. Entrées: $9.95–$13.95. Located across from Star Market, this restaurant is new, clean, and crisp. Open daily for dinner; Monday–Friday for lunch.

Maple Garden, 909 Isenberg Street. 941-6641. Inexpensive

This cozy restaurant has been serving Chinese food since 1975. The cuisine is Szechuan and the menu is traditional. Paintings by renowned Hawai'i expressionist John Young decorate the walls. Open daily for lunch and dinner.

Mariposa, Neiman Marcus, Ala Moana Center. 951-8887. Expensive

Forget you're in a shopping center: the setting and the view, overlooking the beach park from the upper floor of Ala Moana Center, are stunning. Perfectly complementing the open-air vista of palms and sea is a two-part mural by Honolulu artist Yvonne Cheng titled *Hula Breeze* and *Coconut Grove.* Also a sight to behold are the American regional cuisine dishes of chef Douglas Lum, who has won numerous awards. Open daily for lunch, afternoon tea, and dinner.

Matteo's, Marine Surf–Waikīkī Hotel, 364 Seaside Avenue. 922-5551. Expensive

This popular Italian restaurant is designed in the classic style of fine Italian eateries, with rococo decor, intimate tables, and a quiet, dignified ambiance. The food is excellent; favorite menu items include seafood lasagna, osso buco, cioppino, eggplant parmigiana, Maine lobster, and rack of lamb. Complete dinners for $18.95 to $28.95 include soup or salad and coffee. The award-winning wine list has over 800 selections. Open daily for dinner.

Mekong II, 1726 South King Street. 941-6212. Inexpensive

A favorite among the university crowd, Mekong II is owned by Keo Sananikone (see Keo's above) and has equally good food in less upscale surroundings (thus cheaper). Keo's signature dish, Evil Jungle Prince, is delicious here (made with beef or chicken). Other favorites are spring rolls, green papaya salad, Thai noodles with chicken, masaman curry, and, for dessert, tapioca pudding with apple banana. Entrées: $6.95–$14.95. BYOB. Open daily for dinner; Monday–Friday for lunch.

Mermaid Bar, Neiman Marcus, Ala Moana Center. 951-3428. Moderate

With a menu of salads, sandwiches, and hot entrées under the hand of chef Douglas Lum of Mariposa, this casual café is an ideal lunch spot while shopping at Ala Moana. Hawai'i-inspired specialties as well as Neiman Marcus favorites—such as their chicken salad sandwich—highlight the menu (sandwiches: $8–$10). The walls are enlivened with Timothy Ojile's colorful abstractions of sculptures on a beach. Open daily for lunch.

Michel's, Colony Surf, 2895 Kalākaua Avenue. 923-6552. Expensive

A romantic seaside location, fine French cuisine, and impeccable service from tuxedo-clad waiters have made this a favorite for many years. Open daily for dinner.

Miyako, New Otani Kaimana Beach Hotel, 2863 Kalākaua Avenue. 923-4739. Expensive

Situated overlooking the ocean, this traditional Japanese restaurant offers both Western and *tatami*-style seating. Specialties include sukiyaki, *shabu shabu,* and tamaki sushi. Fixed-price traditional *kaiseki* dinners are available as well as à la carte items. Open daily for dinner.

Mocha Java Café, Ward Centre, 1200 Ala Moana Boulevard. 955-4466. Inexpensive

Two restaurants in one, one side offers a coffee bar and pastries, the other a creative, health-conscious menu. Tables are scattered in a central hallway of the shopping center; there are also outside tables. Soups, salads, and sandwiches are available, along with crèpes, frittatas, omelets, and vegetarian chili. Dessert crèpes are delicious. Open daily for breakfast, lunch, and dinner.

Montien Thai, 2671 South King Street. 949-2679. Inexpensive

A typical Thai restaurant menu is prepared in untypical ways, making for an interesting dining experience at low cost. Entrées ($6.50–$8.95) include spicy fried rice with chicken or pork, red and green curries, and a variety of vegetarian dishes. The owner makes his own coconut ice cream, which is a favorite among regulars. Open daily for lunch and dinner.

Mr. Ojisan, 1018 Kapahulu Avenue. 735-4455. Inexpensive

This little restaurant at the *mauka* end of Kapahulu Avenue offers carefully prepared traditional Japanese fare. The *oyako donburi*—tender chicken prepared with onion and egg in sweet sauce

over rice—is outstanding. Tempura comes with a generous variety of tasty vegetables, including Japanese pumpkin, sweet potato, and eggplant. The restaurant is also known for its ramen dishes. The menu is all in Japanese, but the waitstaff offers friendly assistance to *gaijin* (people who are not Japanese). Open Monday–Saturday for dinner; Monday–Friday for lunch.

Musashi, Hyatt Regency Waikīkī, 2424 Kalākaua Avenue. 923-1234. Expensive

Authentic Japanese food is served with a flair at this small jewel of a restaurant in the Hyatt Regency. The waitstaff is clad in kimono, and chefs don samurai garb. The special ten-course *kaiseki* dinner features seasonal delicacies noted for unique and beautiful presentation. The à la carte menu offers traditional dishes like *shabu shabu,* tempura, *teppanyaki,* and sashimi. Open daily for Japanese-style breakfast and dinner.

Neptune's Garden, Pacific Beach Hotel, 2490 Kalākaua Avenue. 921-6112. Expensive

The attraction here is the huge, three-story aquarium with some seventy species of fish. Under new executive chef Eric Leterc, the cuisine is superb, focusing on Continental-style dishes beauti-

fully prepared and artfully presented. Entrées: $24–$32. Open daily for dinner.

Nick's Fishmarket, Waikīkī Gateway Hotel, 2070 Kalākaua Avenue. 955-6333. Expensive

This top restaurant's fine reputation dates back more than thirty years, and it is the winner of numerous accolades. Fresh locally caught fish is brought in daily—*ʻōpakapaka, kūmū, onaga, ulua, mahimahi*—and prepared in more than forty delicious ways. Besides seafood, the menu also offers rack of lamb and chicken and beef selections. A four-course meal featuring Maine lobster is $29.95. Fresh salads, such as Nick's special salad with bay shrimp and creamy spinach dressing, and an excellent bouillabaisse round out the menu. Nick's signature dessert is van-bana pie, a rich creation made of vanilla ice cream, bananas, and hot caramel sauce. After 10 P.M. on Saturday nights the restaurant attracts the young set for a happening nightclub called Twilight. Open daily for dinner.

Ninniku-Ya (The Garlic Restaurant), 3196 Waiʻalae Avenue. 735-0784. Expensive

The aroma of garlic is in the air, and tiny lights sparkle on the outdoor dining lanai (try to get a table here). Everything is prepared with garlic, even ice cream. Not to be missed is an order of garlic toast, a small loaf of French bread laden with savory garlic cloves and butter. The food is delicious, starting with crab cakes or fresh *'ahi* and avocado. Steaks are cooked on a hot stone and brought sizzling to the table for a dramatic presentation. Steak, lamb, and seafood entrées range from $21–$28; pasta entrées are less expensive, starting at $12 for garlic pasta with chili bacon. Open Tuesday–Sunday for dinner.

Olive Tree Café, 4614 Kīlauea Avenue. 737-0303. Inexpensive

Next to the Kāhala Mall, on the other side of McDonald's, sits an unpretentious Greek bistro with a few tables inside and the more coveted seats on a small lanai. You order at the counter and hope for the best in grabbing a table. Fresh fish, chicken, and lamb souvlakis are the most ordered items, with the falafel following up. BYOB (everyone does). Open daily for dinner; Friday–Sunday for lunch.

Onjin's Café, 401 Kamakeʻe Street. 589-1666. Moderate–Expensive

Moderate at lunch with a pricier dinner menu, Onjin's has two distinctive personalities. People

flock here for plate-lunch style food with a flair—gourmet lunches costing little more than fast food. At dinner the table-cloths come out, and chef Onjin Kim prepares exquisite dishes such as crispy *moi*, escargots en croute, and her signature bouilla-baisse with fresh salmon, scallops, king crab, clams, and shrimp in a saffron-flavored broth. Open Tuesday–Saturday for dinner; Monday–Friday for lunch.

ʻOno Hawaiian Foods, 726 Kapahulu Avenue. 737-2275. Inexpensive

In Hawaiian, *ʻono* means delicious, and that describes the food here, simple, abundant, and represen-tative of the foods eaten by ancient Hawaiians and still by many today. Here's a chance to try traditional *lūʻau* dishes, like *poi* and *laulau,* without paying the high prices. You can order à la carte, but the plates are the way to go: *kālua* pig, *laulau,* chicken long rice, or combina-tion ($8.25–$10.50). Open Monday–Saturday for lunch and dinner (until 7:45 P.M.).

Orchids, Halekūlani Hotel, 2199 Kālia Road. 923-2311. Expensive

This lovely restaurant, located on the ground floor and fronting the ocean at the Halekūlani Hotel, has superb food, elegant

ambiance, and first-class service. Orchids consistently receives the AAA Four-Diamond Award. The menu features innovative seafood cuisine, and each dish is meticu-lously prepared using the freshest local ingredients whenever possi-ble. Imaginative dishes include Pacific crab salad with fresh mango, lobster chowder, char-broiled herb-crusted *ʻōpakapaka,* and Peking spiced duckling. Entrées range from $19 to $34.50. Save room for dessert, such as banana-blueberry *lumpia* or chocolate brioche pudding. The lavish Sunday brunch at Orchids is the best in town, featuring their famous popovers served with *pohā* jam as well as numerous buffet stands devoted to American, Continental, and Japanese special-ties. A harp-flute duo performs classical favorites and Broadway tunes for Sunday brunch; evenings vocalists entertain from 8:30 to 10 P.M. The open-air lanai tables offer the best Diamond Head views. No shorts or tee shirts after 6 P.M. Open daily for breakfast, lunch, and dinner.

Padovani's Bistro and Wine Bar, 1956 Ala Moana Boulevard. 946-3456. Expensive

Located across from Hilton Hawaiian Village, this elegant restaurant and bar features the celebrated Mediterranean-inspired cuisine of chef Philippe Padovani, formerly of the Mānele Bay Hotel on Lāna'i. Open Monday–Saturday for dinner; daily for breakfast and lunch.

Paesano, Mānoa Marketplace, 2752 Woodlawn Drive. 988-5923. Moderate

Paesano is one of our favorite neighborhood restaurants—and that of a lot of other people too judging from the crowds at dinner. The decor is pleasing, the waitstaff is friendly, and the food is great, starting with the freshly baked bread that's served warm at each table. Entrées come in two sizes, small and regular. Unless you're a really big eater, the small size is more than ample. The cuisine is Italian, with lots of imaginatively prepared dishes. We like the Kahuku shrimps in spicy sauce for a starter (messy to eat but delicious), the house green salad, and a pasta dish called chicken Paesano, which is chicken sautéed with garlic, peppers, and mushrooms served over linguine. There is a full bar, and the wine list is good. Entrées: $9.90–$15.90 (for the small size). Open daily for dinner; Monday–Saturday for lunch.

Palomino Restaurant Rotisseria Bar, 66 Queen Street. 582-2400. Expensive

The beautiful people of Hawai'i head for Palomino after work (not everyone surfs all day) for drinks, *pūpū,* and dinner. The aroma of spit-roasted meats wafts out to the street, drawing people into this hip, architecturally stunning restaurant, noted for trendy pastas, pizzas, and great crab dip. Open daily for dinner; Monday–Friday for lunch.

Panya Café, 1210 Queen Street. 597-8880. Inexpensive

Another of our favorites, this Japanese bakery/coffee shop is great for an inexpensive meal topped off with sweets from the bakery or for coffee and cake after the movies. Soups, salads, and sandwiches are augmented by the house special meals of curry chicken ($7.95) or oxtail stew ($9.95). Children love the hot dog wrapped in a croissant or the creamy egg salad sandwich on white bread with the crusts cut off. Fresh fruit and vegetable juices are a special treat. Open Monday–Saturday, 6:30 A.M.–midnight; Sunday, 9 A.M.–midnight.

Pavilion Café, Honolulu Academy of Arts, 900 South Beretania Street. 532-8734. Inexpensive–Moderate

A perfect setting in the courtyard of the Honolulu Academy's new Luce Pavilion—amid art, gently flowing water, and exquisite landscaping—makes this elegant café a welcome stop during a tour of the Academy's renowned collections. Sandwiches and salads are imaginatively prepared and generous, and there are daily specials, all under the direction of chef Mike Nevin. Most lunch entrées are under $10. California, French, and Italian wines complement the fine food. This is a favorite place for *kama'āina* to meet friends for lunch, so reservations are advised to make sure you get a table without a wait. Open Tuesday–Saturday for lunch, 11:30 A.M.–2 P.M.

The Pineapple Room, Macy's, Ala Moana Center. 945-8881. Moderate

Here's an opportunity to have Alan Wong cuisine without the very high prices of the King Street restaurant (but not quite as good). Hawai'i regional cuisine is definitely the guideline for the menu, which features pizzas, crab cakes, and great fish preparations. Desserts, prepared by Alan Wong cooks-in-training, are delicious. There's a nice bar—a good place for drinks and a light meal. Paintings and photographs by local artist Doug Young enliven the walls, including a large watercolor of Moloka'i as well as smaller works depicting plantlife. Open daily for breakfast and lunch; Monday–Saturday for dinner. Alan Wong also operates a take-out, eat-in Hawai'i regional cuisine marketplace on Macy's third floor (which may be a Macy's Cellar by the time this book comes off the presses).

Plumeria Beach Café, Kāhala Mandarin Oriental Hotel, 5000 Kāhala Avenue. 739-8780. Moderate

This casual, beachfront café, with very good buffets, is quite affordable in an upscale setting— with far better food than offered by many hotels. Entrées range from $11.50 for a tofu burger to $31.50 for steak and lobster. But it is the buffets that keep people coming back, especially the Thursday night barbecue, the Friday night seafood buffet, and the Sunday night Asian buffet. A twilight dinner, 5:30–6:30 P.M., offers two courses plus the famous dessert buffet for $23. Open daily for breakfast, lunch, and dinner.

Prince Court, Hawai'i Prince Hotel Waikīkī, 100 Holomoana Street. 944-4494. Expensive

Overlooking the picturesque Ala Wai yacht harbor, this casual bistro in the Hawai'i Prince Hotel is popular among *kama-'āina,* especially for weekday lunches and weekend brunches. Chef Goran Streng features ingredients from local farmers and suppliers for his Pacific Rim menu. Favorites are Dungeness crab cakes, sautéed snapper, and grilled prime steaks. Dinner entrées: $22–$34. Open daily for breakfast, lunch, and dinner.

Rainbow Lanai, Hilton Hawaiian Village, 2005 Kālia Road. 946-5336. Moderate

This open-air restaurant offers casual family dining overlooking the beach. An interesting lunch menu offers the likes of Asian duck summer rolls and Portuguese bean soup along with traditional sandwiches and burgers. The international dinner buffets are the best reason to try this restaurant, especially on Friday nights when Hawaiian-style food is served (and you'll have a front-seat view of the Hilton's grand fireworks display). Don't pass up the *lū'au,* which is steamed *kalo* in coconut milk—especially delicious here. Open daily for breakfast, lunch, and dinner.

Rosie's Cantina, Hale'iwa Shopping Plaza, 66-165 Kamehameha Highway, Hale'iwa. 637-3538. Inexpensive

A popular north shore Mexican restaurant, Rosie's is a pleasant place to enjoy a cool drink or hot meal. The menu offers basic Mexican fare. Margaritas are available in many fruit flavors— very refreshing after a day at the beach. Open daily for breakfast, lunch, and dinner.

Round Table Pizza, Hilton Hawaiian Village, 2005 Kālia Road. 944-1199. Inexpensive

Located in the shopping arcade near the entrance to the Hilton Hawaiian Village, Round Table Pizza will deliver to any Waikīkī hotel. Selections include the likes of Maui Zaui (ham, pineapple, bacon, and onions), Gourmet Veggie (artichoke hearts, zucchini, spinach, mushrooms, tomatoes, etc.), and Thai Chicken Supreme (peanut sauce), as well as the traditional. Salads are for dine-in only. Open daily for lunch and dinner.

Roy's, 6600 Kalanianaole Highway, Hawai'i Kai. 396-7697. Expensive

Award-winning chef/owner Roy Yamaguchi's Hawai'i Kai restaurant offers exciting menus that feature Euro-Asian and Hawai'i regional cuisine by one of the founders of that cooking school. What are now old standbys like blackened *'ahi* and ginger-shrimp potstickers were introduced by Roy. His restaurant is consistently included among Hawai'i's top dining establishments by everyone, often heading the list. Dishes, made primarily with fresh local ingredients, are beautifully presented, and service is superb. The open kitchen adds to the drama in this large, bustling room (not the place for a quiet, romantic dinner). Roy's is a must for every visitor to Hawai'i. Open daily for dinner.

Ruth's Chris Steak House

Restaurant Row, 500 Ala Moana Boulevard. 599-3860. Expensive

A version of the famed New Orleans restaurant, this is the top steak house in Honolulu. The ultramodern, pristine atmosphere focuses on one feature: perfectly prepared prime beef. If top-of-the-line steak is your pleasure, you'll love it here. Side dishes—garlic mashed potatoes, broccoli au gratin, asparagus—complement the sizzling beef. Chicken and seafood dishes are also available. All portions are generous, there is an excellent wine list, and service is superb. Open daily for dinner.

Ryan's Grill, Ward Centre, 1200 Ala Moana Boulevard. 591-9132. Moderate

This fun restaurant/bar features innovative American cuisine. Menu items include freshly baked rosemary focaccia, buffalo wings, chicken salad with sesame dressing, Cajun chicken fettuccine, roast chicken Dijon, and crab sandwich. Hawaiian *kiawe* is used for grilling, imparting a rich flavor. Ryan's features one of the most extensive back bar selections in the islands as well as California, French, and Italian wines and a huge selection of beers on tap and in the bottle. For dessert, try their famous key lime pie. Open daily until 1 A.M. for lunch, drinks, and dinner.

Sam Choy's Diamond Head, 449 Kapahulu Avenue. 732-8645. Expensive

Owned by one of Hawai'i's most recognized and accomplished chefs, this Kapahulu restaurant, which opened its doors in 1995, easily places in the top ten best dining establishments on O'ahu. The menu features Hawai'i regional cuisine, and each item uses mainly locally grown ingredients. Menu offerings include fried marlin *poke,* wonton with brie and homemade marmalade, osso buco, seafood *laulau,* and Sam's perfect roasted duck.

Entrées: $20.50–$34.95. All servings, including *'ono* desserts, are large (like Sam), and most people leave carrying a box of leftover food for another meal. Light eaters are encouraged to graze the *pūpū* menu. The studio for the TV show "Sam Choy's Kitchen" is right in the restaurant. Make reservations well in advance. Open daily for dinner; 9:30 A.M.–2 P.M. for Sunday brunch.

Sansei Seafood Restaurant and Sushi Bar, Restaurant Row, 500 Ala Moana Boulevard. 36-6286. Moderate

This seafood restaurant and sushi bar, owned by chef Dave Kodama, known as "D.K.," has received top awards since it opened on Maui in 1996, including Zagat's highest rating for food in the state for two consecutive years. The cuisine is Pacific Rim, influenced by Kodama's Japanese heritage and his travels on the mainland and in Mexico and the Caribbean. The exotic entrées ($15.95–$22.95) include, for samplers, wok-seared fresh Hawaiian *opah* and tiger prawns with shiitake mushrooms, asparagus, and Japanese pepper sauce, or macadamia-crusted Australian rack of lamb with gorgonzola and garlic smashed potatoes and sweet miso sauce. Or you can make a meal from the extensive sushi menu ($3.95–$14.95), with such favorites as mango crab salad roll and panko-crusted *'ahi* sashimi. Sansei serves a great lunch, with Japanese-influenced plate lunches at reasonable prices. There's *karaoke* every night from 10:30 P.M. till closing. Open daily for dinner; Monday–Friday for lunch.

Sarento's, 'Ilikai Hotel, 1777 Ala Moana Boulevard. 955-5559. Moderate–Expensive

At the top of the 'Ilikai, with awesome views from Pearl Harbor to Diamond Head, this Italian restaurant offers excellent food and service. Caesar salad, a variety of pastas, and osso buco are favorite dishes. Open daily for dinner.

Scoozee's, Ward Centre, 1200 Ala Moana Boulevard. 597-1777. Inexpensive

This indoor/outdoor sort-of-Italian café at Ward Centre falls into the fun-dining category. Its menu is reasonably priced, the food is good, and portions are generous. Favorites are *'ahi* cakes, gorgonzola garlic bread, Caesar salad, pasta salad, and cheeseburgers. For dessert try the tiramusu, which they call "Tita I Miss Su." There is sometimes live music at the bar. Weekend

breakfasts are popular. The relatively high noise level makes this a good option when you're with children. Open daily for lunch and dinner; Saturday and Sunday for breakfast.

Shogun, Pacific Beach Hotel, 2490 Kalākaua Avenue. 921-6113. Expensive

Want a short visit to Kobe? This restaurant features elegant Japanese cuisine and service befitting a shogun, plus waterfalls and mermaids. Menu items include assorted sushi, vegetable and shrimp tempura, and sashimi. There are *teppan* tables and a sushi bar. Open daily for breakfast, lunch, and dinner.

Shorebird Beach Broiler, Outrigger Reef Hotel, 2169 Kālia Road. 922-2887. Moderate

This is a fun place to take the family, but only if you don't mind cooking your own dinner with other diners over a large, hot grill. Fish, shrimp kebobs, and steak are the entrée choices, accompanied by a full salad bar, chili, and rice. The open-air restaurant is situated in a lovely spot overlooking the beach, which is lit up at night. Open daily for breakfast buffet and dinner.

Singha Thai Cuisine, 1910 Ala Moana Boulevard. 941-2898. Moderate

Considered one of the top Thai restaurants in Honolulu, this exotic place has a nightly stage show from 7 to 9 P.M. featuring the silk-costumed Royal Thai dancers (be sure to request a table with a good view of the dancers). Specialties include garlic shrimp, blackened *'ahi* summer rolls, and fresh local fish with ginger black bean sauce in addition to traditional Thai curries and noodles. Situated across Ala Moana Boulevard from the Hilton Hawaiian Village. Open daily for dinner.

Sunset Grill, Restaurant Row, 500 Ala Moana Boulevard. 521-4409. Moderate

This award-winning, California-style café is a great place for a relaxing, casual meal. Fish and chicken dishes prepared on the *kiawe* grill are excellent, as are such specialties as hoisin barbecue Pacific salmon and crab cakes with avocado *poke*. Entrées: $14.95–$25.95. Freshly baked bread with a balsamic vinegar/grated cheese dunking sauce is brought to your table at the beginning. The exceptional wine list includes over 200 selections. Dine indoors or out—outside is noisy, but we like it anyway. Open daily for dinner; Monday–Friday for lunch.

Surf Room, Royal Hawaiian Hotel, 2259 Kalākaua Avenue. 931-7194. Expensive

Right on the beach at the Royal Hawaiian Hotel, this restaurant is in the center of everything. It has a big, open terrace under pink and white awnings that block the sun but don't spoil the view. This is a beautiful (though pricey) spot for breakfast. A three-course dinner served every evening but Friday (seafood buffet night) pairs fine wines with each dish ($41.95). Open daily for breakfast, lunch, and dinner.

3660 on the Rise, 3660 Wai'alae Avenue. 737-1177. Expensive

Innovative Euro-island cuisine created by chef Russell Siu has earned this stylish restaurant a number of awards from Zagat, *Gourmet,* Gayot, and others. Situated at the corner of Wai'alae and Wilhelmina Avenues in Kaimukī, it is just a short drive from Waikīkī and well worth the trip. Specials are created daily. A sampling of recent entrées ($19.25–$31) includes pan-seared peppercorn-crusted *'ahi,* tempura farm-raised catfish, choice New York steak, Chinese-steamed island snapper, and *kālua* duck risotto. Open Tuesday–Sunday for dinner.

Tokkuri-Tei, 611 Kapahulu Avenue. 739-2800. Inexpensive

Here is a real find—delicious Japanese food at very reasonable prices. Several set meals are available, but the fun is in selecting from an assortment of delicacies, each of which comes in a small serving mostly priced at between $2 and $5, with a few higher. A couple might order five or six items and share them. Forget preconceived notions about balanced meals and the order in which certain foods should be served. The waitstaff will simply bring you each dish as it comes up, in no special order. The menu is written in Japanese kanji on colorful paper strips attached to the walls, but there is also an English menu, and the exceptional servers are incredibly helpful in explaining and suggesting dishes. Sushi and sashimi are outstanding; skewered chicken is moist and tender; grilled Kahuku corn on the cob (from the north shore) is tasty. For something different, try the tofu steak, which comes in a light but flavorful sauce, and the *tamago-yaki,* a sweet little egg omelet. The ambiance is delightful. There is an assortment of gay paper lanterns in a variety of styles hanging from the ceiling. Along with the mentioned paper strips, testaments from famous visitors, such as musicians Misha Dichter and

Paul Badura-Skoda and football coach June Jones, also are mounted on the walls. Open Monday–Saturday for dinner; Monday–Friday for lunch.

Tokyo Tokyo, Kāhala Mandarin Oriental Hotel, 5000 Kāhala Avenue. 739-1500. Expensive

The exquisite setting, especially the al fresco–inspired dining room, and equally exquisite food make for a memorable dining experience. The menu has been described as "new wave" Japanese, combining the best of East and West. Sushi, wasabi flan, and grilled seafood and vegetables are among specialties. Dining options include, in addition to the patio-like dining room, seating around the *robata,* or grill, and private *tatami* rooms. Open daily for dinner; Sunday–Friday for lunch.

L'Uraku, 1541 Kapi'olani Boulevard. 955-0552. Moderate–Expensive

The cuisine is billed as Euro Japanese at this popular restaurant. The decor is American funk, with brightly colored paintings by Kiyoshi and painted umbrellas suspended from the ceiling. Fish preparations are sublime. Entrées: $15.95–$29.75. You can't go wrong with the steamed *onaga.* The best deal in town is a four-course weekend lunch for $16.

The Veranda, Kāhala Mandarin Oriental Hotel, 5000 Kāhala Avenue. 739-8780. Moderate

We come here for drinks, *pūpū* or dessert, and jazz (Tuesday–Saturday from 7:30 P.M.) in an elegant setting. A classical guitarist plays Sunday and Monday evenings. Food is from Hōkū's (see above) and is superb. A curry buffet lunch on the Veranda ($14.25 up) is a new addition to the dining scene. A special treat is afternoon tea on the Veranda (see page 279). Open daily for lunch, 11:30 A.M.–1:30 P.M., and for tea, 2–5 P.M.

Wai'oli Tea Room, 2950 Mānoa Road. 988-5800. Inexpensive

Open in Mānoa since 1922, this casual restaurant is worth a visit just for the old-style ambiance, reminiscent of days gone by (put away your cell phone and plan to stay awhile, as service is friendly but leisurely). Breakfast, lunch, and afternoon tea are served. There is a reconstructed grass shack on the grounds, supposedly lived in by Robert Louis Stevenson when he visited O'ahu, but that story may be embellished. A small chapel with stained-glass windows is the site of many weddings. The restaurant and chapel are owned and operated by the Salvation Army. Open daily, 8 A.M.–4 P.M.

Keiki-Friendly Restaurants

HAWAI'I IS NOTED for its high regard for the *'ohana,* or family, and most restaurants welcome families with *keiki* of any age. The places included here have highchairs and booster seats at the ready and turn a blind eye to crumbs and worse falling on the floor.

A favorite for families with young children is **Dixie Grill** (404 Ward Avenue; 596-8359), which has a sandbox with toys on the lanai. The food here is southern inspired, with the likes of hush puppies, barbecue ribs, and fried chicken. **All Star Café** (2080 Kalākaua Avenue; 955-8326), in Waikīkī, is noted for its displays of sports memorabilia, especially related to such local activities as surfing and canoe paddling. Teens also will enjoy the upbeat, trendy atmosphere at both the **Hard Rock Café** (1837 Kapi'olani Boulevard; 955-7383) and **Planet Hollywood** (2155 Kalākaua Avenue; 924-7877).

A great eating place for youngsters is the **Oceanarium** (2490 Kalākaua Avenue; 922-1233), in the Pacific Beach Hotel, where diners are seated around the curve of a three-story, 280,000-gallon aquarium filled with fascinating fish.

In Kaimukī, **Columbia Inn** (3221 Wai'alae Avenue; 732-3663) draws the local crowd for its *keiki* menu that includes such Hawai'i favorites as teri chicken and mac salad. Children's meals include steamed fresh vegetables, milk, and a dessert, all for under $5. **Big City Diner** (3565 Wai'alae Avenue; 738-8855) has perhaps the best burgers in town; for the over-21 set, there are beer, wine, and multiflavored margaritas.

California Pizza Kitchen, with one branch in Ala Moana Center (941-7715) and another in the Kāhala Mall (737-9446), has a terrific menu for children and gives each youngster crayons and a placemat to color on.

Zippy's, with twenty-one branches on O'ahu, is Hawai'i's version of McDonald's. Here mainland youngsters can get a taste of what their Hawai'i counterparts like to eat: saimin, fried noodles, fried chicken, cornbread, and Zippy's famous chili. Zippy's has excellent baked goods, and sushi is available in many of their restaurants.

At Ward Centre, **Scoozee's** (597-1777) and the **Yum Yum Tree** (592-3581) appeal to families, as does the **Old Spaghetti Factory** (591-2513) at Ward Warehouse. Everyone in the family can choose a different cuisine at the food courts at **Ala Moana Center** and **Aloha Tower Marketplace**, the latter overlooking Honolulu Harbor. The **Kāhala Mall** also has a small food court.

Glossary *of* Hawaiian *and* Local-Style Words

For fish served in Hawai'i's restaurants, see page 281.

ali'i	ancient Hawaiian royalty
aloha	greeting or farewell; love, kindness, affection, or goodwill
Diamond Head	in the direction of Diamond Head (used in giving directions)
'ewa	in the direction of 'Ewa, a west O'ahu town (used in giving directions; opposite of Diamond Head)
hala	pandanus, or screw pine, tree; it has long, narrow leaves
hale	house, building
hānai	foster or adopted child
haole	foreigner to Hawai'i
hau	lowland flowering tree, often with impenetrable thickets
haupia	coconut pudding or custard
Hawai'i nei	this beloved Hawai'i
heiau	place of worship
hele wiki	quick
'ie'ie	woody, climbing vine
'ilima	shrub with small orange flowers that are used for lei
imu	underground oven
ipu	bottle gourd; drum made of a gourd
kāhili	feather standard, symbolic of royalty
kahuna	priest, minister, expert in any field (pl. *kāhuna*)

kaiseki	a set meal with a variety of small dishes (Japanese)
kalo	taro
kālua	to bake in an *imu*
kama'āina	native-born or longtime Hawai'i resident
kāne	man
kapa	tapa, barkcloth
kapu	taboo, forbidden
katsu	deep-fried chicken, fish, or pork with a savory coating (Japanese)
keiki	child
kiawe	mesquite tree; the wood is often used for grilling
kim chee	highly spiced Korean relish
koa	large native forest tree, valued for its fine wood
koi	carp
kou	tree used by early Hawaiians for cups, dishes, and calabashes
kukui	candlenut tree
kupuna	old person, grandparent (pl. *kūpuna*)
lama	ebony tree
lanai	porch or balcony (*lānai* in Hawaiian)
lauhala	pandanus leaf, used in plaiting

laulau	food, usually pork or fish, wrapped in *ti* or banana leaves and baked in the *imu* or steamed	*muʻumuʻu*	long, loose dress for women, usually made of a bright, flowery print
lei hulu	feather lei	*nēnē*	Hawaiian goose; Hawaiʻi's state bird
lilikoʻi	passionfruit	*ʻohana*	family
lūʻau	Hawaiian feast, named for the *kalo* leaves traditionally served at them	*ʻōhiʻa*	native hardwood tree
		ʻono	delicious (there is a fish named *ono*)
mahalo	thank you		
makaʻāinana	ordinary men and women	*pali*	mountain cliff; precipice
makahiki	annual celebration, with sports and religious festivals, at the beginning of the winter solstice; today the Aloha Festival	*paniolo*	cowboy
		pāʻū	woman's skirt; skirt split down the middle and worn by women horseback riders
makai	toward the ocean, or on the ocean side of the road (used in giving directions)	*pīkake*	jasmine
		pili	a grass formerly used for thatching houses
mauka	toward the mountains, or on the mountain side of the road (used in giving directions)	*pohā*	native gooseberry, used for jam
		poi	food made from steamed and mashed *kalo,* a staple of the Hawaiian diet
maunaloa	vine with blue or white flowers used for lei		
mele	chant, song	*poke*	raw fish seasoned with soy sauce or seaweed (pronounced *pó-kay*)
milo	tree used for shade, wood, and medicine		
		pūpū	appetizer; a *pūpū* platter
mokihana	shrub with waxy leaves and light green berries, used for lei	*shabu shabu*	paper-thin sliced beef cooked at table in a rich broth (Japanese)
musubi	mound of sushi rice topped with a slice of Spam and wrapped with a strip of *nori* (seaweed)	*ti*	woody plant with narrow, oblong leaves; *kī* in Hawaiian
		wahine	woman (pl. *wāhine*)
		wiliwili	native dryland tree; its oblong red seeds are used for lei

Mahalo nui loa to the many individuals who provided invaluable information and assistance during the preparation of this book, most especially William Walters, who wrote the hiking section; my children Robinson and Sarah, who helped in the final stages; and the following individuals:

Charlie Aldinger, Honolulu Academy of Arts; Pam Andelin; Tammi Becker, Happy Trails Hawai'i; Bernie Caalim-Polanzi, Hilton Resorts Hawai'i; Veronica Carmona; Ann Cecil; Robert Chinn, University of Hawai'i; Aulii Chung, W Honolulu; Marlene Donovan, Hawai'i State Archives; Stephen Downes and Mary Kaye Ritz; George Ellis, Honolulu Academy of Arts; Micki Fletcher, Island Heritage; Victoria Gail-White and John Wythe White; Sandra Harms, Hawai'i State Archives; Paula Imamura, Hilton Hawaiian Village; Ralph Kagehiro; Tom Klobe, University of Hawai'i Art Gallery; Roxane Kozuma, Island Heritage; Clarence and Elsa Lee; Deborah Lee, Hawai'i State Archives; Dale Madden, Island Heritage; Joyce Matsumoto, Halekūlani; Victoria Nihi, Hawai'i State Archives; Kelly O'Sullivan, Hilton Hawaiian Village; Aulani Pajimola, Germaine's Luau; Laura Ruby, University of Hawai'i; Allan Seiden, Hawaiian Legacy Archive; Wayne Shek, Color Station; Sandy Shitanishi, Island Heritage; Carol Silva; Cheryl Tsutsumi; Dietrich Varez; Gina Vergara-Bautista, Hawai'i State Archives; Melissa Wageman; Pauline Worsham, Neiman Marcus; Judy and Katsuo Yasutake; and Doug Young.

Picture Credits

Veronica Carmona: cover, back cover (surfers, 'Iolani Palace, Arizona Memorial), pages 4 (pineapples, man with lei, and woman with lei), 5 (woman with lei), 8 (Waikīkī surfing, Contemporary Museum, tea at Hale-kūlani), 9 ('Iolani Palace, Maunawili Falls), 13, 15 (top), 23, 25, 28, 34 (bamboo and *kukui* nuts), 45, 46–47, 48, 49, 52, 53, 54 (top left and bottom), 55 (top right), 60 (top left and bottom), 61 (three zoo photos), 62 (Kapi'olani Bandstand), 63 (War Memorial Natatorium and Sans Souci beach), 74 (top right), 75 (*ti* plant and 'Iolani Barracks), 78 (top), 79 (Washington Place and Marisol sculpture), 80 (bottom left), 81, 82 (State Library and Honolulu Hale), 83 (Charles Watson sculpture, Mission Memorial Building, and Mission Houses Museum), 84 (Kawaiaha'o Church and fountain), 86 (top left and bottom right), 87, 88 (top and bottom), 90, 91 (bottom), 92 (top left and top right, bottom left), 94 (lion dance and herb shop), 96 (bottom), 97 (lion dance and two sculptures), 98 (four photos in right column), 99, 101 (top right), 105, 107, 110, 114, 116 (two photos), 117 (top left and bottom), 118, 120, 121, 126 (Senator Fong), 127 (top right), 128, 129 (bottom right), 132, 133 (top right and bottom left) 134 (top and bottom), 135 (top left and bottom), 136, 137 (two photos), 138 (Ka'ena Point), 139, 141, 142 (three photos), 143, 144, 145 (bottom), 149, 155 (surfer), 156–57 (background), 159 (top), 161, 164, 167, 170, 171 (bottom left), 172–73 (background), 174–75 (background), 175 (bottom), 176 (three inset photos), 177, 178–79 (background), 179, 182, 184, 185, 188, 189 (inset), 191, 194, 196, 197, 201, 205, 212, 216 (background), 218, 220 (top), 222, 223, 227 (top), 228, 230, 231, 233, 234, 243, 253, 254, 257, 279, 288.

Ann Cecil: back cover (Diamond Head), front flap (plumeria), front and back flaps (background), pages 4 (hula dancers, surfers, Aloha Tower, and bird of paradise), 5 (Convention Center), 8 (Chef Mavro), 9 (outrigger canoeists, windward mountains, and Auntie Genoa Keawe), 11, 14, 15 (bottom), 17, 31, 34 (bananas and breadfruit), 44 (top and bottom), 55 (bottom left), 58, 59, 61 (top), 62 (Aquarium), 64 (Diamond Head), 73, 74 (bottom left), 76, 77, 85, 91 (top), 93, 95 (lei), 96 (top), 101 (top left),

102 (top left and bottom right), 103, 111, 117 (top right), 122 (top left), 123 (top), 124 (two photos), 127 (top left), 129 (top left), 130 (two photos), 131 (three photos), 133 (shave ice), 135 (top right), 138 (bottom), 153, 154, 154–55 (background), 158–59 (background), 159 (bottom), 160, 160–61 (background), 162, 163 (two photos), 165 (two photos), 166, 166–67 (background), 168, 168–69 (background), 169, 171 (bottom right), 172, 173, 175 (top), 176 (big surf), 178 (two photos), 182–83, 186, 187, 190, 192 (kayaker), 193 (three photos), 202, 208, 209, 213, 216, 220 (bottom), 221, 226, 227 (inset), 232 (two photos), 237, 238, 239, 240, 241, 242, 251, 268 (two photos), 289, 304.

Hawai'i State Archives: pages 1, 10, 16, 19, 20, 24, 29, 35, 37, 38, 41 (top and bottom), 42–43, 56–57, 63 (bottom right), 73 (background), 74 (Kalākaua Jubilee), 80 (top), 101 (bottom right), 126 (Lunalilo), 152.

Honolulu Academy of Arts: pages 36, 82 (top), 98 (top left), 119, 145 (top and middle right), 146 (two photos), 147, 148 (three photos), 151.

Ralph Kagehiro (illustrations): pages 64–65, 114–15, 122–23.

Dietrich Varez: pages 30, 33, 66, 140, 189 (background), 192 (inset and background), 206, 247, 258–59, 277.

Jim Wageman, Wigwag: back flap (hibiscus), pages 1 (inset), 2–3, 4 (leaves), 6–7, 104, 106, 180–81.

Pam Andelin: pages 95 (top), 127 (bottom); **Don Blanding**, *Vagabond's House:* page 27; **The Contemporary Museum**, Honolulu: page 150; **Halekūlani**: page 263; **Hilton Hawaiian Village**: page 264; **Hawaiian Legacy Archive**: pages 39, 57 (bottom); **Kāhala Mandarin Oriental**: page 272; **Mandara Spa**: page 8 (bottom left); **J.W. Marriott Ihilani Resort and Spa**: pages 214, 271; **McNeil Wilson Communications**: page 211; **Laura Ruby**: page 94 (bottom left); **Sheraton Moana Surfrider**: page 55 (bottom right); **State Foundation on Culture and the Arts**: page 78 (bottom); **University of Hawai'i–Mānoa**: pages 101 (bottom), 109 (top); **University of Hawai'i Art Gallery**: pages 108, 109 (bottom); **Doug Young**: page 89.

index

Note: Where there is more than one page for a listing, boldface refers to the page(s) where the primary reference appears.

Note to the Reader

Every effort has been made to provide accurate, up-to-date information. However, travel information is subject to change. We suggest that you call ahead when making travel plans. We also suggest that prudent care be taken whenever engaging in any outdoor activity and that you be aware of your own limitations. Neither the publisher nor the author can be held liable for errors or omissions herein or for loss, injury, or inconvenience resulting from the use of this book.

We welcome your comments. Please write to:

Essential Guide to Oʻahu
Island Heritage Publishing
94-411 Kōʻaki Street
Waipahu, HI 96797

e-mail:
essentialguides@hawaii.rr.com